When the Fences Come Down

When the Fences Come Down

Twenty-First-Century Lessons from Metropolitan School Desegregation

Genevieve Siegel-Hawley

The University of North Carolina Press CHAPEL HILL

This book was published with the assistance of the Authors Fund of the University of North Carolina Press.

© 2016 The University of North Carolina Press
All rights reserved
Manufactured in the United States of America
Set in Espinosa Nova by Westchester Publishing Services

The University of North Carolina Press has been a member of the Green Press Initiative since 2003.

Library of Congress Cataloging-in-Publication Data
Names: Siegel-Hawley, Genevieve, author.
Title: When the fences come down : twenty-first-century lessons from metropolitan school desegregation / Genevieve Siegel-Hawley.
Description: Chapel Hill : The University of North Carolina Press, [2016] | Includes bibliographical references and index.
Identifiers: LCCN 2015033881| ISBN 9781469627830 (pbk : alk. paper) | ISBN 9781469627847 (ebook)
Subjects: LCSH: School integration—Southern States—History—21st century. | Education, Urban—Southern States—History—21st century.
Classification: LCC LC214.22.S68 S57 2016 | DDC 379.2/63—dc23 LC record available at http://lccn.loc.gov/2015033881

Portions of this book appeared earlier as "City Lines, County Lines, Color Lines: The Relationship between School and Housing Segregation in Four Metro Areas," *Teachers College Record* 115, no. 6 (2013): 1–45; as "Mitigating Milliken? School District Boundary Lines and Desegregation Policy in Four Southern Metros, 1990–2010," *American Journal of Education* 201, no.3 (2014): 391–433; and as "Tearing Down Fences: School Boundary Lines and Equal Educational Opportunity in the Twenty-First Century," in *The Enduring Legacy of Rodriguez*, ed. Charles J. Ogletree Jr. and Kimberly Jenkins Robinson (Harvard Education Press, 2015).

We deal here with the right of all of our children, whatever their race, to an equal start in life and to an equal opportunity to reach their full potential as citizens. Those children who have been denied that right in the past deserve better than to see fences thrown up to deny them that right in the future. Our Nation, I fear, will be ill-served by the Court's refusal to remedy separate and unequal education, for unless our children begin to learn together, there is little hope that our people will ever learn to live together.

—JUSTICE THURGOOD MARSHALL, dissenting opinion in *Milliken v. Bradley*, 1974

*For those who remain behind fences,
and for those who struggle to tear them down*

Contents

Preface xi

Introduction 1
Metropolitan School Desegregation, Past and Present

PART I | *Background*

1. Why Boundary Lines Matter So Much—and What We Have Done about Them 11

2. School Policy Is Housing Policy, and Vice Versa 36

PART II | *Analysis*

3. Divergent Paths 55
   School and Housing Desegregation in Four Southern Cities

4. Divergent Outcomes 73
   The Contemporary Relationship between School and Housing Segregation in Four Southern Cities

PART III | *Solutions*

5. The Choice Conundrum 111
   Challenges and Opportunities for Voluntary School Desegregation Policy

6. Education and the Regional Agenda 133

Afterword with Dr. Gary Orfield 160

Notes 173

Index 215

Maps, Tables, and Figures

MAPS

1. School District Fragmentation, New York/Long Island and Southern Florida 19

2. Elementary School Racial Composition, Richmond-Henrico-Chesterfield, 1992–2009 79

3. Elementary School Racial Composition, Charlotte-Mecklenburg County, 1992–2009 81

4. Elementary School Racial Composition, Chattanooga-Hamilton County, 1992–2009 83

5. Elementary School Racial Composition, Louisville-Jefferson County, 1992–2009 85

6. Elementary School Racial Composition by Black Population Living in Census Block Groups, 1990 90

7. Elementary School Racial Composition by Black Population Living in Census Block Groups, 2000 91

8. Elementary School Racial Composition by Black Population Living in Census Block Groups, 2010 92

9. Elementary School Poverty Composition by Black Population Living in Census Block Groups, 2010 94

10. Elementary School Racial Composition by Black Population Living in Census Block Groups, Richmond-Henrico, 1990, 2000, and 2010 105

TABLES

1. School Boundary Lines and Desegregation Policy 56

2. Student Enrollment by Race, 1992 and 2009 76

3. School Segregation, 1992, 1999, and 2009 88

FIGURES

1. School and Residential Black-White Dissimilarity Index, 1990–2010 96

2. Black Students' and Residents' Exposure to White Students and Residents, 1990–2010 97

3. Percentage Change in Black-White/White-Black Residential Dissimilarity Index, 1990–2000, 2000–2010, and 1990–2010 100

Preface

I began riding a bus to middle school in the fall of 1991. Each morning, at about 6 A.M., it picked us up, rolling over the hilly terrain of Richmond's east end before heading toward the city center. I learned a lot about urban geographic boundaries during those rides—where they were, what they represented, and to whom they applied. I knew, for instance, that when the driver collected the only three white students (myself included) in the heart of an eight-block historic zone, an island of relative white affluence amid government-designed black segregation and concentrated poverty, all of us coming of age on that bus received a message about race and opportunity in our United States.

I learned more about geographic boundaries at my regional high school, a specialty program for government and international studies housed, at the time, on the top floor of Richmond's historic Thomas Jefferson High School. Schoolchildren from eleven participating school districts rode buses far and wide—crossing many a boundary along the way—for the educational opportunities provided by the school. I too crossed over those boundaries as I traveled to athletic games or to stay with friends in suburban and rural communities. A consciousness around the metropolitan dimensions of race, advantage, and opportunity crystallized during those trips.

Toward the end of high school, I became aware of a 1973 court case that, decided differently, would have dramatically reshaped my burgeoning understanding of Richmond's metropolitan landscape. The untapped possibilities of *Bradley v. Richmond*'s failed city–suburban school desegregation plan fueled a decades-long desire to more fully understand what could have been—and what still might be, given the right mixture of political or legal grit—in my community. That desire formed the basis for this book.

I owe an incredible debt of gratitude to many people for helping to make the book possible. A heartfelt thanks goes to Dr. Gary Orfield for his unflagging support and instruction over the course of the original research, as well as for the tremendous amount of wisdom, optimism, and insight he has shared over the years. Many thanks also go to Drs. Patricia Gándara, John Rogers, Leo Estrada, and Stuart Biegel for their thoughtful feedback and direction throughout the writing process.

More recently, Dr. Tom Luce, research director at the Institute on Metropolitan Opportunity, and Dr. Jeffrey Brooks, professor of educational leadership at Monash University in Australia, reviewed and offered valuable suggestions at several stages of this book. It is much stronger because of their gracious assistance.

A delightful cadre of local and national experts also took time out of their busy schedules to read through different chapters of the book. Drs. John Moeser and Tom Shields at the University of Richmond and Dr. Yvonne Brandon at VCU each had recommendations that helped strengthen and clarify the manuscript. Phil Tegeler, executive director of the Poverty and Race Research Action Council, provided thorough and excellent feedback on a number of chapters. David Rusk, founder of Building One America, current consultant on urban policy, former mayor of Albuquerque, and long-time regionalism guru, also sent a number of incredibly helpful suggestions towards the end of the editing process. And as usual, I am indebted to Dr. Erica Frankenberg at Penn State who, in this endeavor as in so many others, provided sage counsel, detailed feedback, and sustaining friendship. Thanks also to my graduate assistant, Stefani Thachik, for her reliable and superb assistance with the endnotes and transcription of the afterword, as well as to Eric Myott, research fellow at the Institute on Metropolitan Opportunity, for his invaluable suggestions regarding the design and presentation of the maps. The team at UNC Press, most especially Joseph Parsons and Alison Shay, has been wonderfully helpful, humorous, and encouraging at every step of the way. Thanks for believing in this book and seeing it through to the end.

Even with such amazing assistance, mistakes are inevitable. These are, of course, my own.

To my parents, who helped ignite a deep commitment to social and racial justice through their own example, thank you. To my husband, who spent countless patient hours and years listening to this project evolve, thank you for your loving support. To my elderly beagles, thank you for being such loyal and relaxed writing partners. And to my daughter, the next generation, thank you for being.

When the Fences Come Down

Introduction
Metropolitan School Desegregation, Past and Present

This is a story of roads taken and not taken—of opportunities secured and squandered—amid the struggle for educational equality in the metropolitan South. At its core is a lesson about what is possible when significant school desegregation efforts come to pass. Because segregation systematically denies minority groups access to mainstream opportunities and resources, policies designed to challenge it remain critical to the expansion of full equality.[1] Tackling the unfinished business of desegregating students in public education, an institution that reaches nine in ten U.S. schoolchildren[2]—shaping minds and hearts along the way—is a fundamental first step on the path toward the full integration of our society.

School desegregation is linked to important academic, social, and civic benefits for students, which include an increased willingness to later seek out desegregated college, work, and neighborhood experiences.[3] In other words, school desegregation can create a perpetuating effect across multiple sectors of society. A key example of these interlocking relationships is illuminated in this book. It shows that metropolitan areas that desegregated schools in districts encompassing both urban and suburban areas saw much faster declines in housing segregation than areas that limited desegregation to central cities. In a still stratified and increasingly diverse nation, surely it is time to pay serious attention to lessons learned from regions that undertook school desegregation across the urban-suburban divide. If we do not, rising inequality and deepening segregation threaten our common future.

Two Roads, Diverged

When the Fences Come Down draws our attention to Richmond, Virginia, where in 1972 a forward-thinking U.S. district court judge ordered the consolidation of the predominantly black city school system with its overwhelmingly white suburban counterparts. Doing so meant that meaningful school desegregation would be possible. Had the judge's decree been upheld in the U.S. Supreme Court, it would have provided school systems around the county with a critical tool to use in the pursuit of integration: the ability to erase or rearrange school district boundary lines with relative ease.

Instead, the case came to represent the road not taken in the Richmond metro area. It also foreshadowed the more nationally significant *Milliken v. Bradley* decision handed down just a few months later. The 5-4 decision in *Milliken*, a lawsuit dealing with the consolidation of multiple school districts in Detroit, made it extremely difficult to combine urban and suburban school systems without proof of intentional segregation in all involved districts. With few exceptions, marshaling such evidence against numerous jurisdictions was beyond the reach of cash-strapped civil rights organizations.[4] *Milliken* thus locked most district boundary lines, and all of the segregation and educational opportunities connected to them, in place. The rulings in Richmond and Detroit would come to signify the end of a very short period of concerted efforts of the federal judicial, legislative, and executive branches to desegregate schools,[5] an endeavor designed to help overcome nearly three centuries of slavery and apartheid.

Despite significant setbacks in the courts, this book shows how a number of southern communities not so far from Richmond traveled down a different road. Such places succeeded in taking down the fences between city and suburban schools through a variety of different mechanisms. In the aftermath of district mergers in these communities, both schools and neighborhoods desegregated with much greater success than in Richmond.[6] Even though the racial makeup of schools and districts remains a central driver of decisions about where to live,[7] residents experiencing city-suburban school desegregation understood they could move anywhere across a broad swath of the region and remain connected to a relatively stable and diverse educational setting. In this manner, the relationship between school and housing decisions began to unravel.[8] *When the Fences Come Down* argues that the successes flowing from city-suburban school desegregation policies provide an example of opportunities within reach for countless other places, even as such stories have been largely forgotten or ignored.[9]

School Boundaries, Segregation, and the Region

Over 80 percent of the U.S. population lives in metropolitan areas today, up from about 66 percent in the 1960s.[10] In most of these communities, school quality and resources, housing stock, municipal services, employment opportunities, accessibility of transportation, exposure to pollution, and tax rates all vary dramatically across a network of invisible political boundaries.[11] Because education is such an important component of social mobility, school district lines matter more than most.[12] These lines create a situation where a large amount of segregation can be attributed to the way students from different racial groups are distributed across districts, rather than to the way they are distributed within a single school district.[13] Said another way, the majority of school segregation occurs because students are enrolled in entirely different school systems, not just in different schools.[14]

Sixty years after the landmark *Brown v. Board of Education* decision, many black and Latino students still attend schools largely separate from those attended by white and Asian students. Nearly 40 percent of black students and 43 percent of Latino students enroll in intensely segregated school environments where whites make up less than 10 percent of the student body.[15] These racially segregated settings cleave along economic lines as well, with the average black and Latino student going to schools with far more low-income students than the typical white or Asian student. According to some measures, today schools are more segregated—both racially and economically—than they were at the time of Dr. Martin Luther King's death.[16]

At the same time, our nation and our schools are growing rapidly more diverse. In 2011, more babies of color were born than white babies—a first in U.S. history. It marked a shift that will reverberate gradually through the population, but somewhere between 2040 and 2050, the United States will become a majority-minority country.[17] Two major regions of the United States, the South and West, already report majority-minority school enrollments, along with a number of large metropolitan areas.[18] As these seismic changes sweep through the country, it becomes ever more important to provide children of all backgrounds the opportunity to learn alongside one another, so that they will be prepared to live and work with one another.[19]

In addition to dramatic shifts in the racial makeup of the country, inequality is deepening. Economic growth over the past three decades has largely benefited the highest earners: between 1977 and 2007, the income of families at the ninetieth percentile increased by an astounding 90 percent, compared to just 7 percent for families at the twentieth percentile.[20] The influence of parental income on student achievement and later earnings is now very high in the United States compared to other developed countries; with that comes much lower social mobility across generations.[21]

Rather than confronting the links between rising inequality, low social mobility, segregation, and school performance, contemporary education reformers largely believe that pervasive achievement gaps between students of different backgrounds stem from low expectations, mismanagement, bloated bureaucracy, and stagnating public school systems.[22] As a result, education policy in recent decades has focused on trying to improve schools by raising standards and expectations, holding teachers and students accountable, and stimulating public school improvement through private sector competition.[23] The prominence of these current policies has edged out the favored reforms of the civil rights era, nearly all of which emphasized a dramatic expansion of access to and equity within elementary, secondary, and post-secondary educational opportunities for historically marginalized groups.[24] Some argue—and evidence supports—that education policymakers would be wise to return to civil rights–era reforms given the segregation and inequality facing increasingly diverse generations of schoolchildren.[25]

Outside the education sector, however, a diverse coalition of environmentalists, smart growth activists, municipal and elected officials, civic, corporate, and philanthropic interest groups, civil rights and fair housing advocates, minority and low-income community stakeholders, and others have thrown their support behind a renewed interest in regionalism.[26] Regionalism pushes for decision-making at a broader geographic level, in order to combat the competitive pursuit of resources that occurs in metro areas divided by numerous political boundaries.[27] Without intermediate governance between the state and fragmented local communities, the thinking goes, decisions affecting the welfare of an entire metropolitan area are made by parochial, self-interested governmental units.[28] As U.S. society grows more urbanized, more diverse, and more unequal, building coalitions dedicated to finding cross-jurisdictional solutions to problems confronting increasing numbers of Americans is crucial.

While regionalism promises to promote the economic and social health of broadly defined communities, many oft-cited examples of regional cooperation fail to directly address educational disparities between cities and suburbs. Education, in other words, frequently has not been at the heart of the regional agenda.[29] Ironically, it is an area in which we have a substantial body of evidence indicating that a regional pursuit of equal educational opportunity is linked to the previously mentioned successes in combating high levels of school and housing segregation.[30]

When the *Milliken* decision put the brakes on most efforts to break down the fences dividing city and suburban school systems back in 1974, its impact reached far into the future. Yet the few places where metropolitan school desegregation did occur, nearly all of which were located in southern or border states, continue to offer tremendously important examples for understanding the possibilities of today's regionalism—but only if education becomes a key focus of the movement.

City-Suburban Desegregation in the Metropolitan South

Educational Regionalism goes into the heart of the contemporary South to draw lessons from the area of the country that engaged most intensely with school desegregation. The book provides an in-depth look at four southern metropolitan areas, ranging east toward Virginia's capitol of Richmond, west to Chattanooga, Tennessee's, perch in the Smoky Mountains, north to the river city of Louisville, Kentucky, and south to Charlotte, near the border of the Carolinas. Each of these communities represents differing and highly illustrative experiences with city-suburban district consolidation and school desegregation policy.

The four metro areas cover a broad spectrum of school district boundary line arrangements, either adhering to the parameters of the *Milliken* decision or overcoming them through various means. The Richmond area offers a key point of comparison, as it came to embody a pattern found in many parts of the country—an urban school system distinct from surrounding suburban ones—in the aftermath of its failed merger. But the other three metro school systems reflect a range of impetuses for consolidation across different time periods. In Louisville-Jefferson County, the federal courts backed a city-suburban merger for the purpose of school desegregation. In the Charlotte-Mecklenburg and Chattanooga-Hamilton County areas, state-level policies helped promote school district consolidations not explicitly related to desegregation.

Though only one metropolitan district, Louisville-Jefferson County, continues to implement a wide-ranging school desegregation strategy, Charlotte-Mecklenburg County employed similar student assignment policies, with shifts occurring during the time period of focus (1990–2010). The Charlotte area thus offers an important "before and after" portrait of a site that engaged with and then retreated from wide-scale school desegregation. After merging, Chattanooga-Hamilton County has pursued both rezoning and an expansion of magnet programs in order to promote diverse schools. Meanwhile, the three Richmond area districts originally slated for consolidation presently do not operate any policies or programs explicitly designed to desegregate students.

Organization and Goals of the Book

The first part of this book sheds light on the major issues involved in understanding the relationship between boundary lines and segregation. Drawing upon evidence from education, sociology, history, political science, and law, chapter 1 argues that politicized, invisible lines give shape to segregation in schools and communities and makes the case for why that still matters. In chapter 2, the reciprocal relationship between school and housing segregation is outlined. Based on the work of noted desegregation scholars, it delves into the theory and research underlying the school-housing link and shows why city-suburban school desegregation policies have been far more effective than policies limited to central cities for integrating schools and neighborhoods. It also draws upon a new base of evidence documenting the long-term and extensive relationship between patterns of metropolitan housing development and school zoning and construction.

 The next two chapters take up the stories and outcomes associated with desegregation policy and district consolidation in Richmond, Louisville, Charlotte, and Chattanooga. Using primary and secondary sources like newspaper articles, school board minutes, policy reports, interviews, and books, chapter 3 outlines key characteristics of each site. Major school desegregation policy shifts are highlighted, and an overview of limited efforts in two of the metros to address housing segregation in conjunction with school segregation is provided. Chapter 4 links the differing city-suburban school district configurations and desegregation histories of the four southern metros to contemporary patterns of school and housing segregation. Most significantly, the chapter shows that metropolitan school desegregation strategies were associated with dramatic declines in both school and housing segregation between 1990 and 2010. The increasingly multiracial nature of school enrollments in the four metros is also emphasized, and key policy changes (e.g., the abandonment of school desegregation policies) are linked to increases in school and housing segregation.

Nearly all of the policy shifts in these southern school districts were related to changing approaches to school choice. And given the direction of the courts over the past several decades, many contemporary efforts to promote diverse schools are in fact voluntary. Today's voluntary integration strategies usually combine some element of family choice with broader goals like ensuring diversity, balancing school enrollments, and considering school proximity to residence. At the same time, school choice was a defining feature of southern resistance to *Brown*'s mandate, and many types of choice continue to contribute to school segregation.[31] Chapter 5 uses the school choice trajectories of the different districts under study to highlight how choice can either promote or undermine school diversity efforts. It also draws upon the experiences of other school systems to illustrate how choice might best be used going forward.

The closing chapter underscores key findings from the original analysis and argues that they strengthen a robust evidence base supporting the need to more strongly insert education into the regional agenda. While the limitations of and difficult politics surrounding metropolitan school desegregation are acknowledged, the conclusion offers solutions targeted toward an array of actors. These overlapping policies would confront school segregation in tandem with the housing, transportation, and employment issues that are often the focus of current conversations about regionalism.

Ultimately, the goal of this book is both to underscore the damages wrought by the segregating impact of school district boundary lines and to raise awareness about regions that have chosen to undermine them. Based on original quantitative research and innovative mapping tools, it shows the remarkable possibilities available to us if we have the courage to act, as well as the deepening costs of our passivity. *When the Fences Come Down* revisits strategies that in many cases were abruptly halted—or never begun—in order to ignite an open conversation about the creation of the healthy, integrated schools and communities crucial to the success of our multiracial future.

PART I | Background

CHAPTER ONE

Why Boundary Lines Matter So Much— and What We Have Done about Them

In many ways, the boundary lines dividing school districts, and schools within districts, are the building blocks of modern-day educational inequality. They help balkanize regions along racial and socioeconomic lines, divvying up students and key educational resources like engaged peers, experienced, high-quality teachers, and challenging curricula along the way. As a result, actions taken to alter school-related boundaries often prove controversial. Consider the following example of contemporary wrangling over school district lines.

Prompted by fiscal concerns related to a shifting political landscape in the Tennessee state legislature, in 2010 the Memphis City School Board voted to surrender the charter governing its school district in order to fold into the surrounding system in Shelby County. In Tennessee, all counties must maintain countywide school districts. Within those large districts, major cities like Memphis often operated separate school systems (Memphis City Schools were incorporated by the state legislature in the mid-1800s). But if city officials and residents agree to dismantle their system, responsibility for administering public education automatically reverts to the countywide district[1]—in this case, Shelby County.

Erasing the lines between Shelby County and Memphis resulted in the largest consolidation in American history, bringing together a city school system that was 85 percent black and 76 percent low income with a suburban one that was approximately 38 percent black and 31 percent low income.[2] Though discussions of altering student assignment policies to promote diversity were not at the forefront, memories attached to the earlier desegregation era echoed through plans for the merger.[3] Proponents of the consolidation hoped it would help create a more unified, sustainable, and highly resourced school system. Opponents feared the loss of control, a depletion of resources, and an erosion of school quality. Many viewed the issues through the prism of racial and economic disparities between the city and suburbs.[4]

Three years later, in 2013, students began their first day of class in the newly unified Memphis-area school system amid signs of revolt from residents in six suburban and predominately white incorporated municipalities. A clash, underway since the early aftermath of the charter surrender, unfolded between the legislature and the courts, with the suburban municipalities eventually winning the right to secede from the newly merged district.[5] The breakaway districts soon became a reality, almost one year to the day when students from the city and the suburbs came together in one system. A single boundary surrounding a system serving all students in Shelby County rapidly multiplied into boundaries dividing the county into seven separate districts.[6]

The purpose of this chapter is to lay the groundwork for our analysis of boundaries, race, segregation, and opportunity in Louisville, Richmond, Charlotte, and Chattanooga—four southern regions that grappled with the issues surrounding school district lines many years before the contemporary struggle in Memphis. It dives deeply into research from a variety of different disciplines to show why school boundaries matter and how they relate to segregation. The chapter then traces the evolution of boundaries in metropolitan areas and describes how the courts almost intervened to remedy the harmful impacts of school district lines. It presents evidence that action to promote metropolitan school desegregation is still warranted, though the issue has been ignored in contemporary educational policymaking. The chapter concludes by examining the promise of regional strategies to promote equity.

Educational Significance of Boundary Lines

Events in Memphis demonstrate how school district boundaries can also become racial and economic boundaries. At the most basic level, once a geographic area defined by a boundary gains a name, it also gains a demographic identity.[7] Those six new suburban districts in Memphis, for example, are now synonymous with whiteness, advantage, and exclusivity. Families and residents with means can look across Memphis, or any other metro area spliced by numerous district boundary lines, and make choices about where to live and send their children to school based on the reputation of the district. Good evidence indicates that the racial and class makeup of a district remains central to that reputation.[8] As people who can afford to relocate begin to sort themselves out on either side of existing or newly drawn lines, important opportunities and resources also go with them. Indeed, our current system of school funding, which relies heavily on local property taxes, compounds the stratification by linking wealthier communities equate to highly resourced schools.[9] One prominent researcher went so far as to call school district boundary lines "social fractures."[10] Those fractures matter today largely because school segregation still matters.

The Harms of Segregation

The consensus of a vast and still accumulating body of social science research highlights the numerous harms associated with high-poverty, high-minority schools. These two layers of segregation go hand in hand nine times out of ten.[11] Disadvantages range from detrimental impacts on teaching and learning to diminished access to key educational resources to damaging social-psychological effects on students. Ultimately, the combination of harms helps produce deeply unequal educational and life outcomes.

Student peer groups—in other words, who goes to school with whom—have an outsized impact on student achievement. Research findings dating back to the famous 1966 Coleman Report, which was commissioned by the federal government to assess the state of equal educational opportunity, show that concentrations of poverty in a school influence student achievement more than the poverty status of an individual student.[12] Updated analyses that rely upon more sophisticated statistical methods have replicated and expanded upon the central findings of the Coleman Report. One such study, published in 2010, concluded, "going to a high-poverty school or a highly segregated African American school has a profound effect on a student's achievement outcomes, above and beyond the effect of individual poverty or minority status. Specifically, both the racial/ethnic and social class composition of a student's school are 1 3/4 times more important than a student's individual race/ethnicity or social class for understanding educational outcomes."[13] The reasons that peer groups can have such an outsized influence on student achievement are many. Going to a school where a majority of classmates normalize regular class attendance, engagement with and follow through on school assignments, and college-going can help instill similar attitudes and goals in other students.[14] Conversely, research shows that a good friend who drops out greatly increases the odds of their close acquaintances not completing high school.[15] Teachers and families who communicate high expectations about schoolwork and homework also contribute to peer group influences.[16]

Excluding peers, of the remaining factors that contribute to academic outcomes within a given school setting, research shows that teachers matter more than most.[17] In segregated schools, teachers tend to be less experienced and less qualified (as in, not as likely to hold a degree in the subject they are teaching) than teachers in other types of school settings.[18] Salaries are usually lower in high-poverty, high-minority schools,[19] which, along with other stresses present in the environment, may contribute to the fact that teachers and leaders frequently leave these schools within a few years.[20] Further adding to the turnover and instability, teacher and staff absences are more frequent and long-term substitutes more common in segregated schools.[21]

Students attending minority-segregated, high-poverty schools often experience watered-down and/or outdated curricula that feels disconnected from their lives. Evidence indicates that segregated schools more often rely upon older textbooks and instructional materials that do not contain information reflective of our rapidly evolving society.[22] Moreover, the increased emphasis on high-stakes standardized testing has corresponded with a rise in "drill and kill" teaching methods to help ensure that all students achieve at the minimum level expected. Many resources—and a great deal of time—are directed toward instilling basic competencies in reading and math, often at the expense of creative and/or otherwise engaging curricula.[23] Advanced placement course offerings, which help boost grade point averages for college applications and offer early college credit, are also more limited (and, in many cases, nonexistent) in segregated schools.[24]

In addition to unequal access to high-quality teachers, challenging peer groups, and strong curricula, the building facilities that house students in segregated high-poverty schools are, on average, inferior to the ones maintained for students in other kinds of settings.[25] Famed civil rights lawyer Charles Hamilton Houston began chipping away at *Plessy v. Ferguson*'s "separate but equal" mantra through his documentation of deeply inadequate school facilities in the pre-*Brown* South. Similar conditions still exist all over the country. Jonathan Kozol, a writer and activist known for his searing portrayal of segregated schooling in the South Bronx, offered the following description of building disrepair in his acclaimed 2005 book, *The Shame of the Nation*:

> I had made a number of visits to a high school where a stream of
> water flowed down one of the main stairwells on a rainy afternoon

and where green fungus molds were growing in the office where students went for counseling. A large blue barrel was positioned to collect rain-water coming through the ceiling.... In another ... school, the principal poured out his feelings to me in a room in which a plastic garbage bag had been attached somehow to cover part of a collapsing ceiling. "This," he told me, pointing to the garbage bag, then gesturing around him at the other indications of decay and disrepair one sees in ghetto schools much like it elsewhere, "would not happen to white children."[26]

Daily newspapers are also rife with stories of crumbling facilities in segregated settings. In Richmond, Virginia, for instance, news accounts describe a "bumper crop of decrepit buildings" in Richmond's racially and economically isolated urban school division. The city system currently needs an estimated $35 million to upgrade its facilities, and is expected to receive roughly $7 million for capital improvements, most of which is already slated for other critical projects.[27]

Within those deteriorating walls, minority-segregated, high-poverty schools often struggle with issues of high student mobility and threats to safety. Both issues strongly impact academic engagement and disrupt the school learning environment.[28] Overlaid onto student safety concerns are the harsh discipline practices that are far more pervasive in racially and socioeconomically isolated schools than in other types of settings. Zero-tolerance policies, which remove any shades of gray surrounding rule infractions, have been shown to dramatically increase student involvement with the criminal justice system, helping contribute to the school-to-prison pipeline.[29]

Incidents within schools obviously do not occur in a vacuum. The neighborhood and societal contexts surrounding schools matter greatly to what goes on inside of them. Deeply entrenched poverty, high levels of unemployment, lack of access to quality, consistent health care, a dearth of healthy food sources, systemic violence, and police brutality are just some of the challenges linked to segregated, high-poverty neighborhoods.[30] These conditions take a corresponding toll on the schools and students situated in their midst.[31]

Educational inequities are on display every time students venture to other schools or districts. Those concrete messages exist alongside the implicit ones students receive from constant teacher and principal turnover, harsh discipline policies, and other facets of segregated schooling, sending sharp signals about race, stigma, and inequality. All help shape student attitudes toward school and society. As Dr. Martin Luther King so eloquently put it, "segregation distorts the soul and damages the personality. It gives the segregator a false sense of superiority and the segregated a false sense of inferiority."[32] Indeed, the harms of segregation very much extend to schools serving isolated white students, who are ill equipped to work, live, and participate in our rapidly diversifying society.[33]

Each dimension related to school segregation contributes to radically unequal outcomes for students of color attending high-poverty, high-minority schools. Test scores tend to be lower and dropout rates much higher in these schools.[34] In the end, levels of educational attainment are depressed, contributing to unemployment and intergenerational poverty.

The Benefits of Integration

While school integration is no longer a popular policy prescription for the persistent educational inequities associated with segregation,[35] it continues to be linked to critical academic, social, and civic outcomes for students of all races. School integration is crucial because it deepens and enriches our concern about the quality of education for everyone's children, not just our own. Ensuring that students of all races are attending the same schools and learning together in the same classrooms helps overcome the long-standing tendency to stockpile educational resources and advantages for a small, privileged segment of the student population.[36] All students benefit from these ties that bind schools and communities together, as James Ryan, dean of the Harvard Graduate School of Education, so plainly laid out in his book *Five Miles Away, a World Apart*.

Still, school integration is not a cure-all for the many layers of inequality in our society. Efforts to promote inclusive and diverse educational settings must be accompanied by strong policies carefully attending to what goes on in the world outside of schools.[37] And within schools, there is an urgent need to guard against the harms of "second-generation segregation" that can undermine even the most well-structured student assignment plan.[38] Widely used policies that sort students along racial lines into different educational tracks (e.g., honors, special education, and ESL programs) fray the ties that bind. Important resources like experienced teachers and stimulating curricula tend to be unevenly allocated to each track, and disparate educational outcomes often follow suit.[39] In essence, bringing students of different backgrounds into meaningful and equal contact with one another must extend all the way into classrooms—even down to the cooperative learning groups formed within classes—to most firmly cement the benefits of desegregation.

One of the more immediate advantages linked to school desegregation relates to heightened academic achievement. Picture a U.S. history classroom composed of students from many different racial, ethnic, and economic backgrounds. The instructor poses a question connecting immigration attitudes at the turn of the twentieth century to current conversations about immigration reform. The ensuing discussion is likely to be rich as students offer differing perspectives based on their own experiences. These kinds of conversations promote critical thinking skills in students by teaching them to examine and evaluate multiple perspectives. This, in turn, is a fundamental component of problem-solving, and strong evidence from the business sector indicates that diverse teams come up with better, more complex and creative solutions than nondiverse ones composed of experts in a particular field.[40]

More narrowly, sophisticated research designs also link racially and socioeconomically integrated schools to higher levels of academic achievement as measured by test scores. Researchers find significant gains in reading and mathematics for black and Latino students in diverse schools, with no corresponding declines for white students.[41] And some major studies do show achievement gains on test scores for white students attending racially and socioeconomically diverse schools, particularly in math and science.[42] Large-scale reviews of the research in this area confirm such findings, indicating that diverse schools are linked to positive effects on academic achievement across multiple subjects and racial groups.[43]

Beyond academic outcomes, desegregated schools are also associated with an amplified ability to communicate and make friends across races, as well as reductions in racial hostilities and students' willingness to accept stereotypes.[44] These social-psychological outcomes are increasingly important in our quickly changing society. Rising generations of students will need to live, work, and govern well with people of many different races and ethnicities, and schools are clearly a crucial place for learning how to do so.

Over the long term, students attending integrated schools report loftier educational and career aspirations, followed by higher levels of educational and career attainment.[45] Occupational attainment for minority students is related to a number of important factors that tend to be more present in integrated schools than in segregated ones. These include higher initial career goals, access to strong educational resources, lessons in how to navigate cultural differences, and linkages to advantaged social networks that pass along informal but key information about job opportunities and contacts.[46] Finally—and perhaps most importantly—graduates of racially diverse schools are more likely to attend integrated colleges and live in racially diverse neighborhoods than graduates of segregated schools.[47] The perpetuating benefits of desegregation, then, unfold across the life cycle.

The research and lived experiences of students clearly indicate that segregation still matters a great deal for educational and life outcomes—and that well-designed, integrated schools can help alter those trajectories. So now we return to one of the chief causes of school segregation and the inequality with which it is associated: district boundary lines.

How Much Do Boundaries Contribute to School Segregation?

District boundary lines like the six new ones in Memphis contribute significantly to contemporary patterns of school segregation. In the not-so-distant past, segregation usually occurred because various policies (e.g., assigning or transferring students to different schools based on race, gerrymandering attendance boundaries around certain neighborhoods, or building new schools in segregated areas) funneled black and white students into separate schools within the same district.[48] Today, however, the majority—between 60 and 70 percent, according to some estimates[49]—of school segregation can be attributed to how students of different races are sorted across district boundaries. Much of this segregation occurs between urban and suburban districts, though increasing minority suburbanization means that it is now also due to the segregation of students among different suburban school systems.[50]

Boundary lines influence school segregation differently across our major regions. The term "fragmentation" is often used to describe the presence of numerous school districts or municipalities in a given metropolitan area.[51] Processes related to the proliferation of new school districts, which contribute to fragmentation, have been called "splintering."[52] Though the splintering of districts in Shelby County illustrates the rise of school system fragmentation in the metropolitan South, metros in the Northeast and Midwest typically have been characterized as the most fragmented. In a recent study of over 300 metro areas, for example, selecting any two

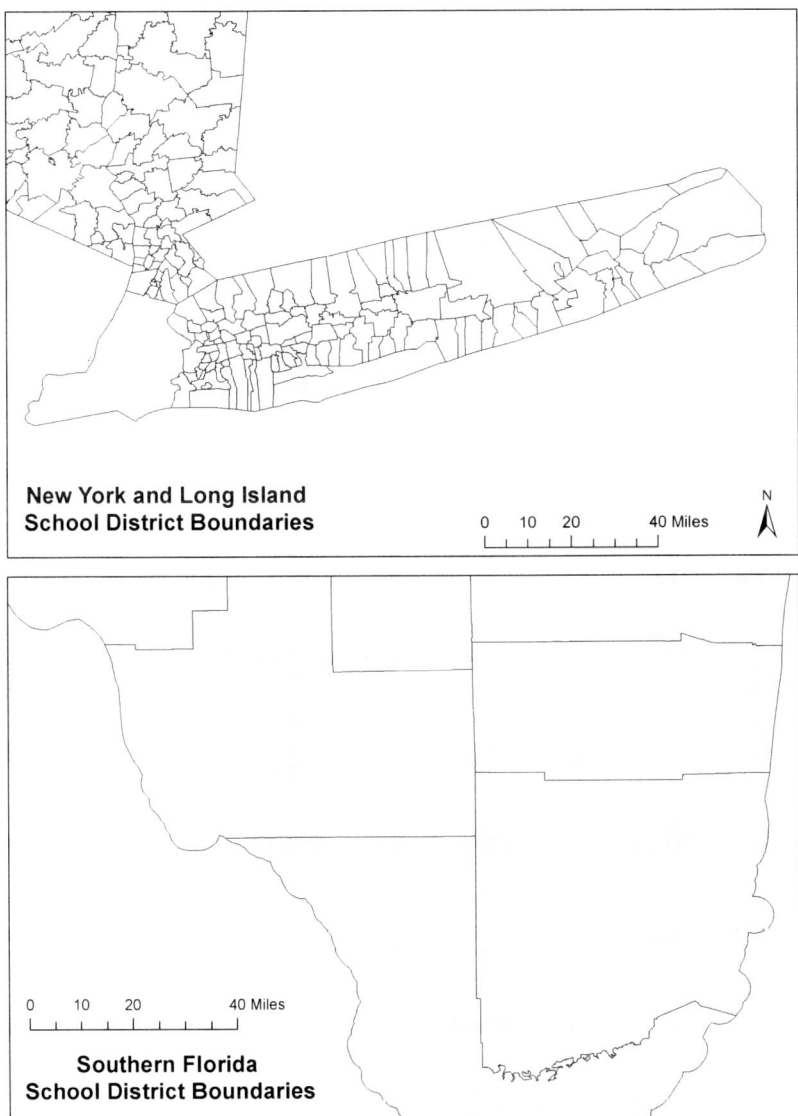

MAP 1 School District Fragmentation, New York/Long Island and Southern Florida. U.S. Census, 2014, TigerLine Shapefiles. For a color version of this map, please visit: http://hdl.handle.net/10156/5060.

students at random was most likely to yield children attending schools in different districts in the Northeast (86 percent probability) and Midwest (74 percent probability), and least likely to do so in the West (70 percent probability) and South (65 percent probability).[53] Students, in other words, were most often enrolled in separate school systems in the highly fragmented metros of the Northeast and Midwest, though the West and the South were not too far behind. Map 1, which shows the high number of school districts in the New York and Long Island area compared to the low number of school districts in southern Florida (near Miami), offers visual confirmation of these trends. Regional differences in school district size largely grew out of historical variations in how U.S. metropolitan areas developed.

Evolution of Boundary Lines in Metropolitan Communities

As different regions in the United States evolved, so did the townships, municipalities, and cities within them. Local economies and settlement histories influenced the contours of governance, as immigrants reached back into their past to find examples for the future. Those local governance structures would, in turn, help dictate the size and set up of many public school districts.[54] It is important to note here that school district lines do not always coincide directly with municipal or county lines.[55] Still, understanding the historical origin and evolution of general government boundaries provides a window into how those lines became so powerfully linked to segregation and unequal opportunity.

In the highly fragmented Northeast, which from the outset relied more heavily on industry and urbanization than the economies of the southern colonies, settlers could easily create small new municipalities under incorporation statutes. America's Midwestern areas followed suit, influenced in part by the creation of townships under the Northwest Ordinance of 1787.[56] These practices tracked closely with the parts of industrial England dominated by towns and urban areas.[57] Meanwhile, in the more agricultural U.S. South (and later, the West), county-based legal structures were imported from rural England.[58] Yet as events in Memphis illustrate, parts of the country traditionally associated with broader boundaries have begun to draw upon old statutes and practices to splinter into smaller, more exclusive communities.

Early on, when cities had considerable power to annex areas beyond their borders, bridging urban-suburban boundaries was relatively easy.

America's urban centers grew rapidly between 1850 and 1910, erasing and enlarging boundaries with every expansion. The contentious politics of urban annexation were ameliorated by the fact that, without being taken over by the city, new suburban municipalities often lacked the capacity to meet crucial infrastructure and service needs like water and sewage lines, transportation and public schools.[59] After 1910, however, resistance to urban annexation increased markedly.

Immigration, both within and beyond America's borders, played a key role in the development of that resistance. The first great migration of African Americans to the urban cities of the North was in the works, fueled by a mixture of "push-pull" factors. The pushes included the ascendance of Jim Crow laws as well as a sudden drop off in the South's cotton production due to the arrival of the Mexican boll weevil. The pulls were the labor demands fueled by the Industrial Revolution and the onset of World War I. More than half a million blacks left the South for cities like Philadelphia, New York, Cleveland, and Chicago between 1910 and 1920.[60] At the same time, a second wave of European immigration brought significant numbers of Poles, Italians, and Jews to the factories of northern cities. These eastern and southern European groups were much less integrated into the social fabric of America's industrial cities than the Irish and German immigrants that preceded them.[61] The surge of different racial and ethnic groups was also accompanied by hardening economic divisions, as industry conditions helped widen the gap between the managerial and working class.

Increasingly, the political lines dividing big cities and their surrounding suburbs came to represent desired barriers that could help seal off affluent white enclaves from rising racial and economic diversity. While whites regularly used violence, rioting, and intimidation to define and control city-suburban boundaries and, where they differed, the lines surrounding growing black ghettoes,[62] they also employed other, less overt tactics. Widespread zoning laws and local ordinances legally sanctioned racial discrimination in housing, persisting even after a 1917 judicial decision declared the practices illegal.[63] Members of neighborhood associations also came together to establish housing covenants, or informal agreements—rarely broken—restricting the sale of homes to members of other races.[64] Special district forms of government also cropped up during this period. These structures paved the way for suburban municipalities to gain independence from cities while still allowing them to reap the benefits of city services through the creation of entities like regional water and sewage agreements.⁶⁵ In the end, the fluidity of the urban-suburban boundary gave way to something much more concrete once the erasure of those lines began to carry heavy racial and economic implications.

Federal housing policies involving the use of boundaries compounded the discriminatory actions of local players. Inequitable government lending policies, dating back to the practice of redlining, were solidified during the New Deal. The 1933 Home Owner's Loan Corporation (HOLC) established the practice of assigning governmental ratings for mortgage assistance on a block-by-block basis. Ratings ranged from the highest level of approval, one, through the lowest, four (ratings of four were drawn with boundaries of red ink, hence the term "redlining"). Two behemoth federal programs, the Federal Housing Administration and the Veteran's Administration, formed to provide mortgage relief to victims of the Great Depression and to returning World War II veterans, subsequently adopted the rating system pioneered under HOLC. Racialized housing discrimination in America's metropolitan areas spread and deepened as newer, white (and increasingly suburban) neighborhoods were continually subsidized as a result of higher federal government ratings.⁶⁶

The Depression and the advent of World War II prompted a second black migration northward, into the now deeply etched urban ghettos of Detroit, Chicago, New York, Baltimore, Cleveland, Buffalo, and others. To accommodate the growing number of black residents, urban real estate agents and developers helped expand the boundaries of segregated black neighborhoods by engaging in a practice known as blockbusting.⁶⁷ Blockbusting began with real estate agents helping a family of color purchase a home on a neighborhood block dominated by white families. Panicked white residents would begin selling their properties at low prices, benefiting the realtors and developers who bought them up—only to turn around and sell them at steep profits to incoming minority residents.⁶⁸ The practice preyed upon the racial fears of whites, at the same time financially gouging first-time minority homebuyers.

Black migration into city neighborhoods coincided with the federally subsidized white migration out of them. Construction of the federal highway system (often through historically black communities) opened up easy access to the neighborhoods beyond the city limits,⁶⁹ but redlining, restrictive covenants, and other discriminatory practices meant that the post–World War II suburban housing boom was largely closed off to buyers of color. Thus, as metropolitan centers became more sprawling, they also became more racially fragmented.[70]

In the 1950s and '60s, federally funded "urban renewal" programs sought to revive downtowns by designating certain areas as blighted and clearing them.[71] Urban renewal forced many black and low-income residents into new, less centrally located—though still within the city limits—high-rise housing complexes increasingly segregated by both class and race.[72] In Indianapolis, for example, the ten low-income public housing projects constructed between 1966 and 1970 were all located within the city limits, and within several years black residents made up 98 percent of the projects' population.[73]

Even as the boundaries defining urban ghettoes expanded, surrounding suburban communities remained overwhelmingly white and affluent. From redlining to highway construction to urban renewal practices, the demographic characteristics associated with urban and suburban life bore the heavy imprint of deliberate government action. As a special Senate committee headed up by Senator Walter Mondale noted in 1972, "The federal government's involvement in residential segregation was not a matter of inadvertence or neglect. It was conscious, stated policy."[74]

Schools, as chapter 2 shows, played a significant and complementary role in the development of segregated neighborhoods throughout the twentieth century. Based on the preceding narrative, though, the basic outlines of the typical American metropolis in the mid-1970s—as the Supreme Court began to deliberate about segregation and the role of school district lines in the milestone *Milliken v. Bradley* case—should be clear. Through concerted action, revolving in many ways around the nature and presence of boundaries, separate central city and suburban school systems were already well on their way to becoming doubly segregated by both race and class. Segregation between school districts, largely unforeseen at the time of the 1954 *Brown* decision, now stood squarely in the way of achieving meaningful and lasting desegregation in most metropolitan areas.

What the Courts Almost Did about Boundary Lines and School Segregation

Over the past half century, the courts have played a central role in expanding and restricting access to equal educational opportunity. This is not, as one prominent legal mind noted, because lawyers were eagerly seeking new areas of business. It is because—as the history of the color lines crisscrossing American cities so amply illustrates—many barriers to full equality of educational opportunity were rooted in law and policy.[75]

By 1973, approximately 70 percent of students attending public schools in the city of Richmond were black. In stark contrast, white students accounted for about 90 percent of the enrollment in the two surrounding suburban school systems.[76] The dramatic differences in the racial makeup of the metropolitan area led *Time* magazine to describe Richmond's suburbs as a "white noose encircling a predominately black central city."[77] Similarly, in the heavily industrialized Detroit region, close to 70 percent of the city enrollment was black, while numerous outlying suburban districts were over 80 percent white.[78] Such patterns were not unique to these two metros.[79] What distinguished Richmond and Detroit from the rest, though, were concerted judicial efforts in the lower courts to remedy metropolitan patterns of school segregation through solutions involving both city and suburban districts.

When it came to school segregation, the U.S. district court judges in the Richmond and Detroit cases felt similarly about the matter of district boundary lines. The judge overseeing the Detroit litigation wrote, "School district lines are simply matters of political convenience and may not be used to deny constitutional rights."[80] In Richmond, Judge Robert Merhige had reached nearly the same conclusion several months earlier. "The proof here overwhelmingly establishes that school division lines between Richmond and the counties here coincide with no natural obstacles to speak of," Merhige stated, "and do in fact work to confine blacks on a consistent, wholesale basis within the city, where they reside in segregated neighborhoods."[81] In ordering city-suburban desegregation remedies, each judge relied on a line of reasoning—heavily backed by precedent—that viewed local units of government like school districts as ultimately having to answer to the state.[82] The state, in turn, was responsible for ensuring that all of its citizens received equal protection under the law as guaranteed by the Fourteenth Amendment. It followed that states had the power to redraw district boundaries if one or more of the districts under their purview acted in a segregative manner.[83]

Yet in 1974, ignoring the careful reasoning of the district courts, along with extensive evidence pointing toward the culpability of an array of state and local actors in fostering residential and school segregation, plans for the metropolitan remedies ordered in Detroit and Richmond came to a screeching halt in the U.S. Supreme Court. A sharply divided Court issued a ruling in the Detroit-based *Milliken v. Bradley* case that has been described as a "tragic decision that in many ways sealed the fate of cities" and "the watershed of racial integration in America's schools."[84] *Milliken* made it extremely difficult, though not impossible, to overcome the lines dividing city and suburban school systems through court-ordered metropolitan desegregation remedies. The Richmond case met with a similar fate. Several months prior to *Milliken*, a tied U.S. Supreme Court let stand the appellate court's decision to overturn the district judge's city-suburban desegregation plan for Richmond.

In both instances, a single vote would have yielded a decidedly different outcome for many American communities. On one side was a group that found the scope of metropolitan remedies too burdensome, noting the "logistical and other serious problems attending large-scale transportation of students."[85] (Notably, though, because the district court's order involved the strategic pairing of smaller urban-suburban segments within the broader Detroit metro, the metropolitan plan would have resulted in less transportation than what ultimately occurred.)[86] On the other stood four justices who agreed with the district court judges on the essential matter of state culpability for patterns of residential and school segregation. Justice Thurgood Marshall summed up this position best when he wrote, "the rights at issue in this case are too fundamental to be abridged on grounds as superficial as those relied on by the majority today. . . . Our nation, I fear, will be ill-served by the Court's refusal to remedy separate and unequal education, for unless our children begin to learn together, there is little hope that our people will ever learn to live together."[87]

Indeed, in many ways, *Milliken* represented the beginning of the end of what turned out to be a short period of concerted judicial action to remedy patterns of school segregation. After numerous years of delay, in 1968 the Supreme Court clearly outlined what a desegregated school system looked like before the law and, in 1971, delineated the tools that could be used to fulfill *Brown*'s integration mandate. The first ruling indicated that separate schools were to be eliminated "root and branch," by ensuring that dual systems of student and teacher assignment, transportation, extracurriculars, and facilities were dismantled.[88] The second held that districts could employ extensive transportation in order to break the link between segregated neighborhoods and segregated schools. In 1973, the Supreme Court also heard the first major desegregation case involving a northern city (where the absence of explicit Jim Crow laws made proving segregative action somewhat more difficult) and found widespread evidence of government discrimination. *Keyes* helped set the standard for proof of intentional school segregation in the North by outlining a number of common school policies that could be considered discriminatory. These included neighborhood assignment plans that maintained segregation, constructing schools and drawing or redrawing attendance boundaries in ways that continued or exacerbated segregation, and student transfer procedures that promoted segregation.[89]

The political winds on the court were shifting, however. In his first term, President Nixon had the opportunity to appoint four justices to the Supreme Court. All eventually sided with the majority in the *Milliken* decision. In documents and recordings later made public, it became clear that President Nixon considered opposition to desegregation-related busing absolutely crucial for his nominees. Hostility to integration was part of Nixon's "southern strategy," an intense campaign to realign American politics by turning out the South for Republicans. An exchange between Nixon and his chief of staff in the early aftermath of the lower court's Detroit decision helps illustrate Nixon's strategy around issues of school integration. "Wait till you get your Court," the aide told the president, "maybe you can get it turned around."[90] Ultimately, the final decision in the *Milliken* case showed that President Nixon's appointees did indeed help reverse the city-suburban merger in Detroit.

Yet the door remained slightly ajar for court-ordered metropolitan desegregation remedies. In describing what prevented them from ordering a city-suburban remedy in Detroit, the justices outlined what would, in fact, be necessary to prove an interdistrict violation of the right to equal protection under the law in other places. Based on the opinions of Justices Berger and Stewart, plaintiffs seeking a desegregation remedy covering multiple school districts needed to prove that:

- Discriminatory policies within one district had "a significant segregative effect in another"
- A state violated the Fourteenth Amendment by deliberately drawing or redrawing school district lines on a racial basis
- Public officials "contributed to the separation of the races ... by purposeful racial discriminatory use of State housing or zoning laws."[91]

Because of the latter points, approaches that sought to tackle school and housing segregation together and/or litigation claiming that a state bore responsibility for any patterns of school segregation existing within its borders were considered viable.[92] In the years following the *Milliken* decision, successful federal cases resulting in metropolitan desegregation remedies were mounted in St. Louis, Missouri; Wilmington, Delaware; Louisville, Kentucky; and Indianapolis, Indiana. In all, roughly fifteen regions comprehensively desegregated students across the city-suburban divide through various means.[93] Many were aided by low levels of local government fragmentation, friendly business and political elites, and/or the presence of countywide school districts.[94] An additional eight metros have engaged in city-suburban student transfer programs for the purpose of desegregation, and several communities, namely in Connecticut, have launched magnet schools that desegregate students across district boundaries.[95] So despite *Milliken*'s limits, a number of locales—including three of the four regions that are the subject of this book—did experience city-suburban school desegregation efforts.

The Feasibility and Desirability of Rearranging School District Boundary Lines to Desegregate

Even in the absence of strong leadership from the Supreme Court, a range of experts and groups, including the mid-1970s-era U.S. Commission on Civil Rights, maintained vocal support for metropolitan desegregation. They viewed it as by far the most effective way to achieve meaningful and stable progress on school desegregation in America's changing metro areas, an effort seen as crucial to advancing equality in areas like employment and housing. Indeed, bridging city and suburban lines for the purpose of desegregation had already proven feasible in a number of locations. William Taylor, a former member of the Commission on Civil Rights, offered a particularly astute analysis of the viability of metropolitan school desegregation. A synthesis of several of his arguments follows.

First and foremost, even without a judicial mandate, school districts had (and continue to have) the power in all but two states to reorganize—and many had already done so in the wave of rural school consolidations that swept the country at midcentury.[96] School system mergers, in other words, were administratively feasible. Indeed, the merger of Memphis and Shelby County highlights the ongoing viability of regional school district consolidation.

Second, in order to address the contentious politics of consolidation—also showcased in Memphis and Shelby County—experts argued that city-suburban mergers need not result in the loss of "local control."[97] While federal efforts to implement *Brown* in spite of fierce resistance at the state and local levels had long meant that local control was a euphemism for preserving school segregation, legitimate concerns about muting community voices in larger regional districts surfaced. This was particularly true in instances when African Americans had finally gained a foothold in city school administration only to face, with the prospect of a merger, the possibility of heavily diluted influence in a broader school system. Importantly, though, the creation of a city-suburban school district did not have to mean the loss of control over key administrative functions like the hiring and firing of teachers, control of the purse, and school curriculum. When it came to desegregation, the only aspect that the regional district needed to control was student assignment. More geographically compact subdistricts could retain power over other aspects of administration.

Third, city-suburban school desegregation did not necessitate extensive transportation policies. Not unlike proposals designed to maximize community voice, many metropolitan desegregation plans called for the division of the larger district into smaller units. In some instances these subdistricts resembled pieces of a pie, with the wedges slicing through portions of a central city and including parts of the outlying suburbs. The subdistricts covered a considerably smaller geographic area and allowed districts to minimize transportation time. For example, the massive Clark County, Nevada (which includes the city of Las Vegas), school district actually managed to decrease student bus times during the implementation of its desegregation plan.

Fourth, metropolitan school districts could promote, rather than detract from, administrative and fiscal efficiencies. Consolidating multiple school systems into one meant that duplicative central office positions could be eliminated and other bureaucratic functions like transportation could be streamlined. In many cases, mergers also opened up the prospect of a larger tax base from which the school system could draw financial support.

Finally, city-suburban school desegregation represented a long-lasting remedy for segregation in public schools. At the time, opponents of school desegregation were increasingly citing concerns about "white flight." The provocative phrase referred to the aforementioned declining white population in many urban centers, along with a corresponding rise in the suburban population. While some influential earlier research attributed white flight directly to school desegregation⁹⁸—and, in doing so, generally called into question the viability and desirability of such efforts—others presented alternative explanations.

In a seminal review of the literature on white flight, researchers concluded that the demographic trends in question were long standing. Desegregation was not related to white flight in smaller cities they found, and while desegregation in large cities might accelerate white flight temporarily, patterns could be expected to stabilize within a year after a desegregation plan was implemented.⁹⁹ Subsequent analyses continued to counter the earlier research, suggesting that it was impossible to parcel out the exact causes of white or middle-class flight, originating in the early twentieth century's "streetcar suburbs" and exacerbated by post–World War II federal policy and demographic shifts discussed earlier in this chapter. Desegregation experts further argued—and this is where the desirability of a metropolitan solution comes in—that by removing the option for a quick exit to a nearby suburb not undergoing desegregation, city-suburban plans helped ameliorate patterns of white flight.¹⁰⁰ Evidence from places that implemented city-suburban school desegregation bore this out.¹⁰¹

Despite the compelling case for pursuing regional school desegregation as a strategy to stabilize rapidly changing schools and communities and, fundamentally, to ensure that equal educational opportunities are available to all students, its successes have been largely ignored. The years leading up to *Milliken v. Bradley* represented a high water mark for desegregation efforts; the years since have been defined by a gradual but steady retrenchment. Today, the subject of school integration is often forgotten in the clamor over testing, national standards, choice, and teacher accountability.

Contemporary Education Policy Ignores the Role of Boundaries in Fostering Inequality

In 1983, the National Commission on Excellence in Education, charged by the Reagan administration to assess the quality of teaching and learning, published an influential report called *A Nation at Risk*. Its provocative opening included the following line, "If an unfriendly foreign power had attempted to impose on America the mediocre educational performance that exists today, we might well have viewed it as an act of war."¹⁰² Those words helped usher in a new era of education reform that continues to the present day.

Written at the height of the Cold War, *A Nation at Risk* suggested that higher educational standards would help the United States regain its competitive edge in the face of what the authors considered evidence of decline. In order to ensure that students were learning new standards, reformers sought to put in place oversight mechanisms to measure and document progress. The most basic form of accountability, adopted first by individual states and later as part of a bipartisan federal law known as No Child Left Behind, took the form of standardized testing. Many of those tests became high stakes for students, with promotion or graduation attached to success or failure.

Efforts to provide families with a menu of school choice offerings, both public and private, appeared alongside the standards and accountability movement. While some forms of choice, like magnet schools, had roots in desegregation, others were holdovers from Massive Resistance, when southern school districts sought to avoid *Brown*'s mandate by offering publicly funded vouchers for white students to attend segregated private schools.[103] Charter schools, generally defined as public schools governed by a chartering organization and granted a large measure of autonomy from existing local and state systems, also gained a foothold during this era. With substantial—and again, bipartisan—federal support, the number of charter schools multiplied rapidly, from zero in 1991 to nearly 6,000 in 2014.[104]

Standards-based accountability and school choice reforms contrast with education policies from the civil rights era, which emphasized the expansion of access to and equity across all levels of schooling.[105] During the 1960s and '70s, educational rights for historically marginalized groups like African Americans, immigrants, students with disabilities, and women were ensured with the passage of key policies and laws, including the Civil Rights Act of 1964, the Elementary and Secondary Education Act of 1966, the Bilingual Education Act of 1968, Title IX in 1972, and the Individuals with Disabilities Act of 1974. Federal dollars flowed to school districts to help support high-poverty schools and spur desegregation efforts, as well as to establish prekindergarten programs in the form of Head Start. The underlying principles guiding many of the education-related policies in the 1960s emphasized schools as instruments of social mobility and opportunity.

Student outcomes from the two different streams of education policy suggest reengaging with the era associated with the expansion of civil rights and equal educational opportunity is crucial. The National Assessment of Educational Progress (NAEP), sometimes referred to as "the nation's report card," offers an important overview of student gains in reading and mathematics since the 1970s. Unlike results from tests administered by individual states, student NAEP data can be accurately compared across the country and over time. NAEP trends indicate two central themes: (1) During what was arguably the height of the implementation of standards-based accountability, between the years 2004 and 2008, the racial achievement gap did not narrow,[106] and (2) achievement gaps between white students and black and Latino students closed most significantly as the reforms linked to the civil rights era took effect.[107]

Of course test scores are just one, limited way of measuring student educational progress. Graduation and college-going rates are also critical. More positive news is available on the high school completion front, as the U.S. recently posted its highest four-year on-time graduation rate since 1976.[108] But those rates dip significantly for historically underserved students identifying as black, Latino, and American Indian. Even starker gaps, by both race and socioeconomic status, emerge when considering overall educational attainment.[109]

A constellation of factors, many of which are related to segregation and the boundary lines that help solidify it, is responsible for the persistence of achievement and opportunity gaps. But the reforms associated with the two recent eras of education policy stem from fundamentally different diagnoses of the causes of inequality in schooling outcomes.[110] Civil rights–era efforts were explicitly designed to address systemic segregation and discrimination, persistent racial and economic inequality, and the intergenerational cycle of poverty. While education was viewed as a crucial element of efforts to combat widespread racial and economic inequality, it was not considered the sole element. Standards-based assessments and the expansion of school choice, on the other hand, target "the soft bigotry of low expectations [for students]" that President George W. Bush famously spoke of, and promote more educational choice to stimulate competition, reduce inefficiencies, and promote higher performance. These market-based reforms view bureaucratic red tape and mismanagement, teachers—and the unions with which they are associated—and underwhelming standards of learning as the crux of the issues confronting America's education system. The narrow focus on such dimensions has effectively promoted the idea that if we can redesign the standards and hold schools accountable for them, in addition to fixing the

Why Boundary Lines Matter So Much 31

bureaucracy and the teachers, deeply rooted societal inequities will disappear. Indeed, contemporary education reforms have occurred in conjunction with policies that have steadily shredded the social safety net.[111] This myopic view fails to take into account the obvious importance of addressing the contextual factors surrounding schools, including distressed neighborhoods, rising rates of child poverty, poor nutrition, lack of health care, and the like.[112]

Today, despite decidedly mixed evidence for current reforms, the policies that evolved out of the *Nation at Risk* report continue to be extended. In the midst of the Great Recession, Obama's Race to the Top initiative dangled billions in front of cash-strapped states willing to adopt his educational priorities. In order to receive the money, states agreed to implement teacher evaluation systems tied to student achievement, expand charter schools, and adopt school "turnaround" models in the face of continual failure to lift student test scores. With the advent of these policies, high-stakes tests for students have become high-stakes tests for educators and principals.

Prompted in part by the federal government, states have doubled down on contemporary reform efforts that largely ignore the link between segregation, opportunity, and achievement. Consider again the example of Memphis mentioned at the opening of this chapter. The state of Tennessee now operates a special district within what remains of the Memphis-Shelby County merged system for schools that experience persistent failure. Established with support from Race to the Top dollars, schools in the so-called Achievement School District are run by a mixture of state-appointed officials or charter school operators. In establishing the Achievement School District, Tennessee drew upon the experience of Louisiana, which created a state-run district in New Orleans consisting nearly entirely of charter schools in the wake of Hurricane Katrina's devastation. Results from both efforts have been ambiguous amid clear evidence that impacted schools are highly segregated.[113] Moreover, in Tennessee, an A–F grading system signifying how a school system's students fared in the aggregate on various standardized tests contributed to the conversations surrounding the city-suburban merger. As noted above, academic achievement is tightly linked to the racial and economic makeup of schools, as well as to the backgrounds of individual students. The A–F system added fuel to the fire for suburban supporters of municipal school districts in Shelby County who pointed to the importance of protecting or creating highly graded school systems.[114] (The simplistic A–F school district metric has recently been expanded to individual schools in Tennessee. Fifteen other states have similar policies.)[115]

As contemporary education reform efforts in Memphis underscore, the United States has been engaged in a three-decade-long effort to make good on the promise of *Plessy*, not *Brown*.[116] Despite some highly publicized beat-the-odds stories, most federal, state, and local efforts to make separate schools equal have met with little lasting or wide-scale success.[117] Yet even though the current stream of education policy has largely turned a blind eye to metropolitan fragmentation and the underlying issues of poverty, racism, and inequality that go with it, other policy arenas are paying attention—and a movement is gaining steam.

Regionalism Seeks to Overcome Boundaries but Largely Neglects Education

Regionalism is not a particularly novel idea. It first surfaced at the turn of the last century as cities were rapidly expanding, and came to light again in the 1960s and '70s around the same time that metropolitan school desegregation was first being discussed.[118] For the last decade and a half, the idea has experienced another resurgence.[119] The basic notion driving today's regional agenda is that cities, suburbs, and exurbs are inextricably connected. Key linkages include housing, commuting, transportation systems, cultural and historical amenities, media markets, sports teams, and other social ties that contribute to the identity of a metro area. In fact, some of these features constitute the very definition of a metropolitan area in federal government terminology.[120]

Regionalists argue that social, economic, political, and environmental issues do not simply stop at any one boundary line in a metro area. Racial and economic segregation in urban cores, deterioration in the suburbs closest to the city, and explosive growth on the exurban fringe that redirects resources away from other struggling parts of a metro all present problems that cannot be solved in isolation. In other words, the health and fate of each depend on the vitality of the other.[121] With more cooperation and sharing of resources across different spheres of a metro, as regional expert Myron Orfield has stated, come "opportunities for economic advancement and social mobility for all citizens."[122]

Operationalizing the concept of regionalism can take many forms. Portland, for instance, started by drawing a bright line around the outer edges of the metro area and prohibiting development past that point. This forced planners and land use zoning committees to think creatively about ways to make the most out of existing spaces contained within the metro limits. Portland's line helped fuel downtown and inner suburban ring revitalization while limiting sprawl and other environmental concerns at the edge.[123] Those efforts were aided by concerted coordination between land use, transportation, and affordable housing policies, all of which have important implications for schools.[124]

Regional governance possibilities also vary. Some places have created regional councils with representatives from smaller communities across the metro in order to make sure all constituencies have a voice. To answer critics concerned with local control, a type of "federated regionalism" seeks to place important decisions affecting the entire metro area at the level of the region, but allows local governments to retain control of other functions. In this manner, it looks much like some metropolitan school desegregation efforts several decades ago. One current example of federated regionalism has cropped up in the Twin Cities, which operates under a tax base–sharing system that mandates that each of the 186 cities in the seven-county area place 40 percent of growth in the assessed value of commercial and industrial property into a regional pot of revenue that is taxed at an area-wide rate. The money is then equitably distributed across municipalities.[125] A Metropolitan Council, which has important regional land use, affordable housing, and transportation planning capabilities, also exists in the Twin Cities, even as smaller, unrelated government units manage aspects of local governance not currently tied into the regional system.[126]

Foes of the regional agenda insist that the presence of clearly defined and independently governed localities offer families and businesses crucial choices. Stakeholders can "vote with their feet" and move to a community that best matches their desired level of government service and taxation.[127] Competition for these people will, in turn, stimulate innovation and improvement in the quality of services, housing, and other amenities offered. But this theory is based on the assumption that all members of a metro area have the ability to move freely. It fails to acknowledge the limitations of poverty and the deeply constricted housing choices that go with it.

Change driven by the regional agenda is occurring. Across the country, downtown revitalizations seeking to build on natural attractions like rivers have taken place. Industrial-era factories are being converted into trendy living spaces that house both young and old. Expanding transportation options like bike and ride shares have taken root. Walkability and liveability are being promoted as key features of communities. Beneath these more surface improvements are efforts to shore up human capital by promoting equality and opportunity.[128]

But while regionalists willingly take on issues of fair housing, transportation, employment, pollution, and public health, education is not often at the center of these conversations. Paradoxically—given the benefits of metropolitan school desegregation laid out here and elsewhere—some speculate that this is related to past scars of desegregation. Given the resistance attached to desegregation efforts, they contend, efforts to cooperate around issues of education will be viewed as too contentious. The Denver area offers an example of this thinking. In Denver, contemporary and hard-won regional cooperation is centered on economic development and access to transportation. But resentments from urban annexation attempts during the school desegregation era still run deep. At the time, the city's efforts to expand met with fierce resistance as previously unincorporated areas incorporated to avoid takeover. A popular vote limiting subsequent annexation efforts was attributed largely to resistance to school desegregation efforts occurring in the city of Denver.[129]

The fact that regional cooperation around issues of transportation or economic development may be less contentious—in Denver and elsewhere—than dealing with how equal educational opportunity is distributed across regions does not make them more impactful. Attempts to overcome school lines remain divisive; the boundary battles taking place in Memphis today amplify this truth. Yet what we choose to do about school district boundaries in the future remains absolutely central to the health of our collective communities.

As this book illustrates, regionalism ignores education to the detriment of the movement. Efforts to reduce the fragmentation and related segregation of school systems are very much related to progress on other key fronts like housing. Indeed, the close interaction between school and housing segregation is influenced by the way the boundaries that help define school and district enrollments are drawn. Understanding just how deeply school and housing policies are woven together is the subject of chapter 2.

CHAPTER TWO

School Policy Is Housing Policy, and Vice Versa

Several years ago, on a bright Southern California afternoon, a professor teaching a graduate seminar on metropolitan inequality posed the following question: "Which should we tackle first, school or housing segregation?" It sparked a fierce debate, cleaving the class roughly down the middle. That same question is now a favorite topic of conversation in my own classes. And each time it is asked, a similar sequence of responses occurs. The first voices usually fall squarely in the housing camp, arguing that sustainable progress on school desegregation will occur only if underlying residential patterns become more integrated. Racially segregated, high-poverty neighborhoods disadvantage students and schools in numerous ways—surely, as a student will put forth, efforts to combat these housing inequities should come first? And when it comes to the benefits of desegregated residential patterns, someone might add that living among people who are different from one another is an important way to enrich and expand notions of community.

But as the conversation takes off in this direction, with many quickly willing to hop aboard the housing train, another segment of the class begins to look thoughtful. After several minutes, one of these thinkers will tentatively raise a hand. "Wouldn't it be quicker to confront school segregation?" the student will ask. Suddenly the mood shifts again as the class sorts through the implications of that question. Student assignment plans that emphasize racial and/or economic diversity in schools, they muse, can be implemented within a single year. Dramatic change is possible in a very short period of time, especially if the plans are implemented across multiple districts. Moreover, as a student is certain to point out, it is change that impacts the youngest members of society. The pros and cons of this piece of the dilemma are then weighed, with one side arguing that exposure to difference at a young age is critical if we want to confront prejudice before it has a chance to take root. But the other side pushes against the idea of so intimately involving our most vulnerable segment of the population—and awakening the protective tendencies of their parents—in the difficult business of righting long-standing wrongs. Finally, as the last gasps of this discussion start to fade, a lone hand will flutter. An encouraging nod from the professor elicits the following:

"Well . . . I guess . . . I mean, shouldn't we be thinking about school and housing issues together?"

As sensible as the suggestion is (and truthfully, the entire session is geared toward this moment of clarity), rarely have we considered school and housing segregation in concert with one another. There are a few important examples of cooperation, to be sure. In the 1970s and 1980s, a handful of communities—including two of the metros studied in this book—designed school desegregation plans that took housing patterns into account. These policies usually exempted stably integrated neighborhoods from transportation requirements and/or released individual students from busing if they made integrative moves with their families. Other places made it clear that government housing decisions that contributed to school resegregation would not be allowed, and worked instead to ensure that public housing was distributed evenly throughout the city or metro.[1] For the most part, though, education and housing stakeholders interested in promoting desegregation have operated independently of one another. This is particularly ironic given that officials in both spheres continue to work together to construct and maintain the color line.[2]

We are at a critical juncture when it comes to issues of school and residential segregation. On the housing front, a broad but commonly used measure of segregation suggests a slow decrease in residential separation between whites and nonwhites over the past century.[3] While the decline may seem encouraging, a closer look at the data and methods used to arrive at that conclusion indicate that caution is warranted. First, while many experts agree that the existence of almost all-white neighborhoods is on the decline as Asian and Latino families have slowly moved in, nearly all-black neighborhoods remain stubbornly segregated.[4] Indeed, a groundbreaking analysis of census data reveals that the vast majority of black residents (roughly 67 percent) living in America's ghetto communities a generation ago continue to live in ghetto communities today.[5]

Second, the relationship between racially segregated neighborhoods and neighborhoods of concentrated poverty in many ways is strengthening.[6] Nearly one out of every four African Americans lived in a neighborhood of concentrated poverty across the 2007–11 time period, compared to roughly one out of every five in 2000.[7] Low-income black families are also almost three times more likely to live in neighborhoods of concentrated poverty than low-income white families. And even for black (and

Latino) families at higher ends of the income distribution, the likelihood that they will live among families with considerably lower incomes persists.[8] Race, then, plays a much larger role in determining the type of neighborhood a family lives in than income.

Third, the general trend toward integration, driven in large part by the growing suburbanization of minority groups, may not be stable. In other words, suburban neighborhoods that appear to be diverse at this moment in time will not necessarily stay that way.[9] Moreover, in high-poverty urban communities, some of the recent good news regarding the decline of segregation can be attributed to the fact that black and Latino families are now living in close proximity to one another in underresourced neighborhoods.[10]

And fourth, even relying on the most optimistic measure, declines in black-white housing segregation are unfolding at a glacial pace. Over the past four decades, the black-white dissimilarity index fell five points per decade, on average.[11] Full integration would take another 120 years at the same rate.

When it comes to school segregation, the picture is even less encouraging. Most experts agree that levels of school segregation now have surpassed those of residential segregation. One study of racial segregation in southern metropolitan areas concluded that the courts' retrenchment on school desegregation policies would have an even more negative impact on segregation in schools were it not for slowly declining levels of residential segregation.[12] Though a debate over the best way to measure segregation emerges here,[13] the fact that black and Latino students remain extremely isolated from white (and, to a similar extent, Asian) students is uncontested. Analyses of the degree to which students of different races come into contact with one another indicate that school resegregation has been on the rise for black students since the early 1990s, and for Latino students since data have been collected.[14]

The purpose of this chapter is to lay out the basic relationship between school and housing segregation. It will show once again the role that school boundary lines play in shaping it, and trace the metropolitan, legal, and theoretical history undergirding the school-housing connection. Acknowledging the deep interrelationship between school and residential segregation is critical to grasping the new research presented in this book and, ultimately, to making significant progress on both fronts.

Basic Relationship between School and Housing Segregation

The common practice of drawing school attendance boundaries to encircle nearby neighborhoods is the main driver of the reciprocal relationship between school and housing segregation.[15] Because attendance zones concretely define the neighborhoods with which schools are associated, disentangling residential decisions from schooling preferences is extremely difficult. These zoning lines structure segregation by helping to ensure that any racial or economic isolation present in neighborhoods will be reflected in school enrollments. On a larger scale, as chapter 1 noted, district lines send demographic signals about entire systems of education. Families with children moving to or across the typical metro thus face a series of racialized decisions between attendance areas and school districts. And while those choices are often billed as free and open, for many families they are dramatically constrained by race and income level.

"Choosing" Neighborhoods and Schools

Families with resources talk about the ability to buy into a better school zone or district, based on the assumption that a wealthy neighborhood means good schools.[16] In many ways, their reasoning is accurate. Property taxes that continue to make up a significant portion of local education funding are related to home values, and housing prices in turn are linked to school districts and school zones.[17] These realities bolster the relationship between educational and housing choices, making it difficult for lower-income families to gain entrance into highly resourced schools.

In addition to the limitation that socioeconomic status places on a family's ability to choose a neighborhood and school, racial disparities related to the accumulation of wealth in America also help define those choices.[18] Data from the 2011 census indicate that the average black household in the United States reports a net worth of $6,314, compared to $110,500 for the average white household. The gap between whites and blacks has actually grown wider in the last decade, exceeding the same gap in South Africa during apartheid.[19]

The wealth gap translates into differential rates of home ownership for racial groups and, relatedly, differential racial access to wealthy neighborhoods and schools.[20] It has important roots in discriminatory federal mortgage practices begun during the New Deal and expanded in the aftermath of World War II. Whites benefited from generous government subsidies for home ownership in new suburban communities. But as the effects of redlining took hold, blacks were consigned to declining neighborhoods in urban cores—and thus systematically locked out of the single greatest opportunity for wealth building in the history of the United States.[21]

Predatory private lending practices compounded rampant discrimination in the public sector. A call to action by *The Atlantic*'s Ta-Nehisi Coates recounts the story of Clyde Ross, an African American man who left the South during the second Great Migration in search of a better life, free from the perils of Jim Crow. In 1961, Ross purchased a home in an integrated area on Chicago's West Side. Yet when a major repair job was needed just three months after the move, Ross discovered that he was not the actual owner of his home. He was paying his mortgage "on contract" to the man who sold the home. "On contract" meant that Ross was responsible for making monthly payments, but could not accrue equity—the central mechanism by which home owners acquire wealth—until the contract was paid in full. Instead, the seller (a middle man who bought the home from the original home owner at a discounted price) collected steep profits and promptly evicted families when they could not pay. A new black family would be brought in, accelerating profits and hardening a vicious cycle. These types of arrangements were extremely common in Chicago (one estimate suggested that 85 percent of black home owners in the city bought on contract) and across the country.[22]

Of course, discriminatory mortgage lending practices continue today. Private lenders still disproportionately deny mortgage financing to minority and low-income home buyers.[23] When these groups do receive assistance, it is often through products with higher interest rates and less-than-favorable conditions.[24] The Great Recession turned on these types of subprime loans, which often operated outside of federal regulations, drawing public attention to a widespread form of contemporary discrimination.

Meanwhile, whites continue to benefit from their historical wealth-building advantages. A series of interviews with more than 200 families in several large American metros uncovered an extensive web of family assistance for young, lower-middle-class white families.[25] Grandparents, for example, would often help place a down payment—sometimes covering it outright—on a home in a school district that would otherwise be out of reach for their children and grandchildren.[26] For families of color who did not have the opportunity to build those resources a generation or two ago, opportunities for home ownership in an expensive neighborhood with well-funded schools are more limited.

Preferences for Certain Types of Neighborhoods and Schools

When it comes to housing, a number of studies have suggested that whites tend to prefer more racially homogeneous areas of residence, while people of color are more likely to be comfortable with diverse neighborhoods.[27] While those two competing preferences do not necessarily align, it is important to understand that the same inclinations can and do shift.[28] Research involving simple visual representations of neighborhoods with varying degrees of racial diversity shows that whites have grown far more comfortable with diverse neighborhoods over the past several decades, even though they preferred Asian or Hispanic neighbors over African Americans.[29] Hispanic and Asian participants reported similar preferences. While blacks continue to express interest in neighborhoods with high levels of diversity, an earlier desire for communities that were evenly split between whites and blacks has shifted to a preference for majority black communities.[30] That change may reflect a certain degree of "integration fatigue," or disenchantment with the prospect of racial equality, as well as a desire to seek safe haven from ongoing prejudice and discrimination.

Housing preferences are more likely to evolve in a positive direction when different groups gain exposure to one another.[31] Though schools would be a natural place for such exposure to occur, race and class continue to play a fundamental role in school choice processes among white and advantaged families.[32] Qualitative studies have attempted to dissect the underlying motivations behind moving decisions among affluent families, finding that interviewees speak knowledgeably about their housing options in relationship to school districts, even down to specific schools within the district.[33] In some cases, white home seekers are guided by perceptions of school quality unrelated to tangible educational characteristics, relying instead upon racially coded information shared among social networks. One researcher conducted extensive fieldwork on white families moving "for the schools" in a Southern California school district. She found that informal conversations passing through friend networks used simplistic labels like "good" or "bad" to describe school settings and that those designations were often strongly related to the racial or socioeconomic makeup of schools (rather than school visits or publicly available data). Such dialogues largely formed the basis for decisions about whether or not a zone or district should be sought out.[34] The cyclical nature of these processes and decisions—whereby segregated white schools attract whites with limited exposure to diversity in their own schooling experiences to segregated white neighborhoods, and vice versa—helps perpetuate racial isolation.

Homes, Property Values, and Schools

Race and racism continue to play a central role in determining access to predominantly white and wealthy neighborhoods and schools, even as our society has become less willing to acknowledge persistent discrimination. One reason for these denials may be related to the subversion of blatant racial hostilities,[35] which, in many cases, have been replaced with less obtrusive—but no less damaging—barriers to equal access to opportunity-rich neighborhoods. An intensive historical case study of Detroit indicated that white home owners became much less likely to express overt racial prejudice in the decades following World War II, relying instead on an ideology linking together home buying, property values, and racial exclusion.[36] This new dialogue around "race, property, and neighborhood integrity" allows whites to shroud racist attitudes beneath the coded language of protecting home investments.[37]

Given the evolving politics around race and home ownership, it makes sense that the racial makeup of a neighborhood or school district appears to impact real estate prices. Majority black neighborhoods exact a cost from homeowners who live there, according to regional expert David Rusk, who calls the disparate home value-to-income ratio a "segregation tax."[38] When it comes to school districts and home costs, a Connecticut study based on data from 1994 to 2004 found that housing prices varied dramatically according to the percentage of Latino students in a school system. After controlling for a variety of neighborhood variables, researchers found that higher home prices were reported in districts with fewer Latino students.[39] Using similar data, a second study found that buyers were willing to pay an average of $7,468 more for a house in order to live near a less diverse school.[40] Further south, North Carolina research examining the Charlotte housing market after the district returned to neighborhood school assignments found that housing prices varied significantly on either side of school attendance boundary lines.[41]

Beyond property values, narrow school achievement indicators like test scores herald a new way of discussing schools and neighborhoods in a coded manner. A by-product of the policy focus on testing and accountability has been the parental capacity to distill the complicated elements that come together to produce a school environment down to a single grade or numerical score. Indeed, test scores became increasingly predictive of housing prices after the passage of No Child Left Behind in 2001.[42]

A Brookings Institution study further illuminated the relationship between test scores and home prices by examining how the two are related to land-use policy. Using a variety of different data sources, the study showed that in the 100 largest U.S. metropolitan areas, housing prices were $205,000 higher, on average, near a high-scoring public school than near a low-scoring public school.[43] These price differences contributed to a situation where the typical low-income student went to a school scoring at a much lower percentile on state tests than the typical middle- or high-income student. Exclusionary zoning practices (e.g., the share of rental housing units in areas with high-performing schools was much lower than in neighborhoods with poor-performing schools) effectively blocked many low-income families' entrance into the highest-performing schools.

Real Estate Practices Rely upon Schools to Steer Clients

Numerous real estate practices are geared toward providing prospective buyers with racialized information about local schools. Any recent familiarity with smartphone applications like Zillow or Trulia illustrates this relationship. A few taps of the finger bring up detailed data on the demographic characteristics of and achievement results for the schools with which a home is associated. The human element also bolsters this information. A probe of real estate sales found that 87 percent of testers were steered into specific neighborhoods, with agents using the racial composition of school districts as a proxy for neighborhood demographics.[44] Because providing direct information about the racial composition of a neighborhood is illegal,[45] housing agents discuss school demographics or quality (which, as we saw, is often conflated with racial composition or test score results) with prospective buyers. Data on school rankings and test performance provide real estate agents with a "legally sanctioned vocabulary" to help steer clients into certain schools and neighborhoods.[46]

Interviewers in hyperfragmented Long Island, New York, found that the relationship goes both ways, with some school officials hosting meetings with realtors to tout the quality of schools in particular districts. Similar findings emerge from metropolitan Hartford, where suburban real estate and school officials worked together to promote specific school zones as high quality, generating intense interest from upwardly mobile white families looking to relocate.[47] Yet when middle-class black families began moving into the suburbs of Hartford, realtors sought to steer them into separate parts of suburbia using school-busting tactics.[48] Reminiscent of blockbusting, the scare tactic designed to facilitate profitable rapid racial turnover in formerly all-white neighborhoods, the school-busting process employs similar mechanisms to flip a whole school zone or district.[49] These efforts provide another contemporary example of close connections between the parties who help link together school and housing decisions.[50] And while those relationships continue to evolve, they are rooted in a long-standing pattern of collusion when it comes to creating and maintaining segregated neighborhoods and schools.

Historical Relationship between Segregated School and Housing Patterns

The historical connection between public and private officials seeking to shape housing and development patterns through decisions involving schools is increasingly coming to light. A growing body of literature places school construction, closure, and zoning decisions at the heart of twentieth-century metropolitan planning and development.

In the 1920s, for example, sites for new schools were increasingly selected in Raleigh, North Carolina's northwestern quadrant as part of an effort to develop whiter, wealthier neighborhoods away from what previously had been a relatively integrated urban core.[51] Adding to the draw of the anticipated new communities, existing and highly popular schools were relocated to the same northwestern part of the metro. A similar situation unfolded in Nashville, Tennessee, albeit with an additional layer of influence from the federal government. A late 1950s document authored by the U.S. Department of Health, Education and Welfare (the precursor to the more streamlined Department of Education) provided communities nationwide with pro-suburban guidelines for selecting sites for new schools. Over 80 percent of the photos included with the guidelines depicted new schools set amid a pristine landscape nearly devoid of surrounding development.[52] Coupled with urban renewal efforts, federal policies helped guide local decision-making that privileged new schools in lily-white suburbs, at the same time serving to concentrate black students in segregated urban cores. Twenty-four new schools were opened in the Nashville area between 1960 and 1972, nearly all of which were located in suburban sections of the metro.

In addition to the role that school-siting decisions played in furthering patterns of metropolitan segregation, processes involving the boundaries drawn around schools also contributed. In Flint, Michigan, for instance, historical evidence points to a widely popular program of "community education" that formally joined patterns of residential and school segregation together. The idea that schools should serve as the hub of community life spread to hundreds of school districts across the country—and remains fashionable today—but was rooted in racist ideologies and practices that actively sought to exclude African American residents.[53] To maintain segregation, school boundary decisions, new construction, and enrollment policies worked in concert with residential practices like redlining and restrictive covenants. In some cases, schools in Flint were more racially isolated than neighborhoods. By intentional design, then, community education meant segregated education.

Intentionality carries with it important legal implications. The de jure (by law) and de facto (in fact) distinction with regard to segregation, as fallible as it is,[54] remains a guiding principle of law. And over time, the judicial system, which we already know has played an outsized role in shaping access to equal educational opportunities, regarded the evidence related to the complex interactions between residential and school segregation in different ways. These shifts influenced both the design of early school desegregation remedies as well as later efforts to scale back those remedies.

The Shifting Perspective of the Courts on School and Housing Relationships

For over four decades, the courts have vacillated between formal recognition that residential and school segregation are linked by virtue of state-sanctioned policies promoting metropolitan patterns of racial discrimination, and a counterinsistence that residential segregation is driven by individual housing choices and therefore not subject to judicial remedy. Embedded within many of the decisions is an acknowledgment that boundary lines, both within and between school districts, play a tremendously important role in either promoting or preventing desegregation.

In the famous 1971 *Swann* ruling involving the Charlotte metropolitan area, Chief Justice Berger described the close connection between housing and schools. "The location of schools may influence the patterns of residential development of a metropolitan area," he wrote, "and have important impact on the composition of inner-city neighborhoods.... [New construction] may well promote segregated residential patterns which, when combined with 'neighborhood zoning,' further lock the school system into the mold of separation of the races."⁵⁵ In order to disentangle residential segregation from school segregation, the justices ultimately ordered a comprehensive transportation plan that balanced white and black students across schools in the merged city-suburban district. The two-way busing strategy meant that some white students were transported to schools in Charlotte's urban core, while some black students were carried out to suburban schools. Though controversial at first, the plan eventually enjoyed widespread support amid evidence that Charlotte's schools were among the most integrated in the nation.⁵⁶

Building upon *Swann*'s early acknowledgment of the influence school-related decisions have on housing patterns, two years later the U.S. Supreme Court clearly delineated the various ways in which school districts might exacerbate residential segregation. In the 1973 *Keyes* case, the Court wrote, "the drafting of student transfer policies, the transportation of students, and the assignment of faculty and staff, on racially identifiable bases, have the clear effect of earmarking schools according to their racial composition, and this, in turn, together with the elements of student assignment and school construction, may have a profound reciprocal effect of the racial composition of residential neighborhoods."⁵⁷

The justices indicated that policies that might reveal intentional segregation included, but were not limited to, constructing schools in racially isolated neighborhoods and drawing attendance boundaries around neighborhoods in a segregating manner.⁵⁸ Furthermore, showing proof of such practices in one part of a community necessitated a remedy for the broader jurisdiction, according to the *Keyes* decision, based on the idea that segregated schools in one area would have a ripple effect on the composition of schools in another.⁵⁹

But shortly after the breakthroughs that these cases represented, political shifts on the Supreme Court altered its position on the school-housing relationship. The lower courts' reasoning in *Milliken*, discussed earlier in the context of district boundary lines, was based in large part on ten full days of expert testimony related to the intentional segregation of neighborhoods in the Detroit area.[60] Yet a Supreme Court majority disregarded the detailed record produced by those experts. One justice went so far as to proclaim that segregation was caused by "unknown, perhaps unknowable, factors."[61] And of course the final outcome of the *Milliken* decision would be associated with exacerbating both school and housing segregation, since white families could easily avoid urban school desegregation by withdrawing to housing in a nearby suburban jurisdiction.[62]

School desegregation in Atlanta, Georgia, proceeded down a similarly bleak path. The Department of Justice brought an intricately documented case against metro Atlanta in 1979, charging that the entire housing structure of the city and suburbs was based on racial hierarchies and outright discrimination. Federal courts dismissed the case as too complex; the judges involved felt the repercussions of a remedy to address existing patterns of metropolitan segregation would have been immense.[63] In the words of the court: "to change the residential patterns which exist would be necessary to rip up the very fabric of society in a manner which is not within the province of the federal courts."[64] The federal district court further suggested that "why people live where they do can never be fully explained."[65] This positioning was heavily based in the early literature, discussed above, dealing with the racial mismatch of preferences for integrated housing. What it failed to consider, though, was the fact that individual preferences for certain types of neighborhoods were inevitably shaped by centuries of government-sponsored racial apartheid and discrimination. The Supreme Court declined to hear the Atlanta case, letting the confusion and inaction emanating from the lower levels of the federal judicial system hold sway.

In another twist involving the judicial position on the interaction between school and housing segregation, a 1985 federal court ruling (later upheld by the Supreme Court) became the first to establish a causal link between the location of public housing and patterns of school segregation.[66] The courts recognized that nearly 100 percent of subsidized housing in Yonkers, New York, was built in one corner of the municipality, thereby confining the vast majority of the area's black residents to that neighborhood and the schools with which it was associated. Based on a nuanced recognition of the state's role in fostering patterns of school and housing segregation, the courts ordered a combined remedy to address both issues.

The pendulum swung back in the other direction with a vengeance, however, as a string of conservative court decisions in the 1990s set the stage for numerous school districts to prematurely be released from judicial oversight.[67] After ruling that a showing of "good faith" efforts to desegregate schools—even if high levels of segregation or resegregation were apparent—could result in the end of court oversight (also known as achieving unitary status),[68] the Supreme Court returned to the position advanced by the majority in *Milliken*. It concluded that residential segregation was primarily the result of private housing choices made without the influence of government policy and, as a result, no longer subject to school desegregation remedies like wide-scale transportation.[69] Again, this theory relied heavily on the social science evidence related to racially disparate levels of comfort with other-race neighbors, disregarding other research suggesting that such attitudes were malleable and influenced by history, law, and policy.[70] It also drew upon a segment of white flight literature to suggest that school desegregation was ultimately unworkable since it had a negative impact on the number of white students available to integrate a district.[71] But as renowned school desegregation scholar Gary Orfield has pointed out, a key contradiction was embedded in these rationales. On the one hand, the court's position assumed school desegregation had a significant impact on the behavior of white families, prompting them to seek housing in suburban districts that were not under court order to desegregate. (This dilemma was in large part of the Court's own making, of course, given *Milliken*'s role in sparing the suburbs from desegregation.) On the other, it suggested that it was impossible to understand the attitudes motivating an individual family's preference for a certain level of homogeneity in their neighborhood.

Despite the convoluted thinking that dominated the Court at the time, some recognition of the research base informing earlier decisions in *Swann* and *Keyes* remained.[72] In the concurring opinion written in the 1992 *Freeman* case, Justice Blackmun discussed the possibility of school racial demographics providing signals to families and exacerbating residential segregation. "Close examination is necessary," he wrote, "because what might seem to be purely private preferences in housing may in fact have been created, in part, by actions of the school district."[73]

The more recent 2007 *Parents Involved* case dealing with voluntary school integration revisited the housing issue once again, with divided results. "Although presently observed [school] racial imbalance might result from past de jure segregation," wrote Justice Thomas, a staunch conservative, "racial imbalance can also result from any number of innocent private decisions, including voluntary housing choices."[74] But while Thomas continued to employ rhetoric reminiscent of the three 1990s-era decisions, the controlling opinion, issued by Justice Kennedy, left open several avenues for continuing to pursue racial diversity—a number of which explicitly acknowledged school policies long thought to contribute to housing segregation. Kennedy asserted that school districts could pursue diversity when drawing attendance lines with recognition of the underlying demographics, or when strategically selecting the site of a new school.[75]

In short, the arc of judicial involvement in the related issues of housing and school segregation has been erratic, connected closely to the changing political composition of the courts. And how the judicial system has looked upon the relationship between the two spheres has made a great deal of difference in determining what should be done about it. The earlier understanding of the complex and reciprocal nature of school and housing segregation resulted in far-reaching school desegregation remedies, to include ones that reached across a joint city and suburban landscape. If present and future political winds on the courts help prompt a shift back to the more nuanced understanding of yesteryear, it would also be important to revisit the theoretical basis for designing metropolitan-wide school desegregation plans. The theory linking city-suburban school desegregation plans to progress in housing desegregation still holds true, offering a key rationale for future efforts in this direction—whether court ordered or voluntary.

Understanding the Dynamics of Metropolitan School Desegregation's Positive Influence on Housing Patterns

It is fairly easy to grasp how housing policy promoting desegregation might positively impact schools. Strategies that offer families mobility into high-opportunity communities place children within reach of resource-rich schools. If the new district operates under a student assignment policy that prioritizes proximity, which, despite the growth of choice and the existence of voluntary and court-ordered school desegregation, is still the overwhelming trend,[76] the student will be able to attend and benefit from such a setting. Highly regarded research confirms this line of thinking. A study of low-income children benefiting from Montgomery County, Maryland's, strong inclusionary housing policy found that they significantly outperformed similar students enrolling in high-poverty schools. Since the early 1970s, the county has set aside 15 percent of any new development for subsidized housing. This practice has given low-income families access to well-off neighborhoods and the schools to which they are connected. Meanwhile, school policy in Montgomery County has dictated that high-poverty settings should receive $2,000 more per child in order to meet the greater set of educational needs within the student population (which helped fund interventions such as full-day kindergarten, professional development for teachers, and tutoring). What made the study unique was its ability to test which strategy better benefited students: socioeconomic school integration or increased funding for high-poverty schools. The findings clearly showed that attending a socioeconomically integrated school impacted student achievement more than funneling extra resources into a school with high concentrations of poverty.[77]

What may be less well understood, however, is how school desegregation policy can impact housing patterns. The relationship is not as intuitive and has often gone unexamined. A handful of studies have found that metropolitan school desegregation plans are associated with lower levels of school and housing segregation.[78] One contribution to the literature also found that the relationship worked in the other direction, citing a causal link between the end of a metropolitan school desegregation plan and the movement of white families into neighborhoods with higher shares of other white residents.[79]

So just how does school desegregation policy drive housing desegregation? As expert Gary Orfield has noted, a central theoretical answer lies in the founding documents of this country. In 1787, James Madison, writing in heated support of the ratification of the Constitution (and thus weighing in on the side of a strong, unified federal government) warned against the dangers of factionalism, which he defined as "a number of citizens ... united and actuated by some common impulse of passion ... adverse to the rights of other citizens, or to the permanent and aggregate interests of the community."[80] The remedy to this type of dissent, he concluded, was to "extend the sphere ... take in a greater variety of parties and interests ... make it less probable that a majority of the whole will have a common motive to invade the rights of other citizens."[81] Madison's "Federalist No. 10" thus outlined a basic but key governmental principle: The most effective way to combat the pursuit of narrow political interests is to broaden the limits of the community itself.

Metropolitan school desegregation is an important example of Madison's theory. Metro-wide desegregation plans are designed to extend across an expansive city-suburban community. Once the boundary lines that separate city school districts from suburban ones are bridged, the constricted interests of white and/or middle-class families seeking more homogenous educational settings for their children can be overcome. Schools across the region may then operate in service of a broader ideal that aims for a unified, integrated, and high-quality educational system benefiting all members of the community.[82]

Another way of thinking about the mechanism behind the success of city-suburban school desegregation is to picture the housing market in a more fragmented metropolitan area. To return to a previous example, think about the six new and racially identifiable municipal school districts in the suburbs of Memphis. These are indeed narrowly defined communities. In the Memphis area, families and real estate agents can easily communicate about school preferences between the larger district and the new breakaway districts without ever having to mention race. These conscious or unconscious maneuvers can occur even though the real estate decisions will, of course, have serious racial implications for both schools and neighborhoods.[83] But in a different metro, one where comprehensive city-suburban school desegregation is carried out in a predictable fashion, the community comes to understand that movement to any part of the metro area governed by the student assignment policy will result in a similarly integrated school—and thus will be connected to the kinds of rich benefits that flow from those environments.

Recall that one of the most important benefits linked to desegregated schools deals with the perpetuating nature of the experience. Graduates of diverse schools are more likely to pursue diverse settings later in life than graduates of segregated schools.[84] The reinforcing and intergenerational nature of this cycle—whereby products of integrated K–12 settings are more likely to seek out integrated neighborhoods, making school integration more likely for their children—supplements Madison's well-articulated rationale for a robust federal government by helping to further illuminate how a long-standing metropolitan school desegregation plan might eventually be linked to advances in both school and housing integration.

It is likely safe to say that both of these dynamics interact to produce the mechanism by which school desegregation policy can become housing desegregation policy. The following two chapters lay out the historical context and results from an analysis of school and housing segregation in four southern regions. Madison's philosophy and prior research and theory is put to a contemporary test, in an effort to understand whether or not metropolitan school desegregation remedies continue to promote school and housing integration across broadly conceived communities.

PART II | Analysis

CHAPTER THREE

Divergent Paths

School and Housing Desegregation in Four Southern Cities

Louisville, Kentucky. Charlotte, North Carolina. Chattanooga, Tennessee. Richmond, Virginia. Four southern metropolitan communities, roughly similar in size and demographic makeup and with a shared history of de jure segregation. Yet each diverged along key dimensions. While all at least considered a regional pursuit of school desegregation, only three actually engaged with it. Among the three metros that did implement city-suburban desegregation, important variations distinguish them. District mergers in these communities occurred at different times and for different reasons. Likewise, school desegregation policy unfolded, evolved, and, in two cases, ended, in distinct ways. The four communities thus offer a critical comparative perspective on the relationship between boundary lines, desegregation policy, and school and housing segregation patterns in the contemporary South.

This chapter outlines the central characteristics of each metro area under study (briefly summarized in Table 1). Differing school district boundary line arrangements are emphasized alongside a discussion of how those arrangements developed. Merger circumstances are then connected to an exploration of how similar early school desegregation histories in the four metros gave way to different approaches to the way students were assigned to schools in later years. Major policy shifts are highlighted, and an overview of limited efforts in two of the metros to address housing and school segregation together is provided. This chapter sets the stage for the key findings related to contemporary patterns of school and housing segregation revealed in chapter 4.

To Merge or Not to Merge? School District Consolidation in Four Southern Metros

School districts in the Louisville, Charlotte, Chattanooga, and Richmond areas reflect a variety of consolidation scenarios. The Richmond area came to characterize the more typical post-*Milliken* landscape after higher courts rejected a consolidation plan, leaving the urban school division

TABLE 1 School Boundary Lines and Desegregation Policy

	Louisville-Jefferson County, Kentucky	Chattanooga-Hamilton County, Tennessee	Charlotte-Mecklenburg County, North Carolina	Richmond-Henrico-Chesterfield, Virginia
School district boundary line arrangement	Merged city-suburban school district	Merged city-suburban school district	Merged city-suburban school district	Failed merger; city school district distinct from two surrounding suburban districts
Origins of merger	Court-ordered merger of city and suburban school systems (1974) formalized by the Kentucky Board of Education (1975)	City school system ceased operations after narrowly approved referendum; folded into surrounding Hamilton County Schools (1997)	Area residents voted by a 3-1 majority to merge the city school system with Mecklenburg County schools (1959)	U.S. Supreme Court allowed lower court ruling rejecting school district consolidation to stand (1973)
Contemporary student assignment policy	Controlled choice to help ensure even distribution of students from neighborhoods of differing racial and socioeconomic makeups; system of magnet programs	System of magnet programs, otherwise student assignment prioritizes proximity	Choice-based policy prioritizing neighborhood schools and system of magnet programs	Open enrollment options in Richmond City; system of specialty centers in Henrico and Chesterfield, regional Governor's Schools (competitive admissions), otherwise assignment prioritizes proximity

distinct from its two surrounding suburban counterparts. The other three metros represent a range of impetuses for city-suburban mergers—explored more fully below—across different time periods. In Louisville-Jefferson County, a 1975 court-ordered merger for the purposes of school desegregation brought down the fences between city and suburb. In Charlotte-Mecklenburg County and Chattanooga-Hamilton County, state law and policy helped promote school district consolidations in 1959 and 1997, respectively, with desegregation as one motivating factor among several. Different points of origin for consolidation efforts meant that school desegregation was a central focus and thrust of the court-ordered mergers in the Richmond and Louisville areas, and merely an underlying consideration for some stakeholders in the voluntary Charlotte and Chattanooga mergers.

Richmond-Henrico-Chesterfield, Virginia:
Desegregation-Era District Consolidation Denied

A fourteen-year delay occurred between the 1954 *Brown* decision declaring separate unequal and the 1968 *Green* ruling clarifying what had to be done to fully desegregate school districts. In the meantime, post–World War II patterns of segregation between cities and suburbs grew and festered. At the beginning of the 1970s, under pressure from ongoing desegregation litigation to meaningfully implement *Brown*'s mandate, the city school board in Richmond began to focus its attention on the issue of metropolitan school district consolidation.[1] Chairwoman Virginia Crockford summarized the growing sentiments of the board in a handwritten note: "In light of increasing numbers of black students in the city, and the counties with practically all white systems, there seems to be no alternative other than consolidation if one is to adhere to the mandate of the Supreme Court, that segregated school systems are inherently unequal."[2] One year after Chairwoman Crockford penned her note, the Richmond City School Board unveiled a city-county desegregation proposal. The plan strategically partitioned the proposed district into separate subdivisions that incorporated a segment of the central city with a portion of the county beyond. Judge Robert Merhige of the U.S. Eastern District Court of Virginia supported the proposal, issuing a 325-page opinion in *Bradley v. Richmond* outlining the rationale for desegregation across a consolidated city-suburban district.[3]

Just six months later, the Fourth Circuit reversed Judge Merhige's decision. The ruling came with the additional influence of a number of national organizations interested in the possible impact of the Richmond case, which was destined for the Supreme Court. The National Education Association, the Congress of Racial Equality, and the American Civil Liberties Union filed amicus curiae briefs in support of consolidation.[4] On the other side, the U.S. Justice Department, with the approval of President Nixon, supported the Virginia State Board of Education and the counties of Henrico and Chesterfield in the appeal against the merger. As discussed earlier, the *Bradley* case presented the first test of a politically reconfigured Supreme Court's position on metropolitan consolidation, an issue with sweeping implications for the future of school desegregation in a rapidly suburbanizing society.[5]

On May 21, 1973, a split 4-4 vote (Justice Lewis Powell removed himself from the deliberations, stating a personal conflict as former chairman of the Richmond City School Board) upheld the appellate court's reversal of metropolitan consolidation. The Supreme Court issued a per curiam opinion, listing no specific author and offering no details other than the statement, "The [Circuit Court's] judgment is affirmed by an equally divided court."[6] The Supreme Court's decision meant that court-ordered desegregation was limited to the city of Richmond.

Louisville-Jefferson County, Kentucky:
Successful, Court-Ordered School District Merger

Around the same time that metropolitan school desegregation first emerged as a possibility in Richmond, the seeds of a similar proposal were taking root hundreds of miles away in Louisville. In 1971, frustrated by the slow pace of school desegregation, several civil rights organizations and families brought suit against the suburban Jefferson County Public Schools district. One year later, plaintiffs filed another suit in federal court against the Louisville school system. In conjunction with the litigation, the Kentucky Human Rights Commission presented a case for a merger of the city and suburban school systems—based largely on their differing racial and socioeconomic characteristics.[7] At the time, the Louisville district was roughly 50 percent black, while schools in surrounding Jefferson County were 4 percent black.[8]

In 1974, just after *Milliken* outlined the difficult legal standards needed to prove an interdistrict violation, the U.S. Supreme Court remanded the Louisville case to the Sixth Circuit Court of Appeals. The Sixth Circuit permitted the lower court to consider an interdistrict remedy since "the situation presented is that of two districts in the same county of the state being equally guilty of failing to eliminate all vestiges of segregation.[9] (This arrangement differed from the Richmond case because the school division boundaries in Richmond, Chesterfield, and Henrico were coterminous with separate city and county governments.) In 1975, the U.S. district court judge ordered the city-suburban merger as a central component of the area's desegregation strategy, one year after the *Milliken* ruling chilled similar efforts across the country.

Charlotte-Mecklenburg County, North Carolina:
Merger absent Desegregation Considerations

Unlike the court-ordered mergers in the Richmond and Louisville areas, city-suburban consolidation in the Charlotte community was put to a public vote. Dating back to the late 1940s, North Carolina residents had generally supported mergers of city and county districts as a means to improve the quality of rural school systems.[10] This proved to be the case in the Charlotte area.

In 1957, as Charlotte sought to enlarge its borders—and economic clout—through an annexation process, city leaders and stakeholders recognized that the operation of two distinct school systems could impede future expansion efforts. Separate school systems also disadvantaged students in the more rural Mecklenburg system, where the tax base continually shrank with each annexation. The Charlotte Chamber of Commerce played an active role in the merger proposal, rolling out an intensive public relations campaign to convince voters to approve the referendum.[11] The chamber, aided by a supportive media establishment, emphasized that district consolidation would spur more efficient administrative and fiscal policies and offer considerable support to rural schools.[12]

As the consolidation proposal proceeded to a vote, some residents of Charlotte, including the superintendent of schools, grasped the implications of the merger for the still-nascent school desegregation process. Still, consolidation had no explicit bearing on what was at the time token compliance with the *Brown* decision. In 1959, Charlotte residents approved the merger by a three-to-one margin.[13] Just two years later, the struggle for meaningful school desegregation began across a consolidated system—replete with the demographic advantages of a merged city-suburban student population.

Chattanooga-Hamilton County, Tennessee:
Late Nineties Merger in the Context of an Urban Renaissance

The merger of Chattanooga City and Hamilton County schools was also brought before the public, but occurred much later than consolidation efforts in the other three metros. In 1997, in the context of a broader renaissance of downtown Chattanooga (funded, in part, by an annexation-expanded tax base), city school board members and residents voted to merge their majority black school system with the predominantly white one serving Hamilton County. The decision to fold into the surrounding suburban system was motivated by several interrelated factors. First, for years the Chattanooga City school system had experienced declining enrollment and diminished revenues. Student attrition was at least in part related to the fact that many urban white students transferred to schools in Hamilton County, according to a complaint filed with the U.S. Department of Education's Office for Civil Rights in the lead-up to the consolidation.[14] Second, as the more recent merger of Memphis and Shelby County illustrates, Tennessee state law requires that county jurisdictions fund and provide educational infrastructure. Handing district operations over to the county, while representing a loss of political control for the city school system, offered the possibility of a newly revitalized, larger, and more racially balanced system that shared the same tax base.[15]

After the vote, a local nonprofit helped convene stakeholders to plan a vision for the consolidated school system. Instead of a simple merger—melding the urban system into the larger county jurisdiction with little regard for the separate histories, leadership, or racially distinctive student populations—residents sought to carve a new, united system out of the two different districts, building on the accomplishments of each. Ruth Holmberg, publisher emeritus of the Chattanooga daily newspaper, recalled the situation: "With the decision by the city to exit the school business, it was possible to merge the city and county systems into the Hamilton County School System. In our case, this was a true merger, not a takeover as had happened in other cities. In Chattanooga and Hamilton County, neither system predominated. A new system was created and a new superintendent hired. It was a formula for success going forward."[16] The district merger between Chattanooga and Hamilton County proceeded, with plans to both build on an existing system of magnet schools and tweak school attendance boundaries in a way that would promote diversity.[17]

These more contemporary student assignment strategies were rooted in historical efforts to desegregate students within the city limits.

Indeed, variations in whether and how our four metros merged their city and suburban school systems should be viewed alongside the development of school desegregation policy. Understanding the interplay between bridging or not bridging boundaries, implementing desegregation plans and contemporary school and housing segregation is at the heart of our study. So with the differing merger histories of the four metro areas in mind, we now turn to an exploration of their desegregation efforts, past and present.

From Resistance to Compliance: Early Days of School Desegregation in Four Southern Metros

School systems in each of the four metros experienced a basic post-*Brown* pattern: resistance and/or token compliance with the decision, followed by a shift toward more comprehensive desegregation efforts after the 1968 *Green* ruling. Take the case of Richmond, Virginia, as an example. Beginning in 1956, a state-operated Pupil Placement Board governed student assignment and transfers. State officials intentionally set up the Pupil Placement Board to delay and impede school desegregation in the Richmond area and across the state of Virginia. Indeed, the *Richmond Newsleader*, widely credited with operating the presses that led the South into a period of Massive Resistance to *Brown*, hailed the establishment of the Pupil Placement Board as the "first line of defense against integration."[18] The defense was so successful that by 1960, less than 170 black students in eleven Virginia school districts (out of more than 200,000) were enrolled in white schools.[19]

Similarly, a 1966 "freedom of choice" plan—legislated by the Virginia General Assembly and implemented by the Richmond City School Board—in reality offered neither freedom nor choice to black students. The plan removed responsibility for integration from school officials, directing it instead toward parents ill equipped to initiate the desegregation of an entire school system. The school board further restricted so-called freedom of choice by offering approval of student assignment on the basis of proximity, availability of space, and students' "best interests."[20] Districts across the South, including Charlotte, Chattanooga, and Louisville, employed similar plans until 1968 brought forth the Supreme Court ruling in *Green v. New Kent County*.

The *Green* ruling dealt specifically with freedom of choice in New Kent County, which lies approximately twenty miles to the south of Richmond. In the years leading up to *Green*, New Kent operated two racially identifiable high schools. Watkins High traditionally served black students, while New Kent High served white students. Three years into the school division's freedom-of-choice plan, no white students enrolled in Watkins and just 155 black students attended New Kent.[21] Drawing upon these figures, the Supreme Court held that freedom-of-choice plans did not sufficiently alter the operation of dual school systems and determined that de jure segregated districts had an affirmative duty to eliminate segregation in the immediate future. "The burden on a school board today," wrote Justice Brennan, "is to come forward with a plan that promises realistically to work, and promises realistically to work now."[22]

The strongly worded *Green* decision encouraged plaintiffs in long-running southern desegregation cases to pursue more comprehensive desegregation plans. Community groups in Louisville, Chattanooga, Charlotte, and Richmond all returned to court in the aftermath of the *Green* ruling. Recall from above that Charlotte and Mecklenburg County schools merged in 1959, nearly a decade before *Green* was handed down. In Chattanooga, residents would not take up the issue of consolidation until the late 1990s. But in Louisville and Richmond, city-suburban school district consolidation for the purpose of desegregation became the key issue confronting the courts in this second wave of litigation. And as we saw, court-ordered consolidation efforts came to pass in Louisville, but not in Richmond. The mid-to-late 1970s, then, marked a real point of departure for school desegregation in these four southern locales. Charlotte-Mecklenburg County and Louisville-Jefferson County began integrating schools across city-suburban boundary lines,[23] while integration in Richmond and Chattanooga was limited to central city districts. Still, in all four locales, pressure from the courts forced districts to set aside ineffective freedom-of-choice plans in favor of mandatory student assignment policies that sought to evenly distribute black and white students across schools.

Mandatory School Desegregation Begins in the 1970s

In the Louisville area, the original city-county desegregation plan was designed to create a system of school clusters, pairing historically black urban schools with nearby white suburban schools. Students were then transported between the paired sites. Like many early desegregation plans, black students bore a disproportionate burden of the transportation required to overcome residential patterns of segregation.[24] In Louisville, black students were bused for up to ten years of their education, compared to just two years for white children.[25] While three African American protesters picketed outside of one of Louisville's historically black high schools on the first day of school to protest the busing plan, the black community, for the most part, was either resigned or supportive.[26]

The initial plan in Louisville-Jefferson County included a stipulation that elementary schools should enroll a student population that was no less than 12 percent black, and no more than 40 percent black, figures that centered on the district-wide average of black elementary school students at the time. Likewise, secondary schools were instructed to maintain a black student enrollment between about 12 percent and 35 percent based on the overall share of black secondary school students.[27] And even though active court supervision of desegregation in Louisville ended in 1978, residents elected to continue a similar version of the student assignment plan.[28]

The 1971 Supreme Court decision in *Swann v. Charlotte-Mecklenburg* produced a groundbreaking two-way desegregation strategy in the Charlotte area. The plan brought wealthy, white suburban students into previously segregated schools in the inner city, and bused low-income, black students out to formerly all-white schools in the suburbs.[29] Similar to Louisville-Jefferson County's student assignment policy, early desegregation in Charlotte-Mecklenburg relied heavily on pairing. Pairing involved expanding the attendance boundaries for two racially identifiable schools in relative proximity to one another and reorganizing grade levels so that the new schools were at capacity. For instance, one school might serve all K-3 students in the enlarged attendance area, while the other would serve all students in grades four-six. Charlotte's early desegregation plan was considered very successful, linked to racial balance and improved academic achievement.[30] The ease with which it was implemented was also a source of civic pride and helped build the area's reputation as a progressive, business-friendly environment.[31]

While desegregation in Richmond and Chattanooga relied on some of the same pairing and transportation strategies found elsewhere, plans in these two areas ended at the city limits. In Richmond, the urban school system was already in the throes of serious racial and socioeconomic transition.[32] Several years into the initial round of desegregation, Richmond's first black superintendent proposed the "K–5 plan" in 1976.[33] Seeking to staunch the suburban flow of middle-class and white families, the new plan allowed elementary school-age children to opt out of the transportation requirements of desegregation in order to attend nearby schools in their neighborhoods.[34] Despite the adjustments, the exodus of white and middle-class families continued. By the mid-1980s, facing the demographic realities of a resegregated, heavily black district, the Richmond School Board sought an end to court-ordered desegregation. In a 1986 motion penned by Judge Merhige, who had once passionately advocated for the consolidation of city and suburban school systems in the area, schools in Richmond City were released from court oversight.[35]

School desegregation limited to the city of Chattanooga ran into the same demographic difficulties as Richmond. Five years after the 1972 implementation of the city's mandatory busing plan, fifteen of the fifty-one schools originally involved in the desegregation plan had closed due to enrollment declines, and the remaining schools were racially identifiable. Nine were majority white schools and twenty-seven were majority black schools. Some of these enrollment patterns were a by-product of swift racial transition, as seventeen of the majority black schools had shifted from majority white educational settings.[36] The transition accelerated over time; by 1985, black students made up nearly three-quarters of the city school system, and the few white students who remained were concentrated in annexed, outlying suburban areas. Amid stark racial segregation, judicial oversight of school desegregation in Chattanooga's central city ended in 1986. Both Chattanooga and Richmond are examples of an early trickle of unitary status decisions in which the courts ruled that dual systems of schooling for black and white students had been dismantled. A steady flow of such cases came after three Supreme Court rulings in the 1990s made it easier for school districts to be released from court supervision—even when patterns of segregation persisted.[37]

In short, the mandatory desegregation era witnessed considerable parallels between the central cities of Richmond and Chattanooga, as well as similarities between the two city-suburban school systems in Charlotte and Louisville. Yet another commonality bound together the consolidated city-suburban districts of Charlotte and Louisville: early on, both broke important and, as chapter 2 makes clear, unusual ground in tying school desegregation to housing desegregation efforts.

Temporarily Linking School and Housing Desegregation Efforts in Charlotte and Louisville

Louisville-Jefferson County was one of the only districts in the country to include transportation exemptions for integrated neighborhoods in its school desegregation plan.[38] Exemptions fell under three categories. First, neighborhoods meeting racial balance goals established in the court-ordered school desegregation plan were excused. Second, black families making an integrative move into a predominantly white neighborhood using housing vouchers were exempted from busing. Third, neighborhoods that evolved into integrated environments were released from transportation requirements.[39] In this manner, officials incentivized residential integration in the metro Louisville area. It worked: research on the time period from 1970 to 1980 indicates that the coordinated school-housing policy was linked to the first decline in area housing segregation in three decades.[40] Despite these positive developments, Louisville-Jefferson County's exemption policies overlooked the critical process of public housing site selection.[41] New public housing could be located in Louisville's historically segregated neighborhoods, requiring transportation to meet the racial guidelines in the school desegregation plan.

Similar to metro Louisville, Charlotte blazed an early path in efforts to link school and housing desegregation policy.[42] The contours of Charlotte's strategy differed widely from Louisville's, however, focusing on the location of public housing instead of the distribution of housing vouchers or certificates. A 1973 lawsuit (filed by Julius Chambers, the same lawyer spearheading the school desegregation case) alleging that officials intentionally concentrated public housing in racially isolated neighborhoods eventually led to a requirement for approximately 900 scattered-site housing units in the metro area.[43] School officials were consulted during the site planning process, prompting a leading researcher to note, "Charlotte was the only jurisdiction I visited [of twelve metros identified as having some model of school and housing coordination] where both planners and school officials mentioned that school integration considerations were a significant concern in the city's planning process."[44]

In the early 1990s, Charlotte's planning commission issued a report titled, "Housing Strategies to Racially Integrate Schools." Some of the more ambitious proposals outlined in the document—beyond an uncontroversial suggestion to enforce fair housing laws—included inclusionary zoning, linkage ordinances, density bonuses, and low-interest loans.[45] The report quickly generated debate, with the Charlotte-Mecklenburg School Board emerging as an ardent backer of the proposed policies. The school board supported the successful creation of a metropolitan Affordable Housing Policy Task Force, the operation of which was subsequently blocked by the city's mayor. Charlotte's planning officials continued to work on housing desegregation issues, but the impetus for real progress had shifted. Support and discussion around the commission's housing report died down as controversy surrounding the school desegregation plan mounted.[46] In the end, the interests of development—and its associated windfall profits—took precedence over equity.[47] In Charlotte, as in Louisville, attempts to link school and housing desegregation dissolved over time. Early efforts to coordinate residential and school desegregation in both metros remain the most noteworthy to date.

Introducing Choice to Mandatory Desegregation Plans in the 1980s and 1990s

While the explicit connections between school and housing desegregation faded away in Charlotte and Louisville (and never occurred in the other two metros), school desegregation policies in all four continued to evolve. Broadly, the eighties and nineties witnessed a shift toward voluntary school integration methods in each locale, with a specific emphasis on creating and expanding magnet schools. These developments mirrored trends in districts across the nation, incentivized by federal policy and funding, as well as a growing emphasis on school choice.[48] Magnet schools were usually located in racially and socioeconomically isolated urban neighborhoods, using attractive themes or programmatic options (e.g., Montessori or the arts) to draw a diverse group of students across traditional attendance zones.[49] Though magnets first gained popularity in northern cities struggling to desegregate, they quickly spread across the country.

When court-ordered desegregation ended in Chattanooga and Richmond's urban school systems, both sought to develop magnet schools. Richmond City's efforts fell far short of the establishment of a system-wide voluntary integration policy.[50] In the late 1980s, a task force researched the feasibility of a broad array of magnet schools in the urban school system. The district went so far as to submit a (failed) application for federal magnet funding. But the superintendent at the time made it clear that he viewed magnets as a way to restructure the school system, not as a way to desegregate students.[51] Early materials related to magnets denied that the programs were designed to draw in a racially diverse group of students, stating instead that they would "allow for a distribution of students without regard to where they live."[52] Over the years, a number of specialty schools or programs (e.g., a regional school for gifted and talented students, a college preparatory high school designed to reach underserved students, and several school-within-a-school International Baccalaureate programs) opened in the city, but no progress was made toward a more systematic implementation of a magnet policy with explicit desegregation goals.[53]

Unlike Richmond's stalled efforts, Chattanooga's early magnets eventually blossomed into an expanded set of programs—supported by two rounds of federal magnet funding—after the 1997 merger.[54] And in the Charlotte and Louisville areas, magnet schools were established alongside choice-based student assignment plans that sought to racially balance schools.

In the early 1990s, the Louisville-Jefferson County school system rolled out Project Renaissance, a student assignment plan based on elementary school clusters. (Elementary schools tend to be the hardest to desegregate because their attendance zones are smaller than middle or high school zones; the small size of the zone tends to concentrate residential segregation in school enrollment.) Students could transfer to any elementary school within their cluster as long as the transfer promoted racial balance. Similar parameters applied to magnet schools.[55] Project Renaissance represented the beginning of extensive controlled choice in the student assignment plan. Controlled choice asked families to rank a set of school choices, with the district making the final assignment decisions in service of creating racially diverse schools. For many years, all Louisville-Jefferson County schools strove to enroll a student body that was 15–50 percent black, amounting to roughly plus or minus fifteen percentage points around the overall enrollment of black students in the district.[56]

In contrast to Louisville's largely successful transition to a choice-based desegregation plan, the expanded emphasis on magnet programs in early-nineties Charlotte signaled the beginning of a slow unraveling of the first completely desegregated school system in the country.[57] The expansion of magnet schools represented a significant change from mandatory student assignment to a more voluntary plan, though the system stipulated that each magnet school needed to serve a student body roughly similar to the district's racial composition (60 percent white and 40 percent black at the time). Despite the racial balance guidelines, no restrictions capped the number of families allowed to leave previously assigned schools to attend a magnet program. White families exited some of the regular public schools for magnet schools quickly, destabilizing racial balance in the process.[58] Undermining desegregation efforts even further, Charlotte-Mecklenburg's teaching faculties grew more racially identifiable over the same time period, a serious issue since faculty composition sends an important signal to families about the racial makeup of a school.[59] Finally, newcomers settling in outlying parts of the metro—many of whom did not understand the historical context for desegregation efforts—may have contributed to the growing political unrest related to Charlotte's student assignment policy.[60]

On the heels of the waning commitment to mandatory desegregation policy, in 1999 the *Swann* case was reactivated after a white family sued the system for denial of entry to a magnet school.[61] The school board and the local media, historically supportive of Charlotte's desegregation efforts, maintained their backing during the new phase of litigation. The Reagan-appointed judge hearing the reawakened lawsuit, however, was a known antibusing advocate who, decades prior, collected signatures for a petition against one of the earlier versions of the desegregation plan.[62] Given Judge Potter's track record, it is perhaps not surprising that in 1999 he declared Charlotte-Mecklenburg schools unitary.

Contemporary Student Assignment Policies in Four Southern Metros

Today, though Charlotte-Mecklenburg County remains a city-suburban school district, it no longer pursues school desegregation. In the early fallout from the 1999 unitary status decision, a majority of Charlotte-Mecklenburg's school board tried to preserve the district's long-standing commitment to desegregation. At the same time, members faced serious urging from powerful business elites in the city to bring rapid closure to the issue. The board eventually caved in to those pressures and settled for a request for increased financial assistance for schools that would resegregate under the neighborhood-driven policy.[63] The new plan helped reconnect patterns of residential and school segregation by emphasizing proximity along with race-neutral choice. After it was adopted, support for the urban-suburban district faded. Though unsuccessful, several movements seeking to secede from the system arose in the outer, predominantly white suburban areas.[64] Overcrowding defined a number of schools in these areas while more centrally located, minority segregated facilities faced declining enrollments and massive closures.[65]

As in Charlotte, contemporary student assignment in the city of Richmond represents a blend of neighborhood schools and choice policies. Until recently, the district was divided into three megazones. An open enrollment policy enabled students to apply to attend elementary schools within their broader zone if space was available after nearby, neighborhood students enrolled.[66] Officials activated a lottery system if an elementary school was oversubscribed. Free transportation was provided to all students enrolling in elementary schools within their megazone. In the wake of the fiscal crisis, however, significant cuts in overall expenditures spelled the end of free transportation for open enrollment students. Controversy ensued, with the head of the local PTA organization accusing the board of authorizing policies that advantaged wealthier families in the city. Perhaps in response to those concerns, in 2009 the school board eliminated the megazones and proposed a new procedure for open enrollment based on enabling transfers from low- to high-performing settings, lottery applicants, and space. The moratorium on transportation for open enrollment students remains in effect.[67] Meanwhile, Richmond's two surrounding suburbs have taken no overt steps to promote diverse schools in the past two decades.

In 1997, Chattanooga City Schools surrendered operational control to outlying Hamilton County, and the merged system was born. Unlike student assignment plans in the pre-unitary-status Charlotte and Louisville areas, though, Chattanooga-Hamilton County schools did not initiate the large-scale transportation of students across the city-suburban district to ensure desegregation. Instead, the superintendent of the consolidated school system supported a rezoning effort that promoted diversity where possible, as well as an expansion of area magnet programs as a means to reduce or eliminate racial isolation.[68] Two federal Magnet Schools Assistance Program (MSAP) grants helped fund initial efforts to grow the magnet program. Initially, the magnet admissions process took students' racial backgrounds into account in order to promote diversity.

More recently, magnet schools adopted a lottery procedure that considered the socioeconomic balance of the student body, a decision spurred in part by federal MSAP funding guidelines under the Bush administration.[69] Funding from a prior MSAP cycle allowed the district to establish a number of central points from which students could be freely transported into different zones. Yet, as in Richmond, transportation cutbacks during the fiscal crisis impacted the district's ability to continue that policy.

The NAACP remains an active watchdog for civil rights issues in the consolidated Chattanooga-Hamilton County system, filing two complaints with the U.S. Department of Education's Office for Civil Rights over the past two decades. One formed a backdrop for the consolidation of the city and suburban school system.[70] The most recent complaint, opened in May 2010, alleged racial bias in school zoning and inadequate funding for renovations to a predominantly black high school, among other issues.[71] It remains unresolved, but is emblematic of ongoing challenges and racial disparities in the system.

Over in Louisville-Jefferson County schools, current school desegregation policy has been heavily influenced by the 2007 U.S. Supreme Court ruling in *Parents Involved*.[72] The controlling opinion in *Parents Involved* struck down the use of the individual race of a student as a deciding school assignment factor in Louisville's (and Seattle's) voluntary integration policy. It left room, however, for the holistic consideration of race as one assignment factor among others in a voluntary plan, particularly if the consideration applied to a group of students (e.g., the racial makeup of school-age children in a neighborhood).[73] In the years following the Court's ruling, Louisville worked with a team of experts to craft a new, legal plan to promote diversity. Relying on neighborhood-level demographics, school officials established guidelines requiring that each school in the district serve a mixture of students from high- and low-opportunity neighborhoods. The criteria for defining neighborhoods expanded the district's original conception of diversity to include income level, the educational attainment of parents, and the consideration of all racial categories (as opposed to the former two-race distinction between African American and white students).[74]

Louisville's broadened consideration of race—beyond the black-white dichotomy that long characterized the South—in its new student assignment policy reflects both an understanding of the new legal context and a growing awareness of the multiracial diversity emerging across the region. Significant demographic changes are underway in each of the four metros and likely require a more nuanced approach to desegregation than in the past.

Concluding Thoughts

School consolidation and desegregation trajectories in the four metros have yielded widely varying contemporary contexts. It is useful to picture a spectrum of merger and desegregation policy circumstances (see Table 1). At one end lies the Louisville area school system, the only district under study that continues to pursue a wide-scale, voluntary school integration strategy. While the city-suburban school system no longer seeks to connect school and housing desegregation efforts, the latest school-related policy does hinge upon existing patterns of residential segregation—seeking to ensure that students from different types of neighborhoods attend school with one another.

Second behind Louisville on the spectrum of current circumstances is Chattanooga-Hamilton County, where the 1997 city-suburban merger yielded new demographic possibilities for desegregation. The consolidation spurred both renewed interest in magnet schools and a redrawing of school zones to promote diversity. Recent shifts related to diversity preferences in the magnet lottery and the availability of transportation, however, may inhibit the desegregating potential of the magnets.

Moving toward the other side of the spectrum, schools in the consolidated Charlotte-Mecklenburg system—once a national leader in school and housing desegregation efforts—have resegregated. Unchecked real estate development, the 2002 implementation of a neighborhood schools-based assignment policy, and the rapid expansion of school choice options all eroded the gains made during the desegregation era.

At the far end of the policy continuum is the Richmond area, where the failure to consolidate Richmond, Henrico, and Chesterfield in the early 1970s locked in the segregating effects of district boundary lines—leaving the city to undertake school desegregation on its own. Even before city schools were declared unitary, the conflicting emphases on neighborhood schools and open enrollment made it difficult to seriously desegregate students in what was, in any case, an already resegregating system. No stated desegregation policy has been pursued in the three major Richmond-area school systems since the mid-1980s.

Keeping this spectrum in mind, we turn to an exploration of the relationship between segregation and the varying city-suburban boundary arrangements and school desegregation policies. Though the long-term evolution of consolidation and desegregation described in this chapter provides important context for more recent developments, in chapter 4 we concentrate on changes in school and housing segregation from 1990 to 2010.

CHAPTER FOUR

Divergent Outcomes

The Contemporary Relationship between School and Housing Segregation in Four Southern Cities

If educational boundaries help structure segregation, and if school and housing segregation are "two sides of the same coin,"[1] then how does the school-housing relationship play out in four southern metros with different boundary arrangements and desegregation trajectories? Given what we already know of the research and theory surrounding the early success of metropolitan school desegregation,[2] we might assume that communities with city-suburban school desegregation plans report lower levels of both school and housing segregation. We have many more issues to layer onto this central assumption, though. What happens to patterns of school and housing segregation when city-suburban school desegregation efforts come to an end, as in the case of Charlotte-Mecklenburg? What about when residents of a metro area consolidate their city and suburban school districts after court-ordered school desegregation has come to a close, as in Chattanooga-Hamilton County? Are Chattanooga's regional magnet schools and rezoning efforts linked to the same kind of desegregation success as Louisville-Jefferson County's comprehensive controlled choice plan? What kind of legacy flows from Richmond's failure to consolidate its city and suburban school districts? Do contemporary patterns of school and housing segregation differ widely for Louisville and Richmond, the two metros at opposite ends of the desegregation and consolidation spectrum? And finally, how does the increasingly multiracial nature of the school enrollment relate to school and housing trends?

These provocative questions form the basis for this chapter. Using education data from the National Center for Education Statistics and housing data from the U.S. Census, it explores school and residential segregation trends between 1990 and 2010 in the Louisville, Charlotte, Chattanooga, and Richmond metros.[3] A quick reminder regarding the use of "metro" or "metro area" to describe the four sites: As used in this study, the terms simply refer to the geographic area covered by the city-suburban school district merger (or proposed merger in the case of the Richmond metro). This is typically much smaller than the census definition of a Metropolitan

Statistical Area.[4] Importantly, though, the metro boundaries in our study encompass only areas directly affected by the school desegregation plan, thus providing the best window into the relationship between consolidation, school desegregation policy, and segregation trends.[5]

As we move through several different ways of thinking about segregation patterns, we will link key shifts in boundary line arrangements and school desegregation policies to changes in school and housing segregation. State-of-the-art maps and graphic presentations of various segregation measures will help illustrate the current landscape of school and housing segregation.

The main emphasis here is on understanding racial segregation between blacks and whites in Richmond, Chattanooga, Charlotte, and Louisville. The South's painful legacy of slavery and Jim Crow, as well as the fact that most school desegregation efforts were designed to redress discrimination against blacks,[6] makes it critical to explore how this history has shaped contemporary patterns of segregation between blacks and whites. That being said, the first and last sections of this chapter address demographic shifts taking place in each of the metros, to include the rapid growth of the Latino student population. Those trends have only accelerated since 2010, the final year of this study, and bear close watching in the future. Overlapping segregation by poverty and race is also addressed, but is not emphasized for the same reasons noted above. One other caveat: The methodology used here cannot prove a causal link between school desegregation policy, district consolidation, and school desegregation. It does, however, highlight deeply important relationships between these different phenomena.

We begin with a brief discussion of school enrollment trends over time in each of the four metros. These numbers inform the maps and measures of segregation that highlight the relationship between boundary lines, school desegregation policy and school segregation in our four metros. The second half of the chapter deals with the way that school district boundaries and school desegregation policy are related to patterns of housing segregation.

Characteristics of Student Enrollment in Four Southern Metros, 1990–2010

From 1992 to 2009, rising levels of racial diversity, driven in most communities by dramatic growth in the Latino student population, characterized school enrollments in Richmond, Louisville, Charlotte, and Chattanooga (see Table 2). The shares of black student enrollment also rose across each southern metro, as did the enrollment of Asian students. In conjunction with these trends, the share of white students in all four areas declined substantially over the twenty-year period. Alongside the racial transformation of schools, the share of students qualifying for free or reduced-priced lunches[7]—a rough proxy for relative poverty—increased in the three metros where longitudinal data were available. Rapid diversification of the school enrollment in each of these metros is emblematic of trends in both the region and the nation as a whole.[8]

The broader Richmond area offers a portrait of a region in transition: The share of Latino students rose from less than 1 percent of the metro enrollment in 1992 to more than 6 percent in 2009. Black students accounted for roughly 38 percent of the metro student population in 1990, rising to about 42 percent in 2009. Meanwhile, the Asian student population doubled to more than 4 percent of the total enrollment over the time period studied. By 2009, white students constituted a minority share of the enrollment—46.5 percent—in the Richmond metro area. According to federal education data, the share of low income students also increased across the metro, from 27 percent in 1999 to roughly 31 percent in 2009.

A more nuanced story emerged from the three Richmond area jurisdictions separated by district boundary lines. Continuing a long-standing trajectory, schools in Richmond city remained extraordinarily segregated by race and class.[9] The share of white students in the city remained below 10 percent, with slight fluctuations over time. Conversely, black students made up the overwhelming majority of city students—about 85 percent of the population in 2009. Also by 2009, Latino students constituted more than 5 percent of Richmond city students. Low income students accounted for more than two out of every three students in the city of Richmond in 2009. As we will see, in this racial and socioeconomic context, structured in part by existing city-suburban boundary lines, marked progress on school desegregation would be very difficult.

In contrast to the stable and extreme segregation of the city school system, a tremendous shift in the racial composition of Richmond's immediately adjacent suburban school systems occurred between 1992 and 2009. In Henrico County, growing racial diversity was largely fueled by an increase in the share of black students attending schools in the county. Rising levels of student poverty occurred alongside the growing

TABLE 2 Student Enrollment by Race, 1992 and 2009

	White Percentage of Enrollment			Black Percentage of Enrollment			Latino Percentage of Enrollment			Asian Percentage of Enrollment		
	1992	2009	Percentage Point Change	1992	2009	Percentage Point Change	1992	2009	Percentage Point Change	1992	2009	Percentage Point Change
Richmond metro	58.6	46.5	−12.1	38.4	42.3	3.9	0.7	6.8	6.1	2.3	4.4	2.1
Richmond city	9.8	8.3	−1.5	89.1	85.2	−3.9	0.5	5.8	5.3	0.6	0.7	0.1
Henrico County	67.5	48.6	−18.9	28.6	39.1	10.5	0.6	5.2	4.6	3.2	7.1	3.9
Chesterfield County	80.3	59.6	−20.7	16.2	28.4	12.2	0.8	8.4	7.6	2.6	3.6	1.0
Louisville-Jefferson County	68.6	53.9	−14.7	30.2	37.4	7.2	0.3	5.8	5.5	0.9	3.0	2.1
Charlotte-Mecklenburg County	56.0	33.6	−22.4	39.7	45.6	5.9	1.3	15.9	14.6	3.0	4.9	1.9
Chattanooga-Hamilton County	70.0	60.4	−9.6	28.5	31.7	3.2	0.4	5.8	5.4	1.1	2.1	1.0
Chattanooga city	39.3	N/A	N/A	59.2	N/A	N/A	0.2	N/A	N/A	1.3	N/A	N/A
Hamilton County	95	N/A	N/A	3.6	N/A	N/A	0.5	N/A	N/A	0.9	N/A	N/A

Source: NCES Common Core of Data, 1992–93 and 2009–10.

Notes: All regular public schools included in analysis. Specifically, alternative, vocational, and special education schools were excluded from analysis; magnet and charter schools (where applicable) were included. American Indian, Alaska Native, or Hawaiian students and students identifying as two or more races were excluded from the analysis due to the small size of the population (less than 1% in each site). Richmond metro numbers for all years reflect the combination of the Richmond City, Henrico County, and Chesterfield County enrollment. Chattanooga-Hamilton County numbers for 1992–93 reflect the combination of Chattanooga city and Hamilton County enrollment.

diversity of Richmond's suburban school divisions. The share of low income students in Henrico County nearly doubled in just ten years. In essence, the boundary lines that had for so long separated a minority segregated, high poverty urban school system from two white and wealthy suburban systems were, by 2009, separating a persistently isolated urban system from two rapidly diversifying county systems.

In Louisville-Jefferson County, Kentucky, even though a regional school district rendered urban-suburban school distinctions less relevant, racial diversity levels still rose sharply between 1992 and 2009. A system with virtually no Latino students in 1992 had become almost 6 percent Latino by 2009, a pattern similar to schools in both the larger Richmond metro and in Chattanooga-Hamilton County. Black students were approximately 37 percent of all Louisville-Jefferson County students in 2009, and Asian students accounted for 3 percent of the total enrollment in the same year. Meanwhile, the share of low income students rose considerably in Louisville-Jefferson County schools, from about 50 percent in 1999 to about 60 percent in 2009—one of the most significant increases in student poverty, and the highest overall figure, in the four metro areas under study.[10]

Of the four regions, the Charlotte-Mecklenburg school system experienced by far the largest growth in the Latino student population. The share of Latino students grew exponentially over the twenty-year period, rising from just about 1 percent of the student population in 1992 to roughly 16 percent in 2009. Similar to trends in the other three metros, shares of both black and Asian students increased in Charlotte-Mecklenburg schools, while the white student population declined. Schools in Charlotte-Mecklenburg County also experienced the greatest surge in student poverty.[11]

In Tennessee, enrollment patterns before and after the 1997 merger of Chattanooga city schools and Hamilton County schools were striking. In 1992, white students accounted for about 40 percent of Chattanooga city's enrollment, and a full 95 percent of Hamilton County's. The combined 1992 share of white students in the two school systems was roughly 70 percent, a proportion that declined modestly after the merger. In short, Chattanooga-Hamilton County's enrollment demographics after consolidation were much more conducive to meaningful desegregation. These enrollment figures help set the stage for further exploration of the relationship between city-suburban school district mergers and school segregation.

City-Suburban Boundaries Linked to More Extreme School Segregation

Multiple measures of segregation confirm one of our main, informed hunches: The district boundary lines separating students in city schools from students in suburban ones are indeed linked to more extreme school segregation. Take the cases of Richmond and Chattanooga.

In the Richmond area, district boundary lines separating Richmond city schools from Henrico and Chesterfield County schools are linked to stark patterns of urban racial and socioeconomic segregation. Mapping these three Richmond area systems over time shows a distinct, if slowly evolving (more on this at the end of the chapter), pattern of segregated minority schools in the city school division cut off from predominantly white schools in the surrounding suburban divisions (see Map 2). The actual numbers linked to the maps further underline the segregation. Roughly 85 percent of Richmond city's black, Latino, and low income students went to an "intensely segregated" school in 2009, a term used to describe a school where white students make up 10 percent or less of the population.[12]

Similar if somewhat less severe trends prevailed during the period when the urban and suburban school systems in Chattanooga remained separate. In 1992, five years before the city-suburban merger, roughly 66 percent of black students in Chattanooga's central city schools attended an intensely segregated school. In the wake of the city-suburban consolidation, about 45 percent of black students enrolled in such schools.

The examples of Richmond and Chattanooga illuminate the divisive nature of district boundary lines. In Richmond, the presence of city-suburban lines has fostered enrollment trends that have long sealed off city students from widespread integration. By contrast, the demographics of the merged school system in Chattanooga-Hamilton County opened up new possibilities for comprehensive and stable desegregation efforts. Opportunity does not always translate into reality, however, which brings us to our next key finding.

Bridging City-Suburban Boundaries a First Step; School Desegregation Policy Still Key

Bringing down the fences between city and suburban school districts can be an important first step toward achieving more diverse schools. At the

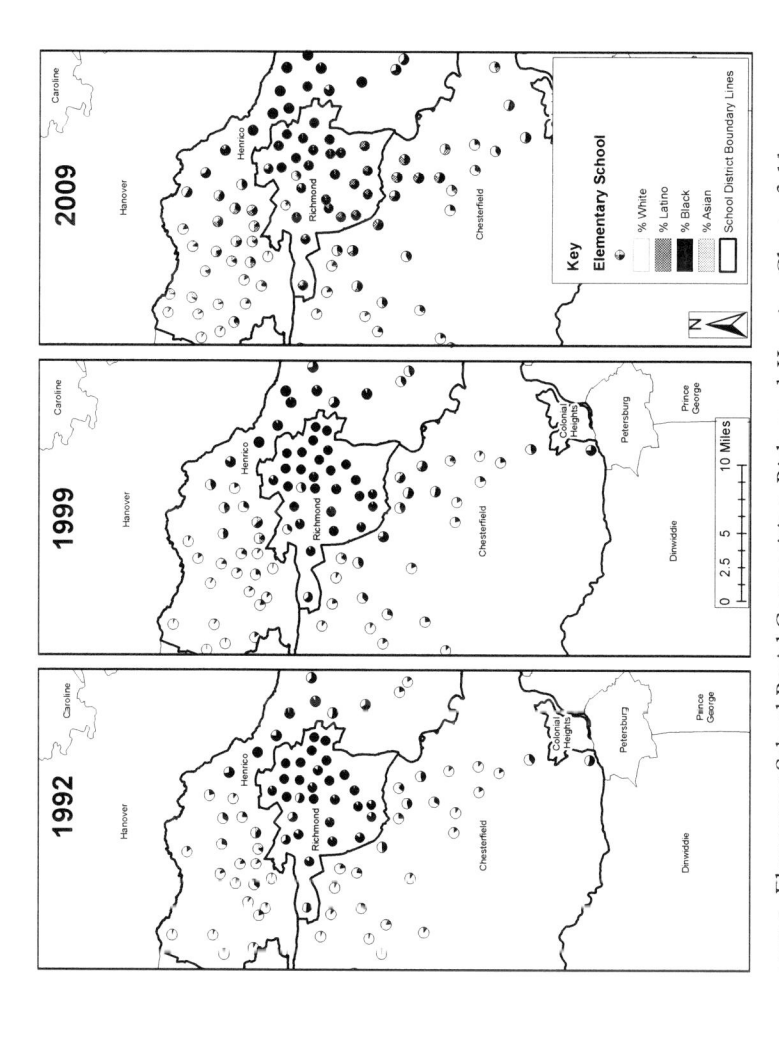

MAP 2 Elementary School Racial Composition, Richmond-Henrico-Chesterfield, 1992–2009. NCES Common Core of Data, 1992–93, 1999–2000, and 2009–10. For a color version of this map, please visit: http://hdl.handle.net/10156/5060.

same time, circumstances in Charlotte-Mecklenburg before and after the courts lifted the school desegregation order show us that policy also plays a critical role. In Charlotte, students still go to school every morning in a district that spans the city-suburban boundary line. But since 2002, the year school officials implemented a plan prioritizing neighborhood-based assignment, school segregation has skyrocketed. According to one popular measure, segregation between the district's black and white students more than doubled after the new assignment policy took effect. In 1992, just 25 percent of Charlotte-Mecklenburg's black students needed to transfer to another school for school-level racial composition to match that of the district, a figure that jumped to 57 percent by 2009. Another way of thinking about these trends is to consider that the typical black student in Charlotte-Mecklenburg attended a school that was 45 percent white in 1992, but only 21 percent white by 2009. (The overall white enrollment in the district also declined during this period, but not nearly as quickly as the share of whites in schools with the typical black student.) The fast-growing Latino student population in Charlotte experienced even more extreme segregation from whites over the twenty-year period.

Map 3 offers visual confirmation of the dramatic shifts underway in Charlotte-Mecklenburg schools. The first two frames show that, during the days of court-ordered desegregation, black and white students were evenly distributed across elementary schools. But the final frame illustrates the relationship between unitary status, the adoption of the new assignment policy, and sharp racial imbalances across elementary schools. It also indicates that black and Latino students are increasingly attending schools together, a trend that bears close watching as stakeholders consider the opportunities and challenges linked to educating two historically underserved groups together.[13]

Other studies document rising racial and socioeconomic segregation in Charlotte-Mecklenburg,[14] in addition to exploring some of the educational and social outcomes associated with the end of school desegregation. Though the black-white test score gap remains unchanged since unitary status,[15] students in resegregated, minority schools have experienced declines in academic performance,[16] decreased chances of attending college,[17] and exposure to less effective teachers.[18] Resegregation is also linked to large upticks in criminality among nonwhite males.[19] Several of these studies established a causal link between the end of desegregation and negative educational and life outcomes. In short, the harms that flow

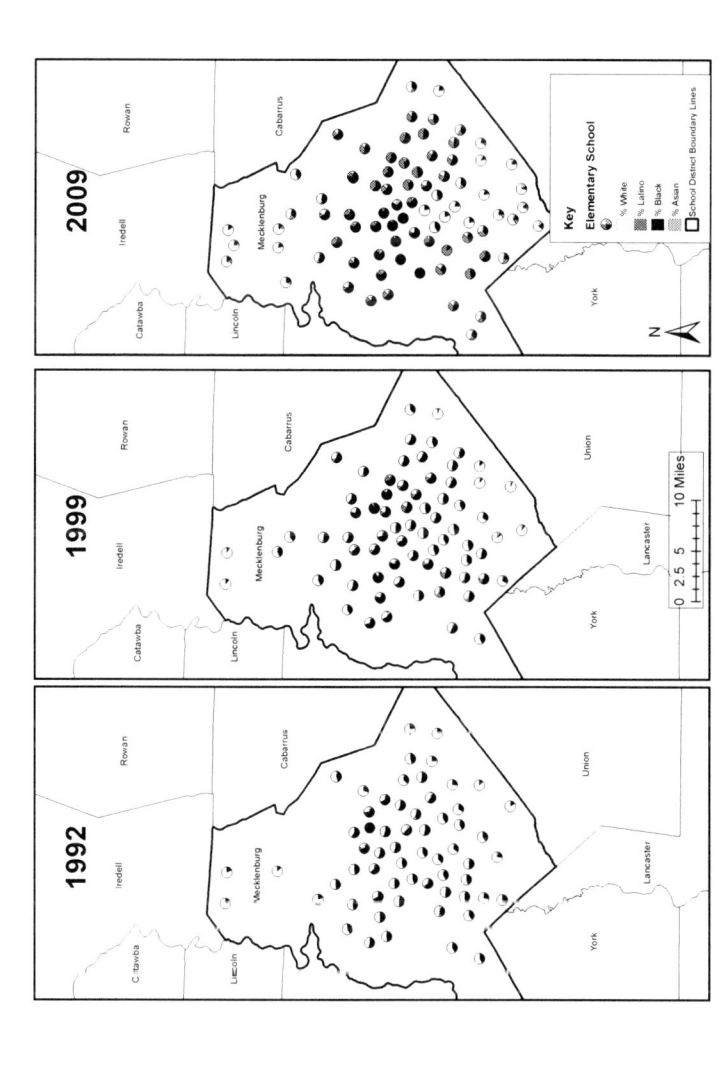

MAP 3 Elementary School Racial Composition, Charlotte-Mecklenburg County, 1992–2009. NCES Common Core of Data, 1992–93, 1999–2000, and 2009–10. For a color version of this map, please visit: http://hdl.handle.net/10156/5060.

from segregated school environments are on full display in postunitary Charlotte-Mecklenburg.

While Charlotte still clings to the demographic advantages of a regional district, ending the district's desegregation policy has led to resegregation and many related harms. The Charlotte case indicates that policies designed to more evenly distribute students and opportunities across schools need to accompany efforts to bring down city-suburban fences. In much the same way that desegregation plans brought students of different backgrounds together in the same school, but often failed to monitor how students were assigned to classrooms within schools,[20] without guiding policy, eliminating district boundaries does not necessarily translate into diversity in all schools.

To really grasp this point, we need to head back over the Appalachian Mountains to Chattanooga. After the 1997 merger in Chattanooga-Hamilton County, the city-suburban district adopted several policies designed to take advantage of new enrollment patterns. Specifically, district officials undertook a modest effort to rezone attendance lines to promote diversity and also to expand the existing system of magnet schools. Over the years, those efforts were associated with declining school segregation (see Map 4 for a visual of the change over time). The share of black students attending intensely segregated schools across the city-suburban landscape fell from nearly 60 percent in 1992 to about 35 percent in 2009.[21] The typical black student across both districts went to a school in which white peers made up about a quarter of the enrollment prior to the merger, compared to nearly one-third of the enrollment a decade after the merger. Still, segregation between black and white students remained high. In 2009, the stark discrepancy between the overall share of whites in the consolidated school system (about 60 percent) and the share of whites in the school of the typical black student (about 30 percent), along with the still-high percentage of black students attending intensely segregated schools (about 35 percent), indicated that, despite marked progress, school segregation by race remained intense.

Racial segregation also overlapped with poverty. In 2009, low-income students made up about 52 percent of the enrollment in Chattanooga. The typical black student, however, went to a school where approximately 68 percent of his or her peers were low income. By contrast, the typical white student went to a school where low-income students accounted for about 42 percent of the enrollment.

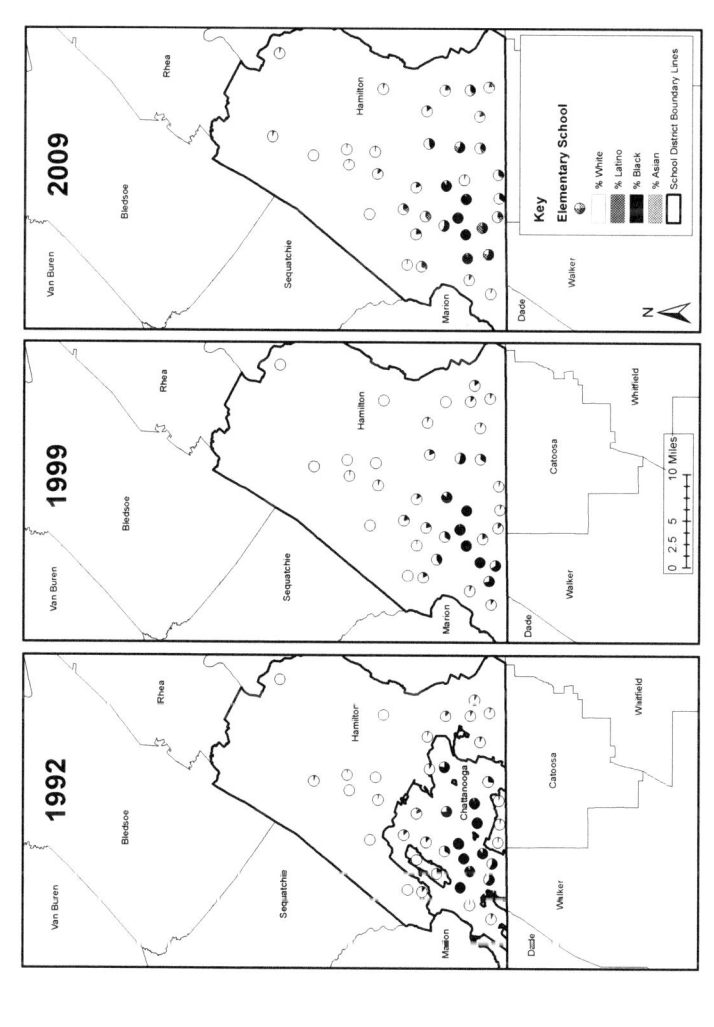

MAP 4 Elementary School Racial Composition, Chattanooga–Hamilton County, 1992–2009. NCES Common Core of Data, 1992–93, 1998–99, and 2009–10. For a color version of this map, please visit: http://hdl.handle.net/10156/5060.

Trends in Chattanooga, then, suggest that the urban and suburban district merger, along with limited school desegregation efforts, were linked to modest progress—with much work remaining. A different comparison of our metros, this time involving Chattanooga and Louisville, underscores another important takeaway: the type of desegregation policy shapes how effectively it brings students of different backgrounds together.

Type of School Desegregation Policy Matters

In postmerger Chattanooga-Hamilton County, rezoning and the expansion of city-suburban magnet programs, which draw students across different attendance zones, are linked to clear declines in school segregation between black and white students. But that improvement, as important as it is, pales in comparison to the stable, long-term, and widespread desegregation for black and white students in Louisville. The differing school segregation trends in the city-suburban districts of Chattanooga and Louisville go hand-in-hand with very different desegregation policies.

The early days of court-ordered school desegregation in the newly consolidated Louisville-Jefferson County district were stained by fear, protest, and violence. Those initial reactions gave way—in relatively short order—to voluntary and comprehensive city-suburban school desegregation. For most of the time period under study, desegregation policy in the Louisville metro called for all schools to maintain a 15–50 percent black population, centered on the overall black enrollment in the district, which remained steady at about 30 percent. During the same period, the introduction of magnet schools and a controlled choice policy brought new options to the school assignment process. Families ranked preferences among a set of schools and the district sought to honor those choices while still ensuring that all schools fell within the 15–50 percent racial guidelines.

Map 5 shows how successful Louisville's controlled choice policy was during the 1990s, when elementary schools across the district served an evenly distributed population of black and white students. (Less than 1 percent of district students identified as Latino at the time.) Segregation figures for Louisville-Jefferson County support the mapping images. Virtually no Louisville-area students of any racial or economic background attended an intensely segregated school (again, defined as 90–100 percent underrepresented minority) between 1992 and 2009.

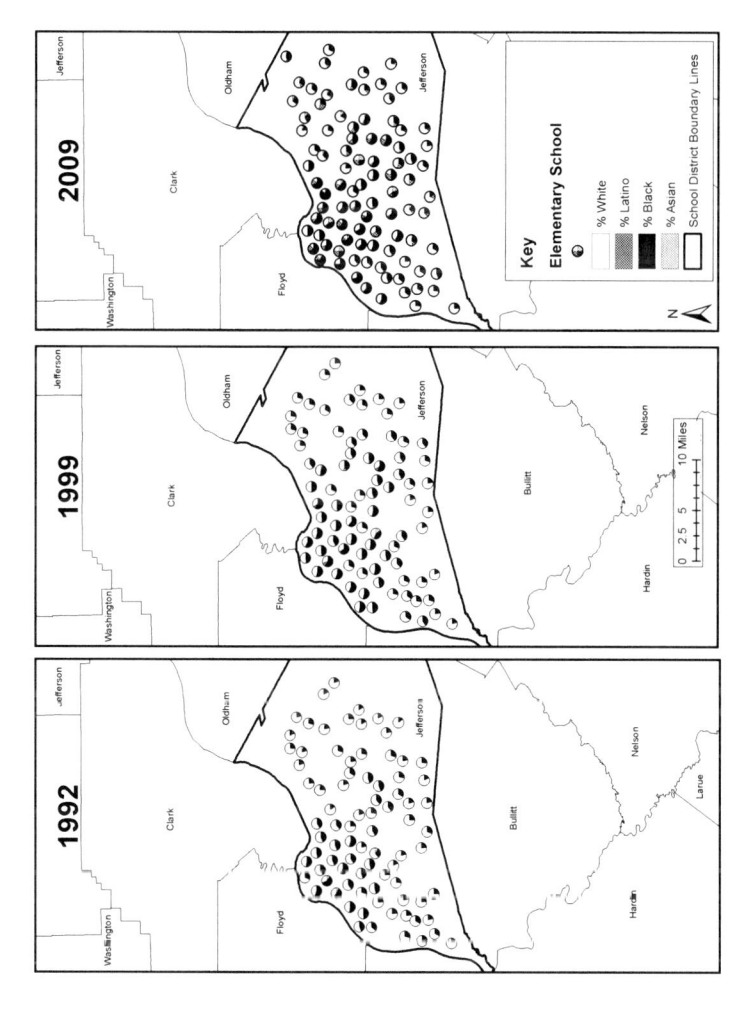

MAP 5 Elementary School Racial Composition, Louisville–Jefferson County, 1992–2009. NCES Common Core of Data, 1992–93, 1999–2000, and 2009–10. For a color version of this map, please visit: http://hdl.handle.net/10156/5060.

By way of comparison, remember that roughly one in three black students in Chattanooga-Hamilton County was enrolled in intensely segregated school settings after the merger. Moreover, black exposure to white students—and vice versa—in Louisville was much higher than in post-merger Chattanooga, as well as far more commensurate with the overall shares of black and white students in the district. Finally, a quick glance back at Map 4 reminds us that a number of racially isolated elementary schools existed in the merged Chattanooga-Hamilton County district, while none were apparent in Louisville. The contrasts between these two consolidated systems indicate that the limited scope of Chattanooga's magnet expansion and school rezoning did not represent the same kind of desegregation as the more comprehensive efforts in Louisville.

School desegregation in Louisville is still remarkably effective in bringing black and white students into contact with one another and, despite numerous political and legal challenges, is broadly supported by the community.[22] A 2011 survey found nine out of ten parents agreeing with the idea that school district guidelines should "ensure that students learn with students from different races and economic backgrounds."[23] Surveys of students also indicate important gains, with large majorities of black and white students reporting that they felt "very comfortable . . . discussing controversial issues related to race" and "working with students from different racial and ethnic backgrounds on group projects." They also felt very prepared to live and work in a diverse society.[24]

In the midst of these successes, the district's student assignment plan experienced another revolution as officials sought ways to bring it into compliance with new legal guidelines. The geography-based plan, which relies on a nuanced understanding of neighborhood characteristics, was in the early stages of formulation and implementation at the close of this study in 2010. Small but noteworthy increases in school segregation for black and Latino students became apparent, along with some concentrations of poverty. Whether Louisville's new policy, which emphasizes multiple facets of diversity—including socioeconomic status and race/ethnicity—can stabilize and address these issues in the coming years remains to be seen.

Origins of District Consolidation Not Necessarily Linked to School Segregation

A related finding involves the relationship between school segregation and the historical circumstances surrounding city-suburban district mergers. Variations in school segregation among the three consolidated school districts of Louisville, Charlotte, and Chattanooga indicate that differences are likely related to the nature of school desegregation policy after the merger, rather than the origins of the merger itself (see Table 3). School trends for the Charlotte and Louisville areas, for example, were remarkably similar in the early 1990s when both districts were implementing comprehensive school desegregation plans. The historical roots of consolidation in the two districts were very different though. Louisville's merger grew out of a 1975 desegregation order, whereas Charlotte-Mecklenburg's consolidation came as a result of a 1959 public referendum. In Chattanooga, consolidation occurred when the city school system relinquished its charter in 1997 and folded into Hamilton County schools. And as we saw, school segregation declined in the merged Chattanooga-Hamilton County district, but not to levels observed in Louisville and preunitary Charlotte. This, again, is almost certainly related to the magnet school and rezoning policies in Chattanooga versus the more wide-ranging controlled choice plans in Louisville and Charlotte. When it comes to school desegregation, it does not seem to matter how city-suburban consolidation occurs, as long as the new, larger district commits to adopting school integration policies alongside the merger. It is important to remember, though, that without consolidation, school district boundaries seal off markedly different populations of students and foster high levels of segregation in the Richmond metro.

We turn now to another fundamental aspect of our analysis: the relationship between city-suburban boundary lines, school integration policies, and housing segregation. Does city-suburban school desegregation help disconnect school segregation from housing segregation? Is metropolitan school desegregation also linked to progress in housing desegregation? And does that relationship differ in communities without a regional school desegregation plan, or in places where a regional plan has ended? The short answers are yes, yes, and yes. But the longer versions offer important lessons about the ways in which a regional approach to school desegregation can extend benefits to spheres beyond education.

Metropolitan School Desegregation Interrupts the School-Housing Relationship on a Regional Scale

Metros with comprehensive school desegregation plans—like Louisville and preunitary-status Charlotte—decoupled school segregation from

TABLE 3 School Segregation, 1992, 1999, and 2009

	Black-White Exposure			Black-White Dissimilarity			Percentage Blacks in Intensely Segregated Schools		
	1992	1999	2009	1992	1999	2009	1992	1999	2009
Richmond metro	28.2	26.6	25.4	0.66	0.65	0.61	36.7	50.9	40.5
Richmond city	8.2	6.1	5.6	0.46	0.49	0.59	69.0	83.6	85.5
Henrico County	44.9	36.1	26.2	0.52	0.59	0.62	10.2	27.2	28.3
Chesterfield County	70.2	60.9	47.4	0.37	0.38	0.39	0.0	0.0	2.7
Louisville-Jefferson County	65.4	59.4	48.3	0.19	0.21	0.26	0.0	0.0	0.0
Charlotte-Mecklenburg County	45.3	40.5	21.2	0.25	0.32	0.57	2.3	2.8	32.4
Chattanooga-Hamilton County	24.9	26.4	31.4	0.77	0.74	0.59	58.3	45.4	35.5
Chattanooga city	19.8			0.64			65.8		
Hamilton County	91.4			0.40			0.0		

Source: NCES Common Core of Data, 1992–93, 1998–99, 1999–2000, and 2009–10.

housing segregation, so that even when residential segregation remained high, students experienced desegregated schools. Most school desegregation plans relied on transportation to accomplish this feat, rendering the yellow school bus a potent symbol of the era.

Mapping the racial makeup of elementary schools on top of the distribution of black residents clearly illustrates how school desegregation policy can help overcome segregated housing patterns. (Elementary schools best illuminate the school-housing relationship because they tend to draw students from smaller geographic areas than middle or high schools.) Maps 6–8 show that, while each of the four southern metros contained segregated urban residential cores, city-suburban school desegregation policies in Louisville and preunitary-status Charlotte were able to distribute students of different racial backgrounds far more evenly across the regional landscape than in Richmond and Chattanooga. Importantly, during much of the time period under study, Charlotte and Louisville had abandoned coordinated efforts to link school and housing desegregation efforts—meaning that school desegregation plans worked alone to desegregate students.

In the early 1990s, sharp contrasts were apparent between the consolidated Louisville and Charlotte school systems compared to the nonconsolidated ones in the Richmond and Chattanooga areas. Note, for instance, that schools were racially balanced even in Charlotte-Mecklenburg and Louisville-Jefferson County's highly segregated neighborhoods (see Map 6). But in the other two metros—Richmond and Chattanooga (premerger)—many students attended segregated elementary schools surrounded by intensely segregated neighborhoods. The presence of urban-suburban district boundaries also meant that the vast majority of these segregated schools and neighborhoods were located within Richmond and Chattanooga's central city school systems.

From the late 1990s to 2010, the Richmond and Chattanooga areas continued to report elementary school enrollments that largely mirrored the racial makeup of nearby neighborhoods. In other words, school segregation overlapped very closely with housing segregation. As Richmond's separate suburban school systems became more diverse, so too did their school enrollments. Increasingly, the predominant pattern of minority segregation in urban schools and neighborhoods extended to parts of the suburbs just over the city-county boundary line (more on this a little later in the chapter). The same trends were evident in Chattanooga-Hamilton County, indicating again that limited school desegregation policy

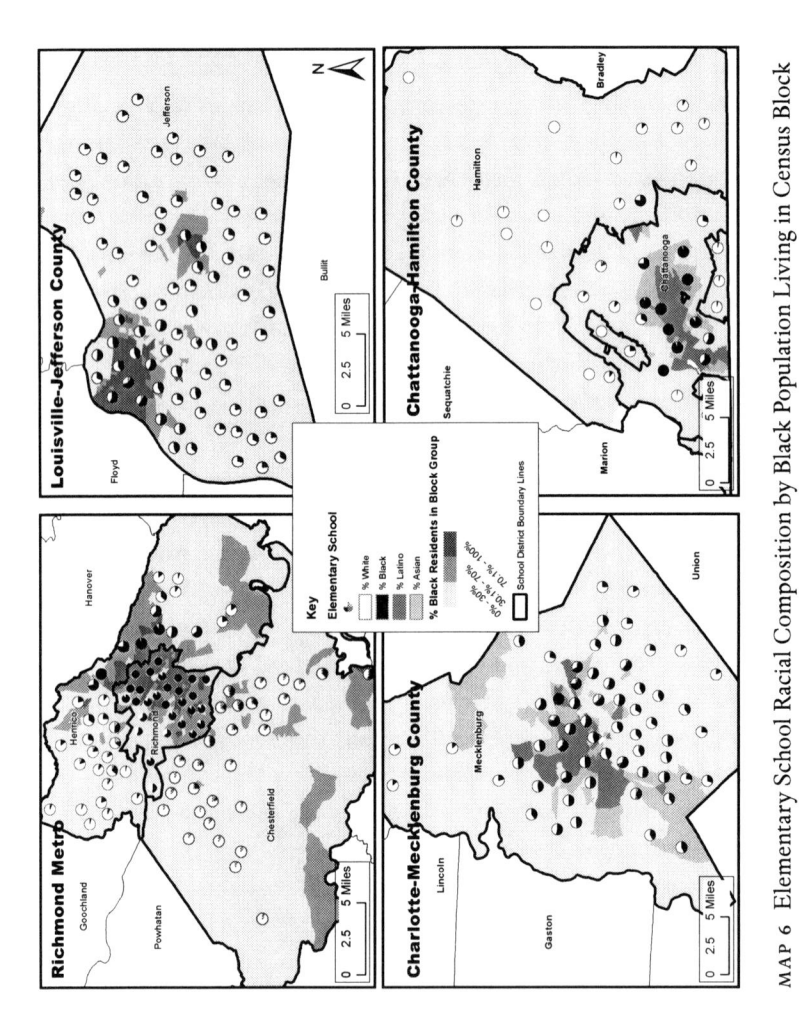

MAP 6 Elementary School Racial Composition by Black Population Living in Census Block Groups, 1990. NCES Common Core of Data, 1992–93; U.S. Census, 1990, SF3, P012. For a color version of this map, please visit: http://hdl.handle.net/10156/5060.

MAP 7 Elementary School Racial Composition by Black Population Living in Census Block Groups 2000. NCES Common Core of Data, 1999–2000; U.S. Census, 2000, SF3, P007. For a color version of this map, please visit: http://hdl.handle.net/10156/5060.

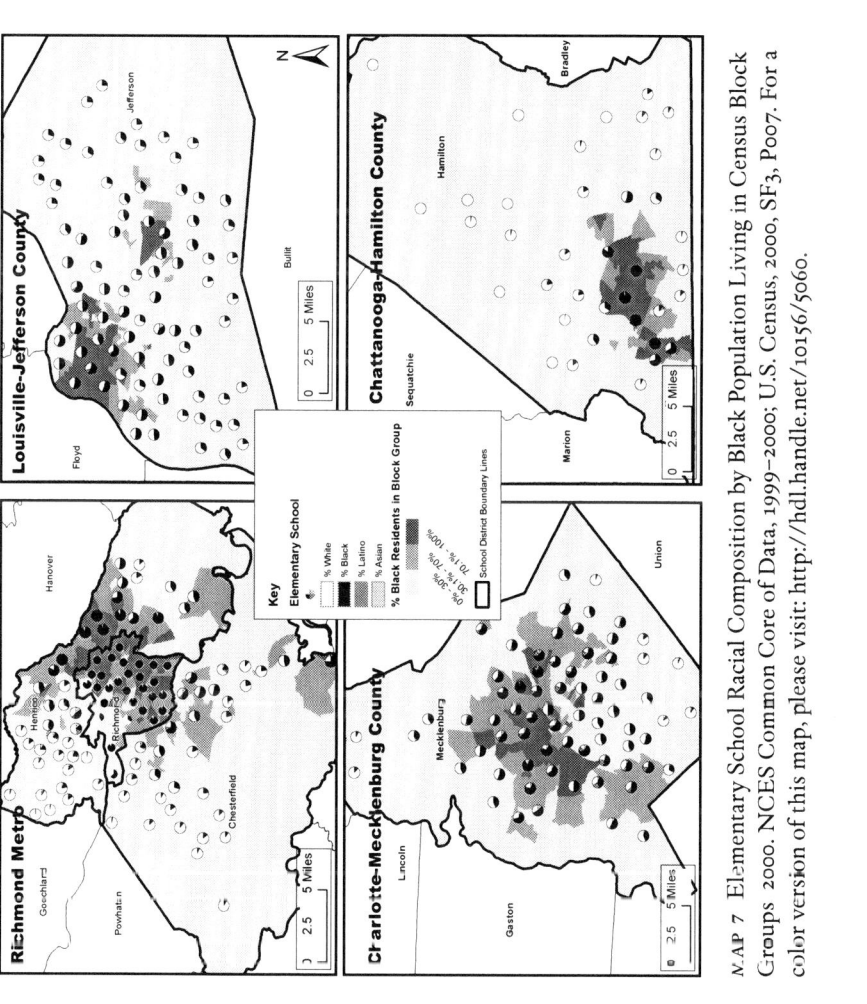

MAP 8 Elementary School Racial Composition by Black Population Living in Census Block Groups, 2010. NCES Common Core of Data, 2008–9; U.S. Census, 2010 redistricting data, P02. For a color version of this map, please visit: http://hdl.handle.net/10156/5060.

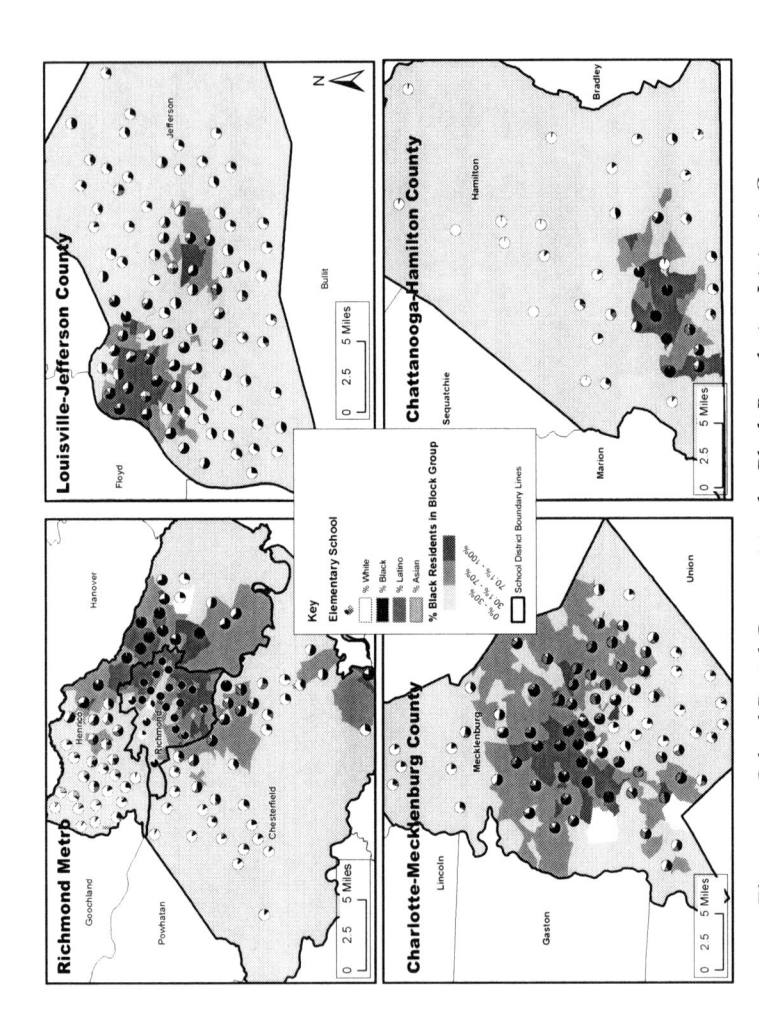

implemented after the 1997 merger did not confront the school-housing relationship as effectively as the controlled choice policies in Louisville and preunitary Charlotte (see Maps 7 and 8).

Charlotte-Mecklenburg's success in disrupting the relationship between school and housing segregation eventually succumbed to mounting political and legal opposition to school desegregation. By 2000, schools in and around Charlotte's urban core, particularly in the western and northwestern quadrants of the city, were beginning to reflect the overwhelmingly black populations of surrounding neighborhoods. Ten years later, Map 8 shows that Charlotte-Mecklenburg school enrollments very much mirrored neighborhood segregation—not necessarily surprising given the postunitary status emphasis on neighborhood schools. The earlier disconnect between patterns of residential and school segregation had all but disappeared.

With these developments unfolding in Charlotte-Mecklenburg, Louisville-Jefferson County became the only metro under study to consistently disrupt the relationship between black-white school and housing segregation. Maps 6–8 display the impact of the metro's ongoing commitment to a comprehensive city-suburban school desegregation policy. Schools across the city-suburban landscape reported roughly even shares of black and white students, reflecting the guidelines in the controlled choice policy. Still, by 2009 several elementary schools in Louisville's still highly segregated inner city had become predominantly black and Latino. This may have been related to the struggle to craft and implement a revised student assignment plan to comply with the 2007 *Parents Involved* decision.

In 2009, it is important to note that intense racial segregation was also linked to elementary schools with high concentrations of student poverty. Map 9 shows that nearly all schools in segregated black neighborhoods contained a majority of students qualifying for free or reduced-priced lunches. Conversely, predominantly nonblack neighborhoods reported schools with much higher shares of students who did not qualify for free or reduced price lunches. These broad trends, which persisted even in Louisville, the only metro with an ongoing, wide-ranging school desegregation plan in 2009, could reflect the historical emphasis on integrating students by race, but not necessarily by class. Louisville-Jefferson County's new, multicriteria student assignment plan—which considers socioeconomic status alongside race—may produce a different set of patterns if it is fully implemented in coming years.

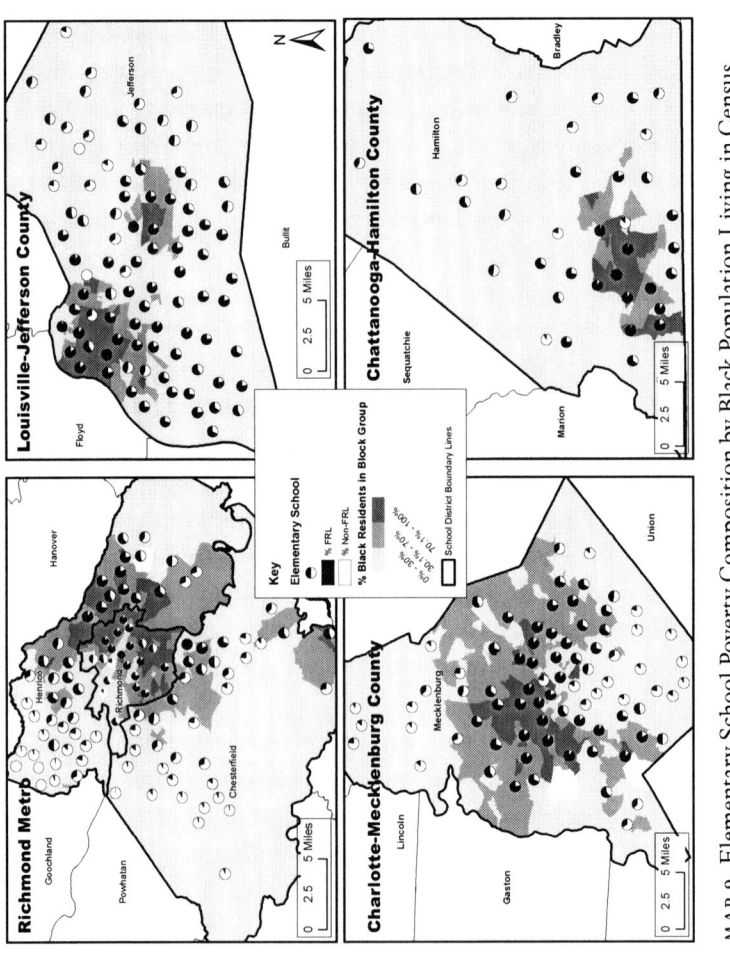

MAP 9 Elementary School Poverty Composition by Black Population Living in Census Block Groups, 2010. NCES Common Core of Data, 2008–9; U.S. Census, 2010 redistricting data, P02. For a color version of this map, please visit: http://hdl.handle.net/10156/5060.

Graphing segregation indices reinforces what we observed in the maps but offers a different way of thinking about the evolution of the school-housing relationship in each southern metro. A measure of how unevenly students and residents are spread out across our metros shows that the connection between school and housing segregation varied widely according to school district boundary arrangements and the presence or absence of school desegregation policy.

In the merged areas of Louisville and Charlotte, the large gap between the lines representing school and housing segregation in Figure 1 indicates that, in the early 1990s, when both metros employed comprehensive school desegregation plans, school segregation between black and white students was low even as residential segregation remained high. About 20–25 percent of black students in both metros needed to change schools to be evenly distributed with white students in the early nineties, compared to roughly 70–80 percent of black residents needing to change neighborhoods. In short, in the 1990s, no matter where you lived in the city-suburban districts of Louisville and Charlotte, you were connected to a desegregated school. That guarantee helped break the link between school considerations and the selection of homes for many families.[25]

During the same time period, Richmond and Chattanooga reported high and deeply intertwined neighborhood and school segregation. Both Richmond and Chattanooga were defined by separate city and suburban school systems and a lack of desegregation policy in the early years of this study. Where you lived in those two metros determined whether or not you went to an urban or suburban school, which closely corresponded to whether or not you attended a racially identifiable black or white school. School and school district names passed along racial and socioeconomic information to families looking for homes, making it much more difficult to disentangle school decisions from housing decisions.

Fast-forward a couple of decades, though, to find a changed landscape in Charlotte and Chattanooga. Between 2000 and 2010, the end of Charlotte's school desegregation plan was linked to rising school segregation that eventually matched the intensity of housing segregation (see Figure 1). Abandoning the school policy, then, reconnected school segregation to residential segregation in an unmistakable way. The renewed emphasis on neighborhood schools in Charlotte meant that existing patterns of residential segregation were mirrored in the enrollment of nearby schools. In Chattanooga, the years after the 1997 merger were defined by rapidly falling school and housing segregation—schools were slightly

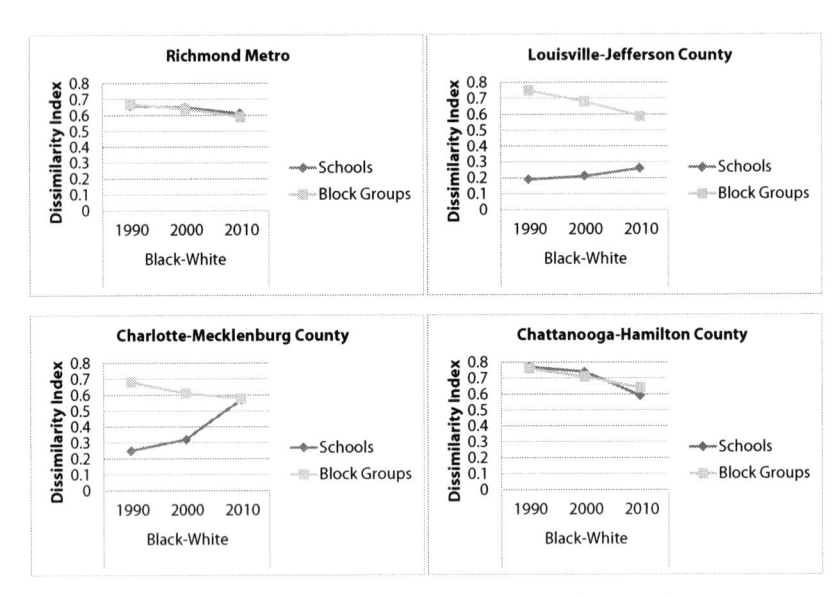

FIGURE 1 School and Residential Black-White Dissimilarity Index, 1990–2010. NCES Common Core of Data, 1992–93, 1999–2000, 2009–10; U.S. Census, 1990, 2000, 2010.

ahead of housing—though the two remained closely connected. We see once again that the magnet school and rezoning policies in Chattanooga did not disentangle school and housing patterns from one another as completely as Charlotte and Louisville's controlled choice plans. At the same time, both school and residential segregation in the Chattanooga area were improving.

Finally, Richmond's school and housing segregation remained very high and entangled over the two decades of study, as no explicit school desegregation policy existed in area school systems divided by urban and suburban boundary lines.

The same general patterns prevailed using a measure of segregation that helps describe contact between different groups of students or residents. Figure 2 shows that black students and residents had little exposure to white students and residents in Richmond and Chattanooga in the years prior to the city-suburban school district merger. In 1990, the typical black student in the Richmond and Chattanooga metros went to a school that was less than 30 percent white (even though whites made up between 60 and 70 percent of the metro enrollment), and the typical black resident lived in a neighborhood that was a little over 30 percent white (even

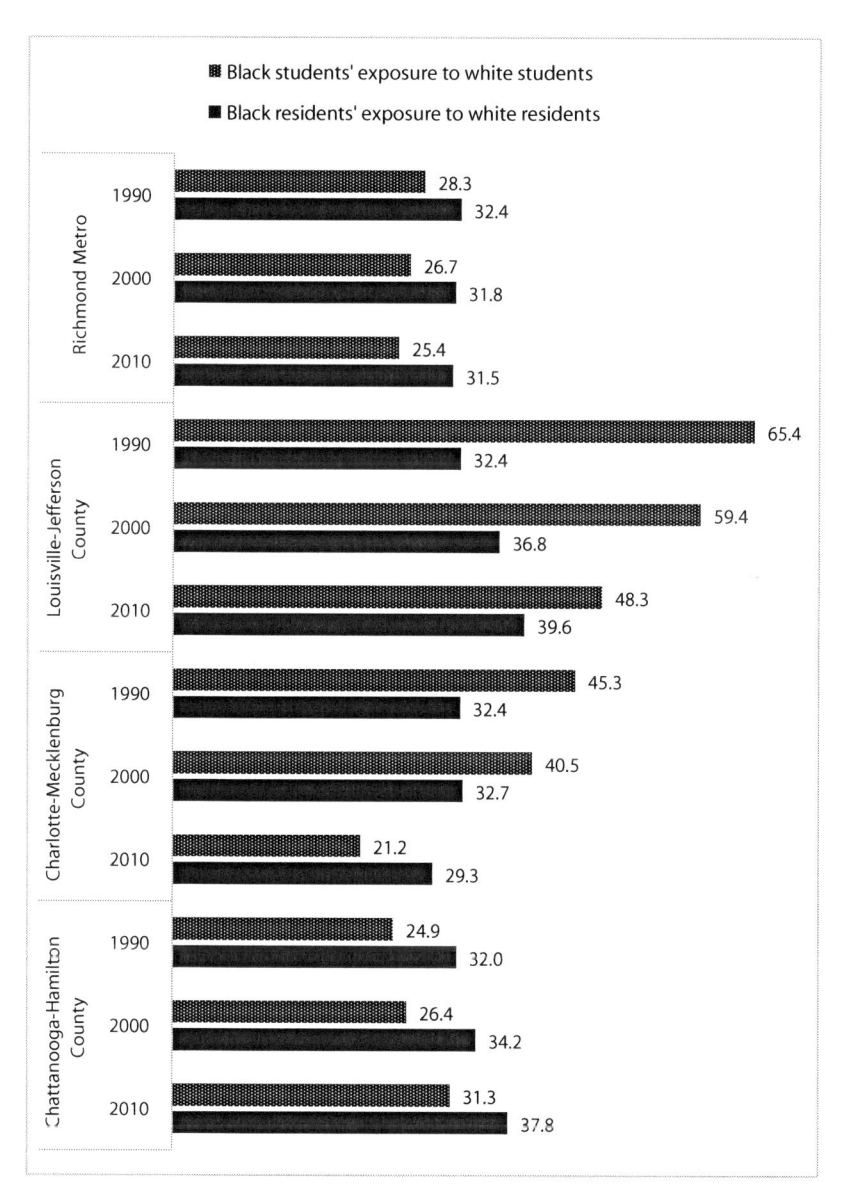

		Black students' exposure to white students	Black residents' exposure to white residents
Richmond Metro	1990	28.3	32.4
	2000	26.7	31.8
	2010	25.4	31.5
Louisville-Jefferson County	1990	65.4	32.4
	2000	59.4	36.8
	2010	48.3	39.6
Charlotte-Mecklenburg County	1990	45.3	32.4
	2000	40.5	32.7
	2010	21.2	29.3
Chattanooga-Hamilton County	1990	24.9	32.0
	2000	26.4	34.2
	2010	31.3	37.8

FIGURE 2 Black Students' and Residents' Exposure to White Students and Residents, 1990–2010. NCES Common Core of Data, 1992–93, 1999–2000, 2009–10; U.S. Census, 1990, 2000, 2010.

though whites accounted for 70–80 percent of the metro population). Twenty years later, Richmond's exposure numbers were slightly lower—likely related to the overall decline in the white population—but, even with similar population shifts, Chattanooga's figures had improved. The typical black student in the newly merged Chattanooga system went to a school that was more than 30 percent white, and the typical black resident lived in a neighborhood that was about 38 percent white.

By contrast, in the 1990s, Charlotte and Louisville reported very high black student exposure to whites, and much lower black resident exposure to whites. In 1990, the typical black student in Louisville-Jefferson County attended a school with more than double the share of whites (65.4 percent) than the typical black resident experienced in his or her neighborhood (32.4 percent). Charlotte-Mecklenburg reported similar trends in 1990 and 2000, though the rapidly increasing Latino population meant that black exposure to whites was somewhat lower than in Louisville.

Later though, a dramatic shift in exposure between blacks and whites in Charlotte reemphasizes the way school desegregation policy can interrupt the link between school and housing segregation—and how the abandonment of that policy quickly restores the relationship. In 2000, just prior to the declaration of unitary status, the average black student in Charlotte-Mecklenburg attended a school where whites made up about 40 percent of the student body. During that time, black residents lived in neighborhoods where white residents accounted for, on average, about 33 percent of their neighbors. But by 2010, the share of white students in the school of the typical black student had been cut in half to about 20 percent, even though whites still made up about 34 percent of the overall enrollment. Charlotte also reported a decline in black exposure to white residents after the district was released from court oversight, though it remained higher than black-white school exposure. What was once known as the "schooling advantage" in the South—shorthand for the idea that school desegregation policies meant that black students were more integrated than the overall black population—faded rapidly in Charlotte, as it did in other communities that abandoned school desegregation.[26]

Metropolitan School Desegregation Associated with Faster Declines in Housing Segregation

Not only did metropolitan school desegregation break the close link between school and housing segregation in our four metros, it also—as prior research and earlier theory have indicated—helped speed up the pace of housing desegregation. A refresher on how this relationship works: in an area governed by a regional school desegregation plan, families find schools of similar racial makeup and quality across a broad swath of the region. School district boundaries no longer fragment communities and schools into racially identifiable spaces, interrupting the feedback loop between residential and school segregation. Freed from the usual calculations about school demographics and quality in the search for new homes, the regional housing market opens up for families to make more integrating residential choices.[27]

Recall also that James Madison outlined the theoretical contours of this process very early in our country's history.[28] In Madison's view of federalism, expanding the boundaries of a community would in turn expand the scope of shared interests and concerns. While he was thinking more along the lines of national boundaries, the same wisdom applies to regional borders. Residents living within a geographic area governed by metropolitan school desegregation are more inclined to view all schools as viable options worthy of the kind of engagement and support that tend to be unevenly concentrated in more fragmented communities.[29]

Another dimension of the relationship between city-suburban school desegregation and faster declines in housing segregation is backed by theoretical and empirical evidence. As originally conceived, perpetuation theory posited that minority students exposed to white students early in their education would be more inclined to seek out diverse experiences later in life—in college, workplaces, and so forth.[30] More recent research indicates that the perpetuation benefits of desegregation flow to both white and nonwhite students, and that those benefits often lead to more diverse residential choices for adult graduates of desegregated schools.[31] Intergenerational impacts of metropolitan school desegregation are thus possible if graduates of desegregated environments choose to live in desegregated neighborhoods and send their own children to desegregated schools.[32] With a renewed understanding of how the link between metropolitan school and housing segregation functions, let us now return to our four metros.

In keeping with national trends, black-white residential segregation, according to one popular measure, declined modestly in all four sites during the time period under study.[33] Yet metros with city-suburban school desegregation reported swifter decreases in black-white housing segregation (see Figures 1 and 3). Between 1990 and 2000, when Charlotte

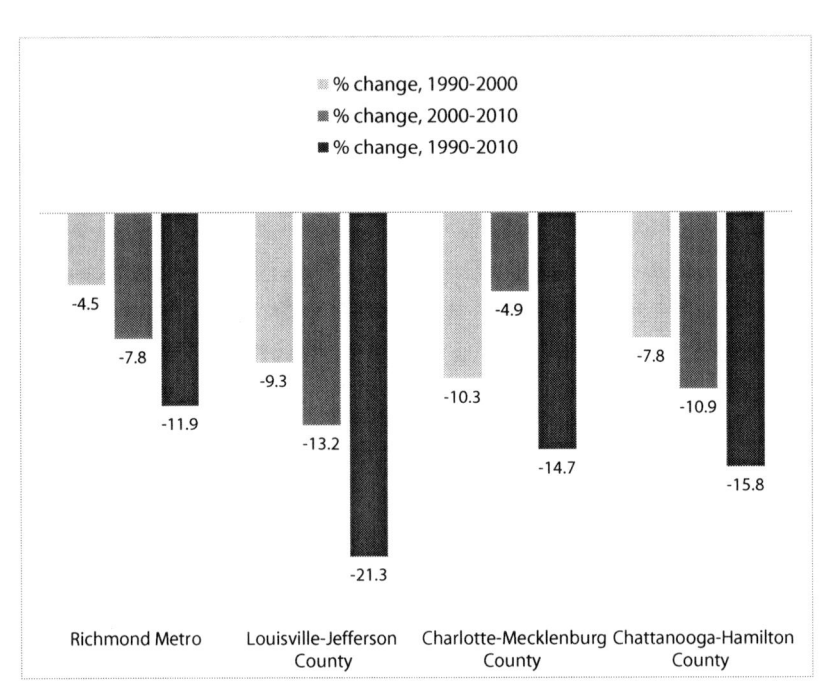

FIGURE 3 Percentage Change in Black-White/White-Black Residential Dissimilarity Index, 1990–2000, 2000–2010, and 1990–2010. NCES Common Core of Data, 1992–93, 1999–2000, 2008–9; U.S. Census, 1990, 2000, 2010.

and Louisville were implementing controlled choice desegregation plans, black-white housing segregation fell by approximately 10 percent, compared to about 5 percent in the Richmond area and 8 percent in Chattanooga-Hamilton County.

In Charlotte, progress on black-white housing segregation slowed considerably in the aftermath of unitary status. Segregation between black and white residents in the Charlotte area declined about 5 percent between 2000 and 2010, compared to over 10 percent between 1990 and 2000, when the school desegregation policy remained in effect (see Figure 3). In just one decade, Charlotte-Mecklenburg County went from leading the group of four metros in residential desegregation between blacks and whites to third from last, just in front of the Richmond area.

In Chattanooga-Hamilton County, housing and school segregation began decreasing more quickly following the 1997 merger and adoption of some school desegregation measures. Between 1990 and 2000, black-white housing segregation declined by just 8 percent. By contrast, from 2000 to 2010, when patterns associated with the late 1990s merger and magnet school expansion were more likely to appear, black-white housing segregation fell by almost 11 percent.

Finally, Louisville-Jefferson County reported the fastest declines in housing segregation out of our four metros. Black-white housing segregation in Louisville-Jefferson County fell roughly 9 percent from 1990 to 2000, and about 13 percent from 2000 to 2010. Findings from Louisville, located at one end of the spectrum of policy and consolidation options, contrasted sharply with figures from Richmond, the metro at the opposite end. Black-white housing segregation in Louisville-Jefferson County fell almost twice as fast as residential segregation trends in the Richmond area (see Figure 3). Evidence from Louisville-Jefferson County underscores the positive relationship between city-suburban school desegregation plans and declining rates of residential segregation between blacks and whites. Interestingly, the success and related public support for the regional school desegregation plan in Louisville also helped promote the consolidation of its city-suburban government.

It is critical to understand that our four metros are by no means an anomaly when it comes to these trends. In a large-scale study of major U.S. metros between the years 1980 and 2010, regional experts Myron Orfield and Thomas Luce showed that diverse neighborhoods were much more likely to stabilize in the fifteen metropolitan areas with regional desegregation plans (including Wake County, North Carolina; Las Vegas, Nevada; Wilmington, Delaware; and Tampa-St. Petersburg, Florida) than in areas without such plans.[34] In other words, during a period when many metros were reporting swift racial transition in their neighborhoods—particularly those located in close-in suburbs—metros with large-scale school desegregation plans were characterized by far more stability. Numerically, this meant that, in 1980, neighborhoods that were more than 23 percent nonwhite in major metros without region-wide desegregation plans were more likely to become predominantly nonwhite by 2009 than remain integrated. By contrast, in metropolitan areas with region-wide desegregation plans, neighborhoods between 23 and 33 percent nonwhite in 1980 were about 50–60 percent less likely to experience racial turnover and resegregation by 2009.[35] Earlier research examining the period between 1970 and 1990 also found that metropolitan school desegregation was linked to rates of decline in residential segregation that were twice as large as rates of decline in areas without metro desegregation.[36] Those numbers dovetail neatly with the differences we observed in residential segregation between the Richmond and Louisville areas during our more recent 1990–2010 period.

Multiracial Change and Blurring the Urban-Suburban Boundary Line

In each of our four southern metros, regardless of whether or not district consolidation occurred, the black-and-white story of school desegregation is quickly giving way to a triracial context. Latino students now account for between 5 and 15 percent of the school enrollment in all four metro areas, representing a significant increase over the past two decades (see Table 1 for exact numbers). Moreover, the Asian share of school enrollment, while still small, is growing quickly in our four locales.

These shifts are part of a broader pattern of multiracial change taking place across the region and the country. Schools in the South and the West are at the leading edge of what William Frey of the Brookings Institution has labeled a "diversity explosion."[37] Both regions now report majority-minority enrollments, with Latino students outnumbering whites in the West and black students in the South.[38] Amid these profound shifts, the share of students qualifying for free and reduced-priced lunch (a common but rough proxy for student poverty) has surged. In 2009, the South was the first region in the country to report that more than half of its students were eligible for the federal free or reduced-priced lunch program.[39] The rest of the country soon caught up: By 2013, 51 percent of the nation's children were eligible for the federal program.[40]

Demographic change raises new questions about how we define segregation and desegregation—to say nothing of integration—in our contemporary society. Is a school that serves a mixture of black and Latino students, as many settings in Charlotte now do, desegregated? How does the fact that these schools are often places of concentrated poverty influence the answer? What about the schools in the western part of the Richmond suburbs serving predominantly white and Asian students, with very few students who qualify for free and reduced-priced lunch? Should they be considered desegregated?

Most experts who grapple with these questions believe that bringing together two or more historically disadvantaged racial/ethnic groups (with the important understanding that much variation exists among groups that fall generally under the heading of Latino or Asian) does not constitute meaningful desegregation—particularly when overlapping and high levels of student poverty come into focus.[41] Desegregation, after all, is about more than simply bringing students of different backgrounds together in the same building. It is also about exposing and linking diverse students to opportunity-rich schools and social networks. Those settings, ties, and contacts help weave a web of life possibilities that look very different than what tends to be produced in low-opportunity contexts.[42]

Because our changing demographics call for a nuanced consideration of the way that race, ethnicity, and socioeconomic status interact to produce opportunity, the exact definition of segregation and desegregation can vary depending on the local context.[43] Decided swings in what the courts view as acceptable remedies for racial isolation further complicate matters.[44] In recent years, policymakers and stakeholders at various levels of government have reacted to demographic change and legal constraints in different ways. Here again, our four metros offer important examples of these varied responses.

In Louisville, when the Supreme Court struck down the former desegregation plan (in part because it disagreed with the simplistic racial categories—black and nonblack—used to make student assignment decisions), the district began to look for new ways to define diversity. The current plan in Louisville considers several different racial/ethnic and socioeconomic factors, which may help the district keep pace with the many changes taking place in the community. In Charlotte, the end of desegregation coincided with the explosive growth of the Latino population. As we saw, black and Latino students in the district are now disproportionately exposed to one another, and to student poverty. Today, Charlotte's Latino students confront triple segregation: by race, socioeconomic status, and language. And in Chattanooga, the district bypassed the issue of racial segregation altogether when it designed magnet school diversity goals based on socioeconomic status. These criteria were developed with guidance from the Bush-era U.S. Department of Education's Magnet School Assistance Program (see chapter 5). The district maintained those economic diversity goals through the time period under study, though the federal government did not renew magnet funding after 2010.

In the Richmond area, where the urban and suburban school divisions remain separate, growing multiracial diversity and other demographic shifts have unfolded across concrete district boundaries. Let us take a closer look at the interaction between those boundaries and racial and economic change—doing so offers an important perspective on what is occurring in many places around the country.[45]

Resegregation across the City-Suburban Boundary Line in Richmond

Today, nearly two decades after Judge Merhige's consolidation order was overturned on appeal, the black-white dichotomy between Richmond's city and surrounding suburbs is less distinct. Growing numbers of black families with the means to cross into the suburbs have done so, rendering inner suburban neighborhoods and suburban schools temporarily more diverse. But in a pattern that has unfolded in a number of close-in suburbs—even more so in the many metros like Richmond without regional school desegregation plans—that diversity gave way, in relatively short order, to resegregation.[46]

Map 10 illustrates the process of racial change and increasing segregation in an inner-ring suburban area just across Richmond's northeastern border. In 1990, two small sections of central Henrico were less than 30 percent black, holdovers from a not-so-distant era when white residents accounted for more than 90 percent of the suburb's population.[47] More predominant, however, were diverse neighborhoods in which black residents made up between 30 and 70 percent of the population. At the same time, black residents accounted for the overwhelming share of residents in a handful of central Henrico neighborhoods, particularly those closest to the city-suburban line, almost mirroring patterns in the city of Richmond. And in conjunction with those neighborhood trends, in 1990 elementary schools serving this portion of Henrico County enrolled large majorities of black students, though several still reported sizable shares of white students.

A decade later, in 2000, larger portions of central Henrico were characterized by growing black isolation. Elementary schools in the area reflected these shifts, nearly all of which were intensely segregated by this point (see Map 10).

By 2010, the movement of blacks across Richmond and Henrico's school district boundary line meant that serious resegregation had taken root in the central portion of the suburb. Black students constituted nearly 100 percent of the student population in central Henrico's elementary schools, almost certainly a foreshadowing of further neighborhood transition to come. Map 10 also shows that Latino students, for the first time, accounted for a small share of students in central Henrico—indicative of future patterns of black-Latino segregation. In another ten years, unless active steps are taken to provide black suburban students

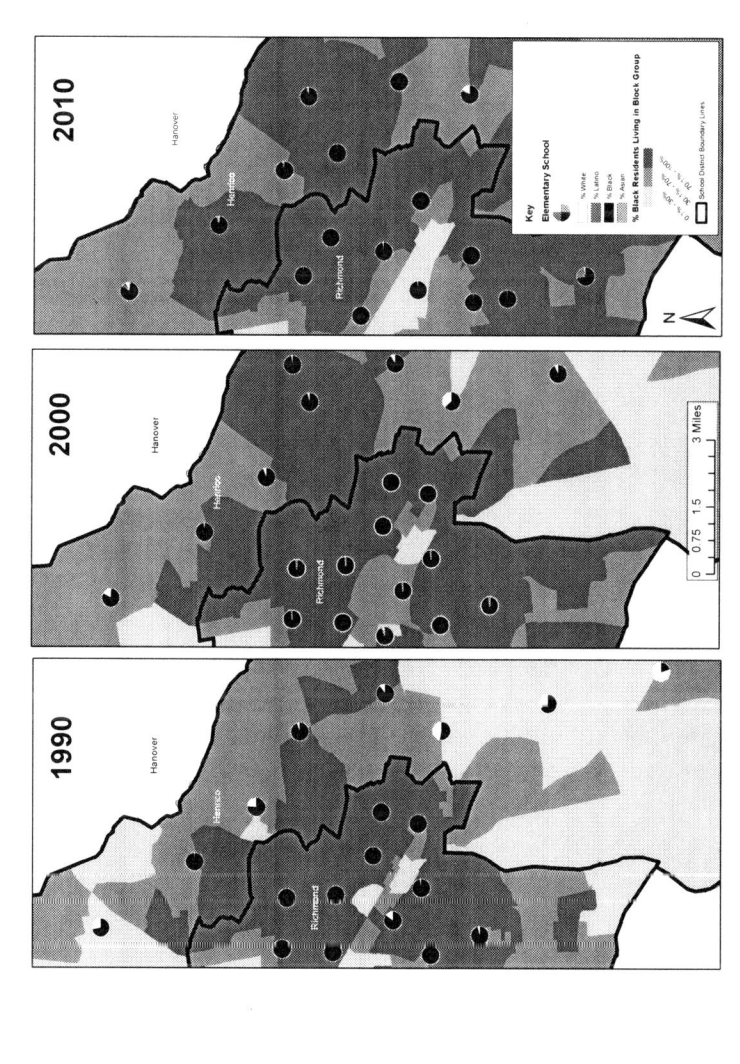

MAP 10 Elementary School Racial Composition by Black Population Living in Census Block Groups, Richmond-Henrico, 1990, 2000, and 2010. NCES Common Core of Data, 1992–93, 1999–2000, 2009–10; U.S. Census, 1990, 2000, 2010. For a color version of this map, please visit: http://hdl.handle.net/10156/5060.

and residents with greater access to other parts of Henrico, large swaths of the county may look a lot like the city's historically segregated neighborhoods.

Conversely, in some limited places Richmond is beginning to resemble the Henrico County of yesteryear. A growing portion of downtown and eastern neighborhoods reported majority white populations in 2010 (see Map 10). That shift likely reflects the leading edge of Richmond's first white population increase in decades, a trend that has intensified since the close of this study.[48] When it comes to schools in and around those gentrifying city neighborhoods, however, little easing of extreme minority segregation is apparent—to date.

The blurring of the boundary between Richmond's urban and inner suburban school systems should be viewed alongside a surge in white residents and students living in the outer suburbs. A 2011 report from the Brookings Institution noted that five of the nation's twenty fastest-growing exurban communities in terms of white population increases were located on the outskirts of Richmond.[49] Put more grimly: white exodus from diversifying communities continues, but the geographic scale of the retreat grows wider. So while shifting student and resident populations in the city and close-in suburbs represent new opportunities to promote school diversity within those districts, the growth of white families on the fringes of metropolitan communities means that thinking about how to bring students together across regions remains absolutely critical. We know from the research and theory surrounding metropolitan school desegregation that systematic efforts to promote diverse schools are most effective when they occur across a significant expanse of a region. Regional plans desgregate schools and stabilize diversifying neighborhoods—so that the process of racial change that we saw in Henrico becomes less likely to culminate in extreme minority segregation.

The Richmond area showcases how significant demographic changes play out in a fragmented context that has chosen to ignore school (and neighborhood) segregation for nearly three decades. While the fragmentation of Richmond differs from our other three city-suburban school systems, it is emblematic of many other parts of the country.[50] Rapid growth and demographic change in most metropolitan communities has occurred largely without accompanying policies seeking to harness the potential of those transformations. Instead, in many ways, law and policy have cemented tremendous inequities into the structure of our cities.

This chapter provides crucial new evidence of the consequences of our retrenchment on policies designed to promote equal educational opportunity across regions. In metros like Charlotte, where desegregation plans have been significantly changed or abandoned altogether, our analysis tells a story of what was lost—but also of what might still be regained. Louisville, which continues to operate under a comprehensive region-wide school desegregation policy, shows us that such plans are linked to more integrated schools and more progress on residential segregation. Louisville points the way for other locales—Richmond, for example—that have not yet adopted policies designed to lessen the impact of boundaries and promote desegregation to examine the consequences of their inaction, and be spurred toward greater efforts.

What those efforts might look like of course will vary according to the local context. There are a number of general policy options and principles to guide interested communities, however. The final section of this book is dedicated to exploring available solutions to persistent patterns of educational inequality in the twenty-first century. It delves first into the past and present circumstances of school choice, as the current state of the courts means that nearly all contemporary school desegregation efforts are voluntary.

PART III | Solutions

CHAPTER FIVE

The Choice Conundrum
Challenges and Opportunities for Voluntary School Desegregation Policy

> The New Kent County freedom of choice plan is not acceptable, it has not dismantled the dual system, but has operated simply to burden students and their parents with a responsibility that *Brown II* placed squarely on the School Board.
> —GREEN V. NEW KEW COUNTY, 1968

> The most compelling civil rights issue of the 21st century is the need to expand school choice and educational options.
> —SENATOR TED CRUZ, 2014

> Parents' confidence in the public school system is in shambles. It's crumbled. So parents are trying to pick among the ruins to find the school districts they believe represent a decent chance for their children to make it safely through school. . . . Zip codes should not act as barbed-wire fences to keep out children whose parents cannot afford homes in that district. . . . Decouple school assignment and zip code . . . then the economic pressure on families would be released almost immediately.
> —SENATOR ELIZABETH WARREN (compiled from various sources)

To understand how the past record of school choice relates to segregation, look no further than to the immediate aftermath of two pivotal school desegregation rulings. School choice designed to resist desegregation was largely forged in the wake of *Brown*, just as school choice designed to promote desegregation was largely forged in the wake of *Milliken*. Arch-segregationists opposing *Brown* used freedom-of-choice plans and private school vouchers to help white families skirt desegregation requirements. Civil rights advocates confronting *Milliken*'s calcified urban-suburban boundary lines expanded choice-based magnet schools to retain and attract white and middle-class families in swiftly resegregating central city systems. In the early aftermath of *Milliken*, a handful of legal victories proving interdistrict violations in Midwestern metros also established school choice policies as a way to help students cross jurisdictional boundaries. The great advance and retreat that *Brown* and *Milliken* respectively represented, then, gave rise to very different uses of school choice.

In recent years, the once clear divisions between school choice policies used to promote or undermine desegregation have been hidden beneath rhetoric claiming that the provision of choice itself will give way to more equal educational opportunity.[1] Senator Ted Cruz's quote above is just one example of a view that conservative and liberal politicians alike have espoused. All sides have much to gain from their positions: political backing for the expansion of school choice extends across a wide array of communities.[2] Many families living in neighborhoods assigned to underperforming schools that struggle with double or triple segregation by race, socioeconomic status, and language latch tightly onto the prospect of educational alternatives for their children.[3] Families living wealthy, predominantly white areas are also typically amenable to the concept of school choice—though many, as Senator Elizabeth Warren suggests, already exercised it when buying a home and do not see the need for an alternate educational system in their own community.[4] Some of these same families also may balk at the idea of providing children from less advantaged neighborhoods access to their schools, resistance vividly illustrated by a spate of criminal charges filed against mothers seeking to enroll their children in affluent, suburban districts other than the one in which they resided full-time.[5] Still, when it comes to the basic principle (if not always the reality) of allowing families to choose among a set of schools, well-off parents tend to be supportive.[6]

School choice can take many forms, ranging from selecting a neighborhood based on the schools with which it is associated to enrolling students in private, charter, or magnet schools. As the courts began to relinquish their oversight of mandatory school desegregation plans, choice-based efforts to promote school desegregation became ever more central. By offering families options beyond their assigned—often neighborhood[7]— school, choice has the power to sever the threads that bind school and housing segregation so tightly together. And when it comes to furthering the regional educational agenda, Senator Warren's quote highlights another key aspect of choice: in the event that the boundary lines between city and suburban districts remain intact, choice can help make them more porous.

Yet fashioning school choice in ways that seek to fairly benefit all students is crucial, and doing so requires a nuanced understanding of the history, theory, and evidence behind the expanding choice movement. A synthesis of those different choice-related dimensions is provided in this chapter. It also draws upon the examples of our four southern metros to show how various types of present-day school choice are linked to segregation and opportunity—in addition to spotlighting several other communities that use choice policies to span existing district boundary lines, as most of our metros have entirely erased theirs. Because the chapter blends findings from the analysis with lessons for city-suburban education policy, it serves as a link between the second and third parts of this book.

Unpacking Values and Assumptions Surrounding School Choice

Our society's support for choice among schools is rooted in a widespread appreciation of choice more generally, something we often associate with the fundamental American values of freedom and liberty. Choice is also a key feature of our economic system, since capitalism relies heavily on the ability of consumers to make choices about products, of businesses to make choices about resources, employees, and products, and of workers to make choices about employers.[8] But there are times when choice and liberty clash with equality, another core American value.

Hold onto an appreciation for the concept of choice in your mind. Alongside it, activate your understanding of the myriad historical reasons a family might immigrate to the United States—to include escaping from poverty, armed conflict, and political and social unrest.[9] Then consider the (fictional) example of a female-headed, non-English-speaking family of three that recently moved to a large urban school system in the United States. The district offers a wide array of school choices, including magnet schools, private schools, regular public schools, and charter schools, each of which is governed by different legal and policy parameters. Confronted with the decision about where to send her two children to school, the mother knows she will need the family car to get to her twelve-hour shift beginning at 6 A.M. Through a phone hotline she sees advertised in two languages on a billboard, she is able to select an option to hear information about enrolling in the district's regular public and magnet schools in her native language. If children live more than a mile and a half from their assigned school, she learns the district will provide free transportation. She also hears that many district magnet schools have competitive admissions processes and do not administer entrance tests in a language other than English. The mother then finds, through a friend, that some local charters provide outreach and application information in multiple languages, but others do not. Charters also do not offer free transportation, though several arrange carpools among families that live in proximity to one another. Also, at a number of charters, parents must sign a commitment form promising to volunteer at least eighteen hours a semester. Finally, she learns from the same friend that private school choices vary widely. Though some offer financial assistance, all charge tuition and do not provide transportation. In this complex choice environment, the mother faces the realization that many of these schooling options are not truly viable given her family's existing constraints.[10]

The two primary theories governing various school choice models take different views of this family's situation. One theory, introduced one year after the *Brown* decision and rooted in American values and assumptions surrounding markets and capitalism, suggests that the presence of so many different schooling options leads to helpful competition that spurs innovation and quality.[11] Consumers of education can "vote with their feet" and make good, informed choices about what is best for their children.[12] Less desirable schools will close as individual preferences help weed out the strong from the weak. These market forces also ensure that our family above ends up in the most suitable environment, regardless of constraining circumstances.

Another theory, concerned both with the appeal of choice and the value of equality, tries to promote school desegregation on a voluntary basis. As desegregation scholar Gary Orfield put it, "Choice in this theory is a noncoercive framework of policies using incentives and other mechanisms to enforce minority rights in a broadly acceptable way."[13] The integration theory of choice flourished in the shadow of *Milliken*, built on growing recognition that future school desegregation efforts, especially in the de facto segregated North, would need to rely heavily on voluntary participation. Free transportation, wide-ranging outreach to diverse constituencies, diversity goals, and noncompetitive admissions policies are hallmarks of school choice based on the integration theory.[14] Yet in a sign of current priorities around school choice,[15] our family did not readily encounter this model during their search—though magnets came the closest of the various options.

Evidence from countries around the world shows that unless school choice is carefully designed, it nearly always exacerbates inequality.[16] As the above example illustrates, important considerations include—but are not limited to—easy access to information about schools of choice, a workable way to get a child to the school of choice, and admissions procedures that allow the family to pick the school (rather than the school picking the family). Even if a choice system tries to take all of those considerations into account, a crucial concern remains. In the current framing of school choice as the civil rights issue of our time, the question of whether or not having more than one school option represents a meaningful path to better educational opportunities often goes unanswered. However, a massive body of research, reviewed earlier in Chapter 1, helped us understand how and why that path tends to track very closely with patterns of school segregation. With this in mind, the remainder of this chapter explores the relationship between school choice and segregation for many popular forms of school choice,[17] using, where possible, the examples of our four metros.

Choice in Free Form: Open Enrollment Plans

Open enrollment is based on the principle that families should be allowed to send their children to any (public) school of their choosing. Like freedom of choice, open enrollment is rooted in avoidance of desegregation. As neighborhoods in many northern cities began to experience racial transition, school districts adopted open enrollment policies to allow white families to transfer into less diverse schools outside their attendance zones.[18] The policy eventually migrated south, as in the case of Richmond. There, an open enrollment plan was adopted in 1977 as part of an effort to staunch the flow of middle-class and white families to the suburbs. Just five years after urban school desegregation began, families had the option to send their children either to the nearby neighborhood school or to another school within the larger "megazone" provided space was available.[19]

Intradistrict (within a single system) open enrollment policies like Richmond's became fairly common in other urban school districts. As is the case with all forms of choice, open enrollment presents families with an opportunity to disentangle serious residential segregation from school segregation. But in many urban systems, including the city of Richmond, equity in intradistrict open enrollment has been undermined by the lack of diversity goals governing student transfers.[20] In Richmond, access to open enrollment policies has been further diminished by the elimination of transportation during the recent fiscal crisis. These characteristics place open enrollment squarely in the market-based theory of choice.

Within Richmond's unregulated market, one researcher documented frequent work-arounds in the enrollment process that gave some families admissions priority through relationships with school principals.[21] Likely as a result, middle-class families in Richmond's struggling urban district disproportionately took advantage of open enrollment to cluster in two to three whiter, more advantaged, and higher-performing school settings.[22] More broadly, because only a very small handful of such settings existed within Richmond, the open enrollment policy fell far short of offering widespread opportunities for all students.

The 2001 passage of the No Child Left Behind Act (NCLB) radically expanded open enrollment policies. Under NCLB, all school districts had to provide families with the right to transfer from a state-defined underperforming school ("in need of improvement" according to the parlance of the law) to a higher-performing one. School systems were also supposed to cover transportation costs.[23] The subsequent spread of intradistrict open enrollment policies to diversifying suburban districts like the two school systems adjacent to the city of Richmond did, in theory, offer students a path to meaningful choice within a single district. Yet there was serious question as to whether or not many families knew about the transfer option.[24] Indeed, estimates of the extent to which eligible students took advantage of intradistrict transfers under NCLB suggested that an extraordinarily low share—less than 1 percent—actually did so.[25] The reasons for this likely involve several critical dimensions that echo through the history of market-based choice: a lack of outreach and information, a design requiring individual families to initiate the transfer, and a decision to accept or reject the transfer left up to leaders in higher-performing schools with limited seats.[26] Before many districts could take firm steps to address those concerns, the policy was being dismantled. During the NCLB waiver process, a number of states abandoned their commitment to the transfer provision.[27]

Our quick review of intradistrict open enrollment plans suggests they are limited in two key ways: (1) They often fail to incorporate key civil rights dimensions like extensive outreach, transportation, or diversity goals; and (2) they tend to constrain students, especially those in racially and economically segregated systems, to a set of school choices that are largely alike in terms of unequal educational resources and outcomes.[28] In response to the latter concern—that intradistrict choice may not provide enough options for higher-performing schools—NCLB allowed for cooperative transfer agreements between districts. But because the law did not provide funding to help districts work out transportation and per-pupil expenditure issues, these cooperative agreements were rarely been established.[29]

Beyond NCLB, most states have adopted between-district open enrollment policies.[30] These policies offer students the option to cross district boundaries in order to access schools in more advantaged contexts. Yet interdistrict open enrollment plans are also limiting in important ways. Many either come with annual academic or behavioral requirements or without extensive outreach, desegregation goals, and free transportation. As such, they often intensify segregation. Using 2006 data from the Denver metro area, for instance, researchers found that white students tended to use Colorado's interdistrict open enrollment policy to transfer from more racially diverse districts to less racially diverse ones. Data also indicated that wealthier students took advantage of open enrollment to transfer from low- to high-income districts.[31] A different analysis of interdistrict plans in Minnesota and Colorado yielded similar results, this time related to achievement. The study revealed that high-achieving students were most likely to utilize open enrollment to transfer to higher-achieving districts.[32] Another comprehensive study of open enrollment in Michigan found that, while more historically disadvantaged students were using open enrollment programs to transfer to a higher-performing district than advantaged students, they were also more likely to exit the program prematurely.[33] Finally, research on interdistrict open enrollment in the Twin Cities found that the majority of student moves increased segregation, with white students residing in central cities likely to transfer to surrounding districts.[34] So while interdistrict open enrollment presents the possibility of regional cooperation around education, without attention to the same civil rights features typically missing from intradistrict open enrollment, it tends to help already advantaged students access better schools.

At the close of this chapter, we will look at other types of interdistrict choice—aside from open enrollment—to consider about how such policies might advance the goals of educational regionalism. For now, though, we turn our attention to the links between magnet schools, controlled choice, and equal educational opportunity. Unlike open enrollment policies, which originated in resistance to desegregation, magnet schools and controlled choice plans were explicitly designed to promote it.

Choice as a Desegregation Incentive: Magnet Schools and Controlled Choice

Most magnet schools are designed to attract a diverse group of families to a school outside of their neighborhood with theme-based or specialized academic programming (e.g., Montessori, International Baccalaureate, or STEM). Controlled choice is a system-wide policy that asks families to rank order a certain set of schools, which usually includes a neighborhood option, and to submit those preferences to the district. The final student assignment decision is left in the hands of the district's central office, whose personnel can take into account any number of factors, including capacity, proximity, and diversity. The central office is well positioned to evaluate how different choices might impact important district priorities like diversity, helping to balance individual preferences with community-wide interests. Magnets and controlled choice plans may operate together (if magnet schools are included as an option that families can rank) or independently of one another.

Magnets and controlled choice plans grew out of a changing legal and political context that emphasized voluntary desegregation efforts. Both try to leverage family interest in choosing from a selection of academic offerings to advance the goal of integration. Said differently, they attempt to harness choice in a way that incentivizes equity and diversity. Doing so means paying careful attention to civil rights standards like desegregation goals, extensive outreach, and free transportation—dimensions that magnet schools and controlled choice plans traditionally have embraced.

Magnet schools and controlled choice plans differ in terms of their ability to pull students across school district boundaries. Magnet schools are well positioned to do so—indeed there are powerful examples of interdistrict magnet schools in Connecticut and elsewhere[35]—as long as participating districts can work out details like funding and transportation. Controlled choice can be more difficult to implement across district lines because it relies so heavily on the judgment of central administrators. However, if multiple districts agree to the creation of an office or administrative position responsible for coordinating the different parameters of the controlled choice system, it is possible. Controlled choice also works well in consolidated city-suburban school systems, as you may recall from the discussion of Charlotte and Louisville's plans in chapters 3 and 4.

In different ways, our metros helps illustrate another key point about controlled choice and magnet schools: They continue to be influenced by rightward-leaning legal and political winds. Those winds have buffeted and reshaped choice with roots in the desegregation era in a number of places, sometimes diminishing the original focus on expanding access and equity. Though both magnets and controlled choice historically enjoyed widespread success as tools for desegregation,[36] unpacking some of the key policy shifts is important to understanding how well they promote integration and opportunity today.

Changing Magnet Schools

By the end of the 1990s, several different court decisions involving magnet schools had begun to curtail their desegregation emphasis. One particularly influential 1999 ruling, known as *Eisenberg v. Montgomery County Public Schools*, involved a white first grader in Montgomery County, Maryland, whose family sought to transfer him from his assigned neighborhood school to a magnet program. In keeping with its voluntary integration policy, the Montgomery school district denied the transfer request on the grounds that it would adversely impact diversity in either the sending or receiving school. Shortly thereafter, the Fourth Circuit Court of Appeals, as part of a much broader turn away from race consciousness in the law,[37] invalidated the district policy and ruled that transfer requests for magnet schools could not be denied on the basis of race.[38] The Montgomery ruling came just three years after a First Circuit decision threw out an admissions policy for Boston's premier exam school that set aside seats for students from five different racial and ethnic minority backgrounds.[39] The legal backpedaling on voluntary race-conscious policies seeking to redress de facto discrimination reverberated around the country, influencing magnet school efforts in any number of districts.

In Louisville, a group of African American parents, dissatisfied with guidelines ensuring diversity at magnet programs in a historically black high school, sued the district. The 1999 lawsuit crystallized a challenge inherent to magnet schools, many of which are located in racially segregated, high-poverty communities. If a magnet theme or specialization is truly attractive, it will draw in students from beyond the neighborhood. But when kids who live in the area—with strong family ties or other connections with the school—are forced to look elsewhere for lack of available seats, tension and anger can ensue.[40] This was indeed the case in Louisville, and it led both to the end of racial guidelines at four district magnet schools and to the lifting of the district's desegregation order. As one observer noted, "Ironically, the special courses provided by the magnet programs, devised as a way to promote desegregation through school choice, had become the potential downfall of the district's busing plan."[41] Further adding to the irony, it was the first time African Americans had brought suit against a school desegregation plan, and they did so against the will of the school board.[42] The litigation undermined diversity at magnet schools, the effects of which are still being felt a decade and a half later as the district debates an extensive review of the magnetic power of its programs. Still, after the dust settled, broad-based support for school desegregation remained in the community, and Louisville continued to voluntarily pursue its controlled choice plan absent a court order to do so.[43]

In conjunction with the courts, shifting federal priorities also helped define and redefine the goals of magnet schools. Dating back to the passage of the Emergency School Aid Act (ESAA) in the early 1970s, federal funding for magnet schools aided districts in financing the materials and teacher training needed to create unique, magnetic programming. After ESAA ended, the federal Magnet Schools Assistance Program (MSAP) began administering the funding in 1985.[44] Over the years, MSAP priorities in the competitive grant-making process have changed depending on the political leanings of the administration in power, as well as the current legal parameters surrounding race-conscious policymaking.[45]

The example of Chattanooga's magnet programs illustrates how the evolution of federal and judicial guidelines can impact magnet schools on the local level. Recall that, after the 1997 merger, Chattanooga sought to expand its system of regional magnet schools. It did so with the help of MSAP funding, which it won several cycles in a row. Federal dollars supported the start-up of a popular museum magnet school in 2002, one of four new magnets opened around the same time in downtown Chattanooga. Students walking through the museum magnet's front door are greeted by a massive aquarium and murals covering the walls, a fitting entry point to an innovative expeditionary learning program.[46] And behind that unique program, and others like it in the district, were efforts to encourage desegregation. Initially, the magnet admissions process in Chattanooga took into account students' racial backgrounds in order to promote diversity. In later years, however, Chattanooga's magnet schools adopted a lottery procedure weighted to produce socioeconomic diversity in the student body—a decision spurred in part by MSAP funding guidelines under the Bush administration (which in turn were influenced by the movement away from race-conscious policies in the law).[47] Most recently, with the loss of federal funding, the district has abandoned diversity goals for magnet schools altogether.[48] The last shift took place just outside the range of years for our particular study, but will likely impact what the data had suggested was a successful—though not comprehensive—school desegregation policy in Chattanooga.

Research supports what most grasp intuitively: Setting desegregation goals that govern magnet school admissions procedures is linked to higher levels of desegregation in magnets.[49] Though current legal guidelines prohibit magnet schools from directly considering the individual race of a student (unless they are part of a school district that is still under court order to desegregate), a number of permissible strategies are still available. For instance, according to jointly released 2011 guidance from the Departments of Education and Justice, magnet schools can craft lottery-based admissions policies that take student background and persistence into account (e.g., extra weight given to applicants from low-performing schools, disadvantaged neighborhoods, lower socioeconomic backgrounds, or homes where English is spoken as a second language).[50] If none of those approaches work to ensure diversity, magnet officials can consider the race of a student as one factor among others.[51] But while federally funded magnet schools are still required to document concrete efforts made toward reducing racial isolation, they only represent a subset of all magnet schools—many of which, as our example of Chattanooga illustrates, no longer have explicit desegregation goals.[52]

When it comes to fostering diversity in magnet schools, other things matter too. The type of magnet theme or emphasis is related to the diversity of the enrollment.[53] Whether or not a magnet operates as a school within a school (which tends to produce a smaller, less diverse school within a larger, more diverse one) or a whole-school program makes a difference for desegregation.[54] Employing a lottery-based admissions policy is connected to more diverse enrollments than a competitive admissions policy—and perhaps in recognition of that fact, virtually no recently funded magnets in the last MSAP cycle relied on competitive criteria.[55] Finally, as we have seen with other types of choice, the presence of transportation provisions and extensive outreach efforts is also positively linked to magnet school diversity.[56]

In listing all of the dimensions related to diversity in magnets, we come to another truism about them, which is that they are a varied group of schools. Even what gets labeled a magnet school is often up for debate. For instance, federal enrollment data indicate that more than a dozen magnet schools exist in the Richmond area, though most desegregation experts (or, for that matter, local education officials familiar with their history) would not use the term to describe the theme-based suburban high school specialty centers that were established to balance enrollment, not to promote diversity.[57]

With that disclaimer in mind, it is still important to understand that past research on the desegregating effectiveness of magnet schools—along with the related academic and social benefits they provide to students— has trended positive.[58] Moreover, under the Obama administration, MSAP grantees have been encouraged to develop more inclusive admissions processes (e.g. lottery-based admissions versus competitive criteria admissions), reduce racial isolation, and allow students to cross district boundary lines to attend magnets.[59] All of this indicates that magnets are worth keeping in the forefront of our minds as we consider which types of choice might best promote educational regionalism.

The Evolution of Controlled Choice

Like magnets, controlled choice plans have been subject to sweeping changes in the courts. We saw above that the 1999 lawsuit brought against Louisville's magnet schools had the potential to radically undermine its broader controlled choice plan. While the narrow ruling—and the lack of further appeal—prevented the case from doing so, it planted the seeds for another challenge to Louisville's student assignment policy.

In 2002, Teddy Gordon, the same lawyer who had represented the African American families in the magnet school case, filed a second lawsuit against the school system. This time it was on behalf of several white parents dissatisfied with the district's controlled choice desegregation policy.[60] The lawsuit made its way through the judicial system, ending up in the U.S. Supreme Court as part of a consolidated case, *Parents Involved in Community Schools v. Seattle School District No. 13* and *Meredith v. Jefferson County* (referred to in shorthand as *Parents Involved*), dealing with voluntary integration in both Louisville and Seattle.

The 2007 *Parents Involved* ruling, as discussed elsewhere in this book, prevented school districts from considering the individual race of a child when deciding where to assign students to schools.⁶¹ In a widely cited statement illustrating the decline of race-conscious jurisprudence, Chief Justice John Roberts wrote, "the way to stop discriminating on the basis of race is to stop discriminating on the basis of race."⁶² That ahistorical perspective, which presumes the arrival of a color-blind society,⁶³ largely defined the *Parents Involved* decision. Even so, a plurality of the justices decided that school diversity remained a "compelling governmental interest"—something worth fighting for within certain constraints—and outlined a number of ways school systems could try to promote it. Districts willing to commit to designing or redesigning student assignment policies to comply with the new standards were thus able to continue to pursue voluntary integration. Louisville was one of those districts.

In the wake of *Parents Involved*, the evolution of Louisville-Jefferson County's controlled choice plan showcased the community's flexibility, creativity, and ongoing commitment to diversity. The year following the ruling, the district considered several possible changes to its student assignment policy. One involved the adoption of a system-wide magnet school plan (in which each school became a magnet); another involved a retreat to uncontrolled choice, and the third involved modifications to the former controlled choice plan.⁶⁴ After deciding that the magnet school proposal was cost prohibitive, and that the community valued school diversity too much to abandon it, Louisville-Jefferson County opted to tailor its controlled choice policy to meet the new Supreme Court standards for voluntary integration.⁶⁵ Guiding principles included diversity, quality, choice, predictability, stability, and equity. School officials divided the city-suburban district into two geographic areas called Region A and Region B. Region A contained more residents of color and more residents with lower educational attainment than Region B. The controlled choice plan then ensured that each school served between 15 and 15 percent of students from Region A.⁶⁶ In short, Louisville's contemporary student assignment policy serves as an example of how controlled choice still can be used to pursue integration on a voluntary basis.

A decade earlier, controlled choice in Charlotte-Mecklenburg went in the other direction. After a federal district court declared Charlotte-Mecklenburg unitary in 1999, steps were taken to dismantle the desegregation plan and implement a race-neutral one instead. In 2002, the Family Choice Plan debuted—a policy that, as the name suggests, was very loosely based on the earlier controlled choice approach. But the priorities of the new plan veered sharply away from diversity and toward proximity, reinforcing the school-housing segregation link. Many questioned whether or not it actually offered choices to all families in the district. In fact, as one leading observer of resegregation trends in the area noted, "the plan allowed relatively little choice because it guaranteed students who chose to attend a neighborhood school a seat at that school."[67] Perhaps in recognition of those shortcomings, by 2004 the district had given the new policy the generic name of Student Assignment Plan.[68] Charlotte, then, offers a portrait of a post-unitary status district retooling its controlled choice policy in a way that undermined the original focus on desegregation.[69]

Older studies examining the popularity and effectiveness of controlled choice as a desegregation policy found largely positive impacts.[70] Though research on the effectiveness of the new geography-based controlled choice plans is limited, one study found that they can help to maintain racially diverse schools, just not quite as much as a race-conscious plan based on the individual race of students would.[71] The accumulated evidence base suggests that, like magnet school options, carefully designed controlled choice policies are worth keeping in mind as a possible lever to promote regional desegregation. However, the story of Charlotte serves as a reminder that not all choice policies are created equal when it comes to advancing the goals of integration.

Choice Will Stimulate Competition (and Maybe Diversity): Charter Schools

Charlotte's reimagining of school choice after it gained unitary status was in line with current streams of education reform that emphasize competition, high standards, and innovation. The idea that providing families with the ability to shop among schools would stimulate competition—and thereby improvement—in existing public schools was the foundation for the expansion of another iteration of choice: charter schools.[72]

Charters are public schools governed by a set of principles laid out in a stakeholder-formulated charter document. The first charter school opened its doors in Minnesota in 1991, just as the push for standards and accountability was accelerating in a number of states. Charters have been broadly supported by both Republican and Democratic presidential administrations and continue to grow rapidly.[73] Between 1999 and 2011, the number of charter schools rose from 1,500 to 5,700 and the percentage of public school students enrolled in charters increased from 1.7 to

5.8 percent.[74] Though still a relatively small proportion of the nation's overall enrollment, the share of charter students has climbed dramatically in a number of large cities. In D.C., for instance, about half of all students enroll in charter schools.[75]

Charter schools, for the most part, are firmly rooted in the market theory of choice.[76] By virtue of the governing charter, they are free from many of the regulations that traditionally apply to public schools. Supporters tout this flexibility as key to innovation in public education, suggesting that lessons from charters will eventually extend to other schools.[77] This thinking dovetails neatly with notion that bureaucratic bloat and mismanagement, union restrictions, and the like are largely to blame for poor performance in U.S. schools—rather than persistent segregation, rising inequality, and a tattered social safety net.

Nevertheless, a small handful of charter schools and networks have begun to tout diversity as an important goal.[78] Formed in the summer of 2014, a group called the National Coalition of Diverse Charter Schools has committed to sharing best practices for the creation of diverse charters. These include thoughtful site selection, careful recruitment, weighted lotteries that take into account student socioeconomic status or neighborhood context (e.g., zip code), and the establishment of curricula and/or school culture that embraces diversity.[79] Note that such elements are very similar to the ones employed by choice policies rooted in the desegregation era. The coalition only contained fourteen charter schools and networks at the time of its inception—a proverbial drop in the bucket of around 6,000 charters nationwide. Yet the existence of the group is a new direction for the charter movement, and may suggest the beginning of an important shift in its goals and values.

In theory, when it comes to overcoming school district boundary lines, charter schools—like magnet schools—are easily able to do so. An important example of a regional charter school can be found in Rhode Island. Blackstone Valley Mayoral Prep offers a lottery for students from four different city and suburban school districts. As a report (expanded into a book called *A Smarter Charter*) from the Century Foundation explained, "The school enrolls equal numbers of urban and suburban students, and the first 60 percent of seats in the lottery are reserved for low-income students. As a result, Blackstone Valley Prep serves a socioeconomically and racially diverse group of students."[80] So Blackstone Valley not only draws students across city-suburban boundaries, it also employs a weighted lottery to ensure diversity.

Yet despite the potential for charter school diversity, it is impossible to deny evidence that charter schools as a whole are characterized by extremely high levels of segregation. One study indicated, for instance, that in 2007 fully 70 percent of African American students attended an intensely segregated charter school (90–100 percent minority).[81] Similar statistics emerge from other research, which also documents serious discrepancies in the shares of low-income, English learners, and special education students in charter schools versus regular public schools.[82] Importantly, charter school segregation tends to be a mixed bag, with significant numbers of minority-segregated, high-poverty charter schools set alongside many white-segregated, low-poverty charters.

Charlotte again emerges as a key example here, as it was the only one of our four communities with a substantial number of charter schools during the time period under study. (Tennessee, since winning federal Race to the Top dollars in 2010, has rapidly expanded its charter sector.) In Charlotte, the number of charter schools increased from five in 1999 to sixteen in 2010. The charter school surge began just as the district implemented the Family Choice Plan and continued as serious patterns of resegregation began to emerge in regular public schools. Still, along several dimensions, charters managed to be more segregated than regular public schools for both black and white students. In 2010, roughly 60 percent of Charlotte's black charter school students attended an intensely segregated minority school, compared to 33 percent of Charlotte's black regular public school students.[83] Meanwhile, the typical white charter school student in Charlotte headed to a school where his or her peers were about 77 percent white, compared to the typical white regular public school student, who went to a school where 65 percent of his or her peers were white.[84] Charlotte illustrates how charter schools can be places of serious white and minority isolation,[85] alongside a regular public school system that also was becoming radically more segregated.

Even though a small chorus of voices is slowly beginning to raise the importance of fostering diversity in charter schools, advocates face a number of hurdles in and outside of the government. As currently imagined, many charters set up significant barriers to access, entry, and retention by not providing transportation, suspending and expelling students at startlingly high rates and routinely requiring things like family interviews, extensive paperwork, parental time commitments, and behavioral contracts.[86] Professor Kevin Welner at the University of Colorado at Boulder counts some of these issues among a list of twelve documented practices (he calls them the "dirty dozen") that help ensure that charter school populations do not reflect the broader public school population.[87] These practices are exacerbated by the fact that little organization and oversight of the maze of existing policy and law has guided charter school enrollment.[88]

At the federal level, funding flows to support the expansion of charters through the Charter School Program. (Not incidentally, federal magnet funding has remained relatively flat at about $100 million per year, while federal charter funding has skyrocketed, going from next to nothing in 1996 to over $250 million in 2010.)[89] For many years, guidelines for receiving federal start-up funds did not permit the use of anything other than a straight lottery, preventing awardees from weighting for student socioeconomic, racial, or geographic attributes.[90] Though that changed in January 2014, federal charter school grantees may only weight lotteries to advantage low income students—which may in some cases prevent schools from flexibly maneuvering to promote economic diversity.[91] And when it comes to the competitive federal grant competition for charter school funding, the Obama administration has offered points to charters that sought to promote diversity, though a far greater number of points have been awarded to charters that serve low-income populations.[92] In June 2015, Obama's Department of Education released new set of priorities for the Charter School Program that contained strong language in the introduction and in two of the nine priorities regarding the importance of fostering diversity in charters.[93] This may be read as a small but significant step forward in federal leadership on charter schools and integration.

At the state level, statutes governing charter school enrollment vary widely. Some stipulate generally that charter schools should not discriminate; some require that charter schools not interfere with existing desegregation orders; and a handful actually promote the idea that charter schools should be diverse.[94] On the other hand, a number of states—including Virginia, North Carolina, and Tennessee—explicitly prioritize the establishment of charters that serve low-income, at-risk, or minority students.[95] Irrespective of whether or not they incentivize diversity, little oversight generally has been given to existing regulations, as the presence of numerous racially isolated white charter schools in Charlotte, North Carolina, helps illustrate.

A final layer of influence on diversity in charter schools is the outsized role of foundations. Similar to federal and (some) state policies, many foundations channel funds to charter schools and management organizations that exclusively seek to serve specific segments of the student population—often poor and/or minority groups. Though an admirable goal, it flies in the face of the overwhelming evidence indicating that, on average, racially and economically segregated schools will remain unequal schools.[96]

In keeping with the concrete research showing that the charter school sector as a whole is more segregated than our already segregated public schools—a phenomenon that is then related to many different layers of inequality—evidence regarding student achievement, graduation, and attrition in charter schools is decidedly mixed.[97] On balance, research indicates that we have been pushing steadily forward to expand a market-oriented form of choice that has produced unreliable results along a number of different dimensions. But if charter schools are here to stay, and it would seem that they are, advocates working to advance equal educational opportunity across city and suburban lines might consider the "smarter charter" model à la Blackstone Valley Prep Mayoral Charter in Rhode Island. These charter schools would balance the prevalent market-based orientation of charters with important equity-based lessons from the civil rights era in order to meaningfully expand educational opportunity.

Thus far, our four metros of Richmond, Charlotte, Louisville, and Chattanooga have helped illustrate the various ways in which the design of school choice might help or hurt efforts to promote educational regionalism. Examples of open enrollment and what gets labeled as a magnet school in the Richmond area, magnets in Louisville and Chattanooga, controlled choice in Louisville, and charters in Charlotte all contributed to a broader narrative showcasing significant distinctions between choice rooted in the goals of desegregation and choice rooted in the goals of the market. The evolution of school choice in the four metros further highlighted how legal and political currents can dramatically influence the goals and design of choice policy.

There is one final type of choice for us to consider (with the understanding that we have not covered all possible choice mechanisms here, just those that are public, relatively prevalent, and lend themselves to city-suburban possibilities).[98] In our earlier discussion of interdistrict open enrollment, the idea that interdistrict choice with desegregation goals existed in certain places was introduced. These city-suburban transfer plans, crafted specifically to overcome—but not erase—district boundaries, offer important insight into how regional choice plans might work best. They cannot be found in any of our southern four metros, however. Three have already eliminated their city-suburban boundary and thus do not need to rely on such plans. The fourth, Richmond, has not yet chosen to pursue any equity-based interdistrict strategy. So in the final section of this chapter on choice, we look elsewhere to examine the history, goals, and evidence related to interdistrict school desegregation plans.

Existing Regional Choice Imbued with Equity: Interdistrict Desegregation Plans

Across the country, eight different interdistrict desegregation plans, or what some scholars term "collaboratives," are currently in operation.[99] These collaboratives can be found in places like East Palo Alto, Minneapolis, Omaha, Milwaukee, St. Louis, Hartford, Rochester (New York), and Boston. They came into existence under a variety of different circumstances, but all were initiated as a result of grassroots efforts to offer students in deeply segregated, struggling schools the chance to transfer across district boundaries to less-segregated, higher-opportunity schools.[100] In response to those mobilizations, three interdistrict desegregation plans were court ordered based on language dealing with the right to education in state constitutions, while three others were court ordered based on proof of an interdistrict violation of the Fourteenth Amendment to the U.S. Constitution.[101] The remaining plans came about as a result of state legislation.[102] Though firmly grounded in choice, most of the interdistrict collaboratives were established during the civil rights era, designed first and foremost with desegregation goals and equity provisions like free transportation and student support services in mind. These characteristics distinguish them from interdistrict open enrollment policies.

The collaboratives have dealt with the central but thorny issues of funding and transportation between different school districts in various ways. The most effective route to ensuring broad participation among suburban communities, according to researchers, is to craft financial incentives—above and beyond per-pupil funding amounts—for enrolling students from urban school systems.[103] Not all of the interdistrict programs operate under such incentives, though, sometimes offering just the per-pupil funding for transfer students, and in other instances providing a set amount that may be less than the actual costs per pupil. It is also helpful to offer a certain level of compensatory funding to the urban systems facing a loss of students.[104] (In several cases, though, the interdistrict programs are two-way, meaning that some suburban students cross the boundary into city schools, bringing dollars with them.) State financial support can assist with these costs, and is often necessary to ensure that all students have access to interdistrict transportation—something that each existing collaborative provides.[105]

The interdistrict desegregation transfer plans are further characterized by an emphasis on providing emotional and logistical support for the students who spend their days navigating many different political and cultural boundaries. These students, who have taken advantage of the opportunity to access more highly resourced schools in communities far from their homes, often confront stereotypes and microaggressions from peers and teachers. As scholar Susan Eaton, who interviewed sixty-five graduates of Boston's city-suburban transfer program described it, "Differences between the communities where they lived and the communities where they were schooled meant that as children and teens, these adults lived in what they often termed 'two worlds.' These worlds were marked most obviously by distinct speech patterns, tastes, habits and social behavior with friends."[106]

In order to help smooth the transition between the two worlds, a number of the interdistrict transfer plans offer counseling services for participants. The St. Louis program, for instance, has an office dedicated to recruitment, outreach, and support. Two social workers, a guidance counselor, and a student services administrator help serve students participating in the Boston program mentioned above.[107] Boston's interdistrict transfer students also are paired with a host family that serves as a home base in the receiving suburban district on occasions when extracurricular activities or events might require extended after-school stays.[108]

Governing interdistrict desegregation cooperatives requires a careful balance of representation, agility, and expertise in navigating the political interests of a number of different groups. The governance structure of the interdistrict collaboratives varies. One is governed by appointed school board representatives from each participating district, while another brings superintendents from the participating districts together with nonaffiliated leadership in charge of administering the program. The most recently established interdistrict collaborative, in Omaha in 2007, is governed by a mixed board of electoral district members, school board–elected members and nonvoting school board–appointed members.[109]

A study dealing in part with the effectiveness of these three types of governance found, through a series of interviews with key policymakers and stakeholders, that the structure of governance impacts both political support for the programs and the nature and quality of decision-making.[110]

For instance, places that have implemented the one-district, one-vote model—without regard for the size of the districts—may struggle with buy-in from the large, urban district losing students. And communities that offer a limited role to superintendents may encounter difficulties when trying to make decisions that require expertise in school administration. Yet the need to balance these representation considerations against the importance of a streamlined governing body that can efficiently make decisions is also present.[111]

Though careful attention to governance structure can bring with it some built-in political support, interdistrict desegregation collaboratives have faced numerous political and legal hurdles over the years. The rise of market-based choice options like charters, an education policy conversation that has largely turned away from desegregation, and a judicial system that has continually constricted efforts to confront racial discrimination head-on have at times threatened the very existence of these programs. Yet, for the most part, they have persisted (though one, Indianapolis, has been in the process of phasing out its program since the courts lifted the authorizing desegregation order), with the help of steadfast support from key policy and administrative actors and grassroots coalitions.[112] The transfer programs are also continually in high demand; many have long waiting lists of thousands of students.[113] And even with the many logistical and social/emotional challenges, research has shown that the long-term impacts—like the ability to move comfortably across racial lines, connections to higher-opportunity social networks, and a longer-term willingness to seek out desegregated environments—for participating students are beneficial.[114]

As powerful examples of choice used to spur regional cooperation around issues of educational equity, these interdistrict desegregation programs deserve our close attention. But they tend to be small in nature—perhaps not surprising given the lack of attention and support most have received in the past several decades—impacting anywhere from 500 to 10,000 students.[115] Obviously, a central policy recommendation related to such programs would involve expanding them to serve many more students.

Other considerations, largely dealing with aligning the interdistrict collaboratives to fit the demands of contemporary law and policymaking, are also important. For regions no longer under court order to operate the city-suburban transfer programs, current legal standards restricting the consideration of an individual transfer applicants' race apply. Yet in order to continue to differentiate these programs from general open enrollment policies, targeted efforts to attract and enroll historically disadvantaged populations remain critical. These might involve considering the characteristics of neighborhoods where transfer applicants live, their past enrollment in a chronically underperforming school, or whether English is spoken as a second language in their homes—or some combination of all of the above. Experts have also noted that providing temporary "safe havens" when it comes to state or federal sanctions for poor performance on tests may be an important way to ensure the ongoing participation of suburban districts.[116]

The desegregation goals—and what the collaboratives have done to make sure they are realized—at the heart of these interdistrict agreements offer important reminders of the broader policy lessons of this chapter on school choice. The theory and history grounding different types of choice, along with the evidence base regarding the relationship between choice policies and segregation, makes it clear that choice governed by appropriate civil rights standards is a worthy, though at times imperfect, policy tool for those interested in expanding equal educational opportunity across boundary lines. The same evidence also indicates that simply offering school choice of any kind, regardless of its accessibility, quality, or relationship to segregation, does not amount to civil rights progress. Ultimately, we saw that the best kind of school choice for promoting desegregation systematically weighs the impact of individual choices to ensure that the collective goal of diversity is met. It is important to keep these lessons in mind as we turn to chapter 6, which deals with regional policy options that include school choice, but that also extend beyond it.

CHAPTER SIX

Education and the Regional Agenda

"Community" is attached to any number of definitions. Many emphasize groups with shared interests, concerns, and responsibilities. Some highlight fellowship; others talk about a sense of collectiveness. Though all contain crucial tie-ins to regional school desegregation, perhaps the most relevant comes from ecology. Here, "community" means "a group of interdependent organisms of different species growing and living together in a specified habitat."[1] This definition underscores the importance of recognizing how decisions made about the education of children in smaller parts of a community impact the education of children across the larger whole. More than ever before, the segregation and related inequalities that track along urban, suburban, and exurban lines means that we need to peer over existing fences to see into the shared space of a broadly defined community. Refusing to do so now jeopardizes our ability to grow and live together—successfully—in the future.

One of the central messages of *When the Fences Come Down* is the urgency of looking closely at the triumphs and failures of our recent past to better inform our unfolding present and not-too-distant future. The book seeks to recenter our gaze on what has been, for many years, a lost conversation about the benefits of city-suburban school desegregation—even as a deeply important dialogue has reemerged around the advantages of regionalism more generally. Given the myriad but largely forgotten advantages of metropolitan school desegregation, the momentum gathering behind regional equity movements related to jobs, housing, transportation, and the environment must expand to include education.

The story of our four metros demonstrates that efforts to eliminate the fences between city and suburban school districts, especially when they are accompanied by strong desegregation policy, bear important fruits. Yet our four regions also highlight the great reversal that takes place when city-suburban school desegregation efforts are abandoned, as well as the dangers of doing nothing in the face of deepening segregation.

This book is written for those who wish to think about how we might replicate, regain, or expand the opportunities presented by metropolitan school desegregation (which we will rebrand here with the twenty-first-century moniker "educational regionalism"). The following pages discuss various ways we can begin to do so. Before delving into the different policy, legal, and advocacy options for pursuing educational regionalism, however, a review of the central arguments and key findings emerging from this book is in order.

The Argument for Educational Regionalism

Forming high-quality educational communities where children from different walks of life learn with and from one another on equal footing was a central goal of school desegregation. It did not always live up to that ideal—especially when desegregated school communities were undermined by processes that sorted students of different backgrounds into separate classes[2]—but remained a guiding principle of the movement. Given the still wildly incomplete status of school desegregation, it remains a principle worth fighting for. As famed African American historian John Hope Franklin once said, "The merit is not in going back or holding back and becoming and remaining segregated. The merit is in making desegregation work. Making desegregation work. That's where the merit is. We didn't work to do it. We haven't worked to do it—not hard enough. We haven't pressed our government. We haven't pressed our communities. We haven't pressed our educational systems to stand up and do what they're supposed to do."[3]

Today, the wide range of student backgrounds that make up the nation's school enrollment would probably astound the nine justices who unanimously handed down *Brown v. Board of Education* in 1954. During that time of blossoming and widely shared prosperity, it probably also would have been hard for the justices to imagine the scope of contemporary poverty and economic inequality. Sixty years later, in order to harness the strength of our growing diversity—and combat the trend toward polarization—we urgently need to get serious about realizing the vision of *Brown*.

For decades, however, officials in many places have neglected to put school desegregation at the center of education reform, replacing it with efforts to make separate schools equal through standards, accountability, and market-based initiatives. Those efforts have been buttressed by law and policy that largely sought to "save the city and spare the suburbs," as James Ryan so forcefully argues in his book *Five Miles Away, a World Apart*.[4] That is, after *Milliken* spared the suburbs from school desegregation, extra resources were allocated to save city schools struggling to serve high and climbing shares of disadvantaged students. Since then urban schools have experienced one wave of reform after another. Many major city systems are now waist-deep in the privatization and charterization of failing public schools—failures blamed not on racial and socioeconomic segregation fueled by the wholesale abandonment of cities, but on poor leadership, management, and teaching.[5]

Thus far none of these "separate but equal" reform strategies have worked to scale.[6] Yet many well-intentioned stakeholders have held out hope that each new round of efforts will yield the next great solution for racially and economically isolated urban—and now close-in suburban—schools. All while allowing the most advantaged schools in many suburban and exurban districts to operate virtually untouched by the layered churn of reforms. (This is not to say that we should leave off with trying to make separate schools equal—indeed we must continue to do so as long as our schools remain segregated—but our end goal should be ensuring that the number of separate schools dwindles.)

This book shines a spotlight on an education reform that works by defining community broadly and spreading opportunity across it. City-suburban school desegregation overcomes district boundary lines and brings together students from various corners of a region, which in turn brings together the interests and resources of many different families and stakeholders. And the plans have not only led to stably desegregated school systems after a year or two, they have also helped decouple the relationship between segregated school and housing choices in dramatic fashion. The Louisville area's regional approach to school desegregation, remember, was connected to far faster decreases in housing segregation between blacks and whites than the nonconsolidated Richmond area. Even when school and housing choices remain largely entangled, as seemed to be the case with Chattanooga's more recent city-suburban merger, swift progress on residential and school segregation was evident.

Two of our four metros also displayed a rare—if short lived—commitment to explicitly linking school and housing desegregation efforts. Louisville designed policies that incentivized integrating housing choices by offering exemptions from the transportation required to desegregate schools. Charlotte, on the other hand, tried to ensure that public housing was distributed in a way that would foster school desegregation, rather than exacerbate segregation. While those efforts were not maintained, they offer a reminder that it is powerfully possible to coordinate school and housing policy to promote integration.

Yet the successful example of city-suburban desegregation in Charlotte eventually came to represent the challenges of sustaining support for the policy in a nationally hostile political and legal climate. After court-ordered desegregation was lifted, the once-friendly business community, worried that turmoil would detract from Charlotte's desirability, moved against pursuing a voluntary policy.[7] Those actions turned out to be shortsighted. Evidence from the years since regional school desegregation ended tells an unforgiving story of resegregation and diminished opportunity for Charlotte's rising majority of nonwhite schoolchildren. (On a positive note, however, the Charlotte community began to revisit issues of student assignment and diversity in the summer of 2015.)[8]

In Richmond, a similar story played out three decades earlier, after the higher courts rejected a much-needed metropolitan remedy for discrimination in the former capital of the Confederacy. The failure to erase the lines separating the predominantly black urban school system from the more than 90 percent white suburban ones accelerated an existing pattern of white and middle-class flight as families opted out of a city-only school desegregation plan that sought to upend the former social order. Today, evidence of that earlier default on the vision of *Brown* can be seen on a much larger scale. Schools in the city of Richmond remain heavily segregated by race and class; the two overwhelmingly white suburban school systems slated for consolidation are coping with rapid increases in student poverty and have either reached or are close to reaching majority minority status; and Richmond's outer exurbs are experiencing significant white population growth.[9]

Though many places around the country have taken Richmond's path, doing little or nothing to advance regional cooperation around educational equity, an opportunity to reignite such efforts now presents itself. Linking the current regional agenda, which emphasizes fair housing policies, inclusionary zoning, reinvestment in closer-in communities, limits to sprawl, and revenue sharing across the metropolitan landscape,[10] among other things, to education represents an absolutely critical way forward. In keeping with that forward focus, we must begin to imagine a twenty-first-century version of metropolitan school desegregation that not only builds on the examples of the past, but that also expands and improves upon them.

The Elements of Educational Regionalism

A movement toward contemporary educational regionalism would recognize the ongoing and fundamental role that segregation by race, poverty, and language plays in limiting opportunity. Given existing inequities between city, suburb, and exurb, today's educational regionalism would emphasize expanding educational access and equity across a broadly defined community. It would likely hinge on elements of school choice, though the door for the courts to provide new leadership on these issues remains open. The movement would emphasize connectivity and the importance of overcoming racial, linguistic, and social class boundaries as well as geographic boundaries. It would recognize and celebrate voices from many different corners of a region and use a federated system of governance to ensure that all groups are fairly represented.[11] Twenty-first-century educational regionalism would likely centralize the distribution of students and revenue in a regional office, but leave other important administrative duties like personnel and curricular decisions to smaller subunits.[12] Transportation, a crucial component of any regional education effort, would be free and available to all students, with routes carefully designed to maximize efficiency. In order to foster the kind of long-lasting benefits linked to successful school desegregation, a movement for educational regionalism would prioritize bringing students together in schools across a broad community—but would also ensure that they begin learning together in the same classrooms.

In talking about what educational regionalism should do, it becomes important to understand what it should not do. First, efforts to promote educational regionalism should not preclude efforts to promote school desegregation within existing districts. Redesigning student assignment plans, rezoning for diversity, or expanding school choice with civil rights protections are still important policies for individual school districts to consider, especially in light of rapid demographic changes. We do not focus on them here, however, because the evidence flowing from this study and others indicates that such policies are more effective when they include large portions of a metropolitan area.[13] Second, any movement for educational regionalism should recognize that education alone cannot produce social mobility.[14] Past experiences show us the challenges of sustaining stable, successful school desegregation policy without considering housing, land use, or transportation policies alongside it. For decades, school desegregation shouldered much of the burden of remedying a society founded on racial discrimination. Racial and economic inequality has many roots, and we need to marshal all of our resources to combat them. This is not to say that stand-alone regional school desegregation policies are not worthy of consideration on their own merit—they are, and we will consider them—but rather to underscore that the positive impacts of such policies will be greatly amplified in combination with other efforts to combat metropolitan inequality.

It is easy to see how existing components of the regional agenda lend themselves to supporting the goal of spreading equal educational opportunity across broadly defined communities. Opportunity-based housing policies and enforcement of fair housing laws offer a critical long-term path to inclusive communities and schools. Accessible regional public transportation systems would make it easier—and less expensive—for students to get to metropolitan schools. Land use policy limiting the sprawl that makes it more difficult for students to come together is just good sense. And a strong regional jobs training program can help foster social mobility for residents who have aged out of the K–12 public education system.[15] Yet despite the obvious benefits these policies would have for promoting equity and opportunity, a regional vision for K–12 schooling is still imperative. Public schools in our metropolitan areas reach the overwhelming majority of the next generation of Americans.[16] Strong systems of public education prepare students for tomorrow's economy and offer an important path to greater mobility. Weak systems of education, by contrast, represent dead ends and stilted growth.[17]

How to Advance Educational Regionalism

The major elements of educational regionalism can be advanced through policy, law, and advocacy—in other words, reversing the ravages of metropolitan and educational fragmentation requires that we go through the very same channels that helped produce it.[18] Many levers for change exist at the federal, state, and local levels, and many different actors should help pull them.

Policy

This book has primarily dealt with the important benefits linked to city-suburban school desegregation plans, and thus we begin by considering how similar policies might be enacted today. It is important to emphasize again that while these recommendations are worthy of advancing by themselves, they will be most powerful in conjunction with the school-housing policy recommendations that follow—in addition to other regional policies promoting land use reform, inclusionary zoning, housing mobility, transportation, and employment. In each of the subsections below, we explore the basic parameters of a series of research-backed policies and then consider different federal, state, and local avenues for pursuing them.

REGIONAL EDUCATION POLICY

Since school district boundary lines remain a central hurdle for regional educational efforts, successful policies must find a way to overcome them. These policies generally fall into two categories: elasticity or permeability. The first is arguably more difficult but, as the example of Louisville and preunitary-status Charlotte illustrate, can produce powerful results.

Erasing School District Boundaries (Elasticity) When school districts reorganize with an eye toward facilitating desegregation, stakeholders are required to embrace the idea of "elasticity," to borrow a term from the regionalism literature.[19] Applied to school systems, elasticity asks citizens to view district boundaries as malleable rather than immutable, evolving rather than permanent—in service of the broad-minded ideals of educational equity and opportunity. To ensure those ideals begin to translate into reality, the newly consolidated school system must pursue a student assignment plan that includes promoting diversity as one of its priorities.

Voluntary school district consolidation is possible in virtually every state,[20] though the reorganization process varies around the country. A sampling of these processes from two states, one southern and one northern, demonstrates this variation. In Virginia, where city and county lines are coterminous with school district lines, the school boards of participating school systems and their respective governing bodies must approve a merger, which then goes to the state board of education for a final seal of approval. In more heavily fragmented New York, where many smaller districts flourish within and across municipal boundaries, more than one option for district reorganization is available. School systems can expand either through consolidation or annexation processes, with interplay between the state education commissioner and local voters impacted by the changes.[21] Whatever the path, once prointegrative district reorganization occurs, student assignment policies can be taken up by local school boards.

While school system consolidation processes and desegregation policies almost always develop through state and local channels, the federal government can play a vital role in shaping perceptions of, and providing financial support and incentives for, district elasticity and school diversity. Federal planning and monitoring grants to states willing to assist regions in merging a metropolitan group of school districts for the purpose of promoting school diversity could go a long way toward incentivizing educational regionalism.[22] Funds would be used to lay out a vision for systems of shared governance, student assignment, transportation, and teacher and staff training for newly diverse schools. Federal dollars would also facilitate data collection and evaluation of efforts to promote elasticity and diversity—building our knowledge of what works and what needs to be changed in the future. The nation's ten federal Equity Assistance Centers, which were established under the 1964 Civil Rights Act to help implement school desegregation, could help disseminate best practices and provide technical assistance to other regions. In years past, the idea of federal tax breaks to promote voluntary school desegregation has also been floated.[23] That idea could be expanded to include voluntary participants in regional desegregation strategies. Finally, Congress could lift the ban, passed at the height of the national debate about busing, prohibiting federal financial assistance for the school-related transportation costs so critical to educational access and equity.[24]

Many of these suggestions do, of course, run counter to the education policymaking emanating from Washington since Nixon's Southern Strategy began to turn the tide against federal support for school desegregation. Still, under the Obama administration, resistance to taking leadership on such efforts may be softening. The administration has continually appointed well-credentialed, tireless civil rights advocates to key positions in the Department of Education's Office for Civil Rights and the Department of Justice's Civil Rights Division.[25] In 2011, the two departments released joint guidance to school districts affirming the importance of reducing racial isolation and promoting diversity in schools.[26] Also in 2011, then secretary of education Arne Duncan used his bully pulpit to express support for voluntary city-suburban desegregation in Raleigh-Wake County.[27] Two years prior, Secretary Duncan's Department of Education offered a modest technical assistance grant competition for school districts interested in redesigning their student assignment plans after *Parents Involved* (though subsequent studies of the grant indicated that more guidance on the importance of diversity was sorely needed).[28] The Obama administration also sought to preserve the desegregation goals attached to federally funded magnet schools in a changing legal context and created a "diversity preference" in its competitive funding priorities for discretionary grants programs (note, though, that promoting diversity was entirely left out of the massive Race to the Top stimulus spending).[29] More recently, in the proposed 2016 budget, the administration requested a substantial funding increase for the Office for Civil Rights. Finally, the appointment of Deputy Secretary John King to replace outgoing Secretary of Education Arne Duncan touched off a flurry of media attention surrounding the possibility of an explicit federal commitment to school integration for the first time in decades.[30] Much of the speculation was based on the fact that, as New York commissioner of education, King initiated a noteworthy effort to promote educational regionalism. Yet even if these hopeful trends at the federal level do not strengthen or continue, there are options at the state and local levels.

Like the federal government, state governments are capable of taking leadership and incentivizing roles encouraging school district elasticity and desegregation. Since school system reorganization processes generally require state-level involvement or approval, state action nudging local systems toward consolidation and/or elasticity would be powerful. A first step might be to order a state-funded evaluation of the feasibility and desirability of policies that would foster school district elasticity. Three decades ago, the North Carolina legislature offered a path toward school system elasticity in the Raleigh metro area, passing a key measure facilitating a merger between Raleigh and surrounding Wake County in the name of more effective desegregation.[31] (Numerous other city-suburban school district mergers have occurred in the state due to a favorable legislative atmosphere.)[32] More contemporary examples of state leadership around consolidation, which have occurred amid education policymaking that largely ignores segregation, tend to emphasize fiscal and administrative efficiencies. Using the power of the purse, New York governor Andrew Cuomo has consistently urged small school districts and municipalities to consolidate services to ease financial concerns. He first tried to pressure municipal and school district consolidation by withholding funding from struggling localities.[33] Later, with the help of a significant state surplus, he went in the opposite direction, seeking to incentivize municipal consolidation with the promise of additional funding.[34] While the example of New York does not involve school district elasticity—which would recognize the potential for desegregation—it certainly highlights a strong state role in facilitating district reorganization.

Local governments obviously have the most direct involvement in matters of school district elasticity. In some cases, they may confront a threat to their very existence—if consolidating means dissolving the current system of government in favor of a new, more inclusive one. The task of framing the political debate surrounding district elasticity and desegregation in terms that are agreeable to populations that have often been pitted against one another is immense, but not insurmountable.[35] (Note that these kinds of political challenges at the local level make strong leadership at the state and federal level essential.) District elasticity requires that narrow notions of neighborhood and community be expanded to include a diverse cross-section of interests and needs. Referendum campaigns that explore the basic interests of the targeted communities and devise their political strategy accordingly have a higher probability of winning public support. Strong local leadership and agenda setting from business, media, and community stakeholders is also critical.[36] Local officials will need to carefully consider what will be gained by sharing power and provide strong leadership around issues of equity and voice. They are best positioned to listen to community concerns and offer suggestions for preserving elements of local control in the context of a broader system of governance.

Of course, in the absence of state, local, or federal efforts to actually eliminate school district boundary lines, other alternatives that ease segregating effects of those lines should be considered. Policy options for promoting more permeable school district boundaries on a regional scale are considered below.

Bridging School District Boundaries (Permeability) School district permeability involves carefully constructed school choice policies that help students transcend existing boundary lines. It seeks to foster cooperation and collaboration between multiple school systems in a metropolitan area with a central goal of connecting students confronting layered disadvantages with high-opportunity schools.[37]

One way to achieve permeability involves updating the policy of pairing schools, a desegregation strategy used by many districts in years past. Twenty-first-century pairing would combine school attendance zones for two schools in close proximity to one another but separated by district boundaries. These might be urban and suburban schools or inner-ring and outer-ring suburban schools. The paired schools would share a broad attendance zone spanning district boundaries. One might serve K–third graders living in the zone and the other might serve fourth and fifth graders (or some other grade configuration depending on whether elementary, middle, or high schools were being consolidated). This seems especially commonsense in instances where two nearby schools, separated only by a political boundary, confront over- and undercrowding that could be alleviated by distributing students more evenly across the districts through transfer policies.

Another permeability option involving student transfers would be to expand the nation's eight interdistrict desegregation programs, in addition to revising existing open enrollment policies to reflect civil rights considerations. The majority of states already have laws on the books that allow students to transfer to other school districts. As chapter 5 noted, however, many interdistrict open enrollment policies lack basic provisions that would put such options within reach for low-income families. Updating state-level open enrollment policies with transportation and outreach provisions would considerably expand their potential as a vehicle for permeability. At the federal level, student transfer provisions in the 2015 Every Student Succeeds Act (ESSA) include funding for outreach and transportation, and should be used to deliver interdistrict permeability.

Beyond transfer policies, initiating and expanding systems of regional magnet schools that attract students across district boundaries could promote permeability. Connecticut, for example, has developed a set of regional magnet schools in its major metros for the purpose of racially integrating students across districts. Regional charter schools, imbued with appropriate civil rights protections like free transportation, extensive outreach, and admissions processes that are not overly burdensome to families and students, might also offer integrative possibilities. Metro areas with high percentages of English language learners could consider establishing regional dual-language magnet or charter programs, which would foster both integration and academic development.[38] And even if schools do not formally adopt a magnet or charter designation, interdistrict possibilities may appear if under-capacity urban schools commit to opening up their doors to the children of workers commuting into downtown areas. Albuquerque successfully experimented with such a model, using money from the city government to subsidize an extensive after-school program for students.[39]

As promising as many of these popular choice-based permeability options may sound, each stumbles into the same key hurdle. Because they do not seek to alter the basic structure of school district boundaries—or the student assignment plans within those boundaries—they likely will not reach all students in a region. And, as noted in chapter 5, unless the policies are very carefully structured,[40] interdistrict choice may increase stratification rather than ease it.

More far-reaching school district permeability is possible to envision, though. A cooperative agreement between multiple school systems in a metropolitan area could leave school boundary lines in place, along with district leadership and central offices that would continue to administer key functions like the budget, curricula, hiring and firing of personnel, scheduling, and professional development. But school systems involved in the cooperative agreement would be governed by a new regional body in charge of developing and overseeing a student assignment plan to promote diversity, as well as distributing revenue and resources more equitably across the districts. This is not a pie-in-the-sky idea. In fact, it adheres very closely to the parameters of a 2007 agreement in Omaha called the regional Learning Community.

In Omaha, eleven school districts came together around the goals of equity and diversity. The desegregation component of the agreement hinges on distributing economically disadvantaged students evenly across the Learning Community.[41] At the same time, the Learning Community establishes wraparound academic, social, and health support services in a number of high-need elementary schools. To promote equity, the agreement relies heavily on a revenue-sharing mechanism that allows the regional body to issue a common levy. Taxes based on property wealth across the eleven districts are pooled together and then shared among the participating districts according to need. (Higher-wealth districts are permitted to tax residents at somewhat higher rates in order to maintain advantage.)[42] The Omaha Learning Community is still in the early stages of existence, and continues to run into a number of political and implementation hurdles along the way.[43] These difficulties illustrate the challenge of balancing the interests of still-separate district entities with the needs of the region. Though imperfect, the basic structure of the cooperative agreement in Omaha offers an important and creative model for other metropolitan areas.

Perhaps more so than school district elasticity, signs indicate that government officials at different levels are taking note of the importance of school district permeability. The growth and popularity of school choice has likely contributed to that interest, as well as the fact that existing policy frameworks like open enrollment make it easier to advance permeability than elasticity.

The federal government has room to nudge the needle on permeability through several channels: guidance and regulations surrounding ESSA, the 2015 retooling of the major federal education law formerly known as No Child Left Behind, as well as funding and guidelines for federally backed magnet, charter, and turnaround schools.[44] Federal guidance and regulations regarding ESSA should promote the critical importance of offering students options to transfer to schools in other districts under Title I, in addition to the availability of funding for interdistrict transportation and communication. Federal guidelines should also require districts to provide outreach in multiple languages. Finally, as noted researchers Jennifer Jellison Holme at the University of Texas at Austin and Amy Stuart Wells at Columbia University, among others, point out, high opportunity school systems participating in interdistrict efforts under Title I should be given a temporary reprieve from accountability provisions that might penalize them for accepting previously low-achieving students. These are the students targeted under the new federal transfer provisions—rightly so—but they will have difficulty accessing schools in higher-performing districts if those districts fear sanctions upon accepting them.[45]

As far as federal magnet and charter funding and guidelines go, the Department of Education could encourage educational regionalism by awarding extra points in the grant competitions to applicants who propose interdistrict programs. There is some indication that the Obama administration has placed value on such applications, at least in the magnet school competition. Surveys of federally funded magnet school leaders indicate an increase in interdistrict awardees in the last grant cycle.[46] Similar merit should be given to interdistrict charter applications—in addition to markedly increased federal attention to the civil rights protections needed in the charter sector.

School Improvement Grants—which involve all three major levels of government since the federal government distributes the money to the states, which in turn distribute it to local education agencies—could, as the U.S. Department of Education stated in a 2015 guidance document, also incentivize the creation of regional magnet or charter schools by holding them up as school turnaround possibilities (more on how this might work based on the example of New York below). And when it comes to these different federal possibilities for promoting permeability, government-funded research could help build more support for the potential expansion of such programs.

States can also promote permeability by adjusting or revisiting time-tested policies. Given the large number of states that already allow students to cross district lines through open enrollment, reworking these plans to look more like interdistrict desegregation programs seems within reach. The same goes for state charter school law and policy, which should value both diversity and regionalism. Additionally, states can direct funds to school turnaround efforts that foster those values. Using federal School Improvement Grant money, in 2014 New York adopted a "socioeconomic integration pilot program," which offers up to $1.25 million to applicants who propose programs that will increase integration across district boundaries in the state's lowest-performing schools.[47] Several years ago, Ohio adopted a more comprehensive permeability policy that applies to both regular public and charter schools. It encourages interdistrict transfers and regional magnet schools and offers guidance on student assignment plans that reduce racial isolation and concentrations of poverty.[48] Like the federal government, states are generally well positioned to incentivize the participation of a range of students and districts in permeability efforts by offering additional per-pupil funding, supporting transportation costs, and fashioning accountability measures that do not penalize high-performing districts for accepting low-performing students. Finally, states can offer funding incentives for regional cooperation more generally, with extra points awarded to applications that seek to address education. Virginia had such a competition in the mid-1990s, though it has since gone by the wayside.[49]

At the local level, leadership around issues of equity and access is critical. High-ranking school officials should remain open and committed to collaborating across district lines, and support their personnel in efforts to ensure that schools are inclusive and welcoming for all students. Outreach and support offices affiliated with the regional programs should be well staffed and able to communicate and disseminate information in multiple languages.

REGIONAL EDUCATION AND HOUSING POLICY

The close relationship between school and housing segregation patterns has surfaced throughout this book on educational regionalism. From the interrelated choices that families make about schools and neighborhoods, to the idea that the presence or absence of boundary lines can shape those decisions, all the way to evidence showing that regional school desegregation can interrupt the school-housing relationship, the importance of considering the two together is clear.

For much of the time period under consideration, school desegregation policy bore the full weight of responsibility for interrupting underlying patterns of residential isolation in our metros. Given the success of those largely one-dimensional efforts in the Louisville and preunitary Charlotte areas, it is perhaps difficult to comprehend the power of a joint school and housing desegregation strategy. Early, pre-1990s evidence from the same two metros provided extremely rare examples of coordinated school and housing desegregation efforts.[50] Lessons from Charlotte and Louisville, along with a handful of other places, suggest that voluntary school integration plans should offer transportation exemptions for families making integrative moves, in addition to providing exceptions for students living in stable, diverse communities. Such plans would require an awareness of underlying demographic trends—which, given the trend toward geography-based integration, should not present too much of a problem—and be developed in collaboration with housing officials.

On the housing side, subsidized efforts to provide housing for low-income families should be guided by school considerations. Scattered site housing proposals and planning for new mixed-income communities must prioritize proximity to high-opportunity schools that offer a realistic path to higher education. Likewise, Section 8 housing choice vouchers and the Low Income Housing Tax Credit should be disbursed in ways that promote affordable housing in high-opportunity areas—attached to high-opportunity schools—throughout a region. Such actions would represent a marked departure from the segregating ways these low income housing subsidies have traditionally been disbursed.[51] Moreover, all new developments in metropolitan areas should be required to provide a certain share of affordable housing to low income families.

The federal government can support a coordinated approach to school and housing segregation by establishing a high-level commission to uncover and study potential avenues for doing so. It could model collaborations for state and local governments by establishing partnerships between the Departments of Education, Transportation, Housing and Urban Development, and Treasury. Such partnerships would allow for consideration of school racial isolation and capacity alongside decisions about the siting and distribution of subsidized housing—as well as any related infrastructure upgrades to transportation or water and sewers.[52]

One concrete outcome for these kinds of partnerships might come in the form of a new pilot program based on lessons from older mobility programs like Chicago's court-ordered Gautreaux Project, the federal Moving to Opportunity housing experiment, and interdistrict school desegregation plans.[53] A coordinated school-housing mobility program would include thorough outreach and ongoing counseling for relocating families about neighborhoods and schools, school transportation, regional administration, and suburban participation, some of which is already occurring in cities like Baltimore and Dallas.[54]

Within metropolitan communities, there is a basic need for expertise in the areas of housing and schools to flow across districts and agencies. Local housing programs develop and shift—as do student assignment plans and building and rezoning decisions—with little knowledge or discussion about the two related processes within the different sectors.[55] And community planning and development often occur without input from school systems that need to consider how resulting changes might impact school capacity. Local governments should put public officials into place to help bridge these gaps. These officials should convene regular, data-driven meetings between regional school and housing stakeholders with an eye toward creating and implementing joint plans for growth, development, and revitalization. In San Francisco, for example, former mayor Gavin Newsom created a special advisor in charge of education and families. She sat on the school board and helped coordinate communication between school and housing officials, keeping them abreast of new housing developments that would present opportunities to create more successful and diverse schools.[56]

San Francisco aside, very few examples of sustained coordination between school and housing officials exist, making it difficult to know how to proceed. A few more steps in this direction, in a few key places, could help build our knowledge base and offer models for the future.

Law

Again and again, this book has highlighted the integral role of the courts in both advancing and impeding the goal of equal educational opportunity. Since the need for educational regionalism remains rooted in acts of government-sponsored discrimination, it is useful to consider what the role of the courts might be going forward.

Developments regarding the constitutional rights of gays and lesbians have stirred up old arguments about judicial intervention in normed patterns of social behavior. One camp believes that the courts should stay out of such matters, leaving the public to wrestle with them at the voting booth. This, advocates assert, is the only way to bring about lasting change. But the other camp argues, as one commentator put it, that "the courts are where the least powerful and least accepted members of society can seek recourse."[57] From this perspective, the courts have an essential role to play in advancing the rights of minority groups—especially in the face of majority resistance.

This debate carries over into matters of school desegregation. Some legal scholars suggest that the failure to fully achieve the ideals of the *Brown* decision is grounded in the judiciary's limited power to mandate societal change.[58] They remain largely dismissive of any future role the courts might play in furthering school desegregation, on a regional scale or otherwise. As in other debates about the courts and social change, though, the opposing side views the prospect of meaningful, positive judicial engagement in matters of school desegregation more hopefully.[59] Among this group exists an explicit understanding of the many ways conservative headwinds began to reshape the courts in the late 1960s and early 1970s.[60] It follows that a different judiciary, born out of an alternate set of political circumstances, may produce different rulings.

Though valid points emerge from both sides, the durability of educational inequality along racial, economic, and geographic lines suggests that it would be foolish to rule out an entire branch of government—particularly the one that initiated the call for change—when it comes to the prolonged denial of *Brown*'s promise. A number of viable, if largely underutilized, legal avenues related to the pursuit of educational regionalism remain.

One judicial path to educational regionalism weaves through our state court systems. In many states, education is a fundamental right, one that is enshrined in constitutional law. (By dint of the same conservative judicial majority that derailed *Milliken*, education is not a constitutional right under federal law.)[61] Legally speaking, once states view education as a fundamental right it no longer becomes necessary to prove intentional discrimination. A case can more easily be built on the basis of whether official knowledge—and subsequent inaction—resulted in racially unequal educational outcomes. Indeed, a number of civil rights lawyers and organizations have used state constitutional language regarding the right to education to argue for adequate or equitable school funding formulas.[62] But these school finance cases that define the legal remedy for discrimination in terms of dollars might well redefine it in terms of desegregation.[63] As we have seen, the two aspects are not unrelated since resources—financial, human, and political—flow differently to schools segregated by student race, ethnicity, and socioeconomic status. Pulling students of diverse backgrounds together also pulls the resources together.

As it happens, this legal approach has already worked to significant, positive effect in Connecticut.[64] The long-running *Sheff v. O'Neil* case, opened in 1989 and still active today, has been celebrated for inspired grassroots organizing and masterful legal strategizing.[65] It has led to the gradual implementation of an interdistrict remedy for school segregation. Connecticut's major metropolitan centers have established a number of regional magnet schools that draw students across district boundaries. Though Connecticut's constitution, by outlawing de facto discrimination, offered a particularly good opportunity for a case of this sort, a modified version of the legal strategy could be applied in other states.[66]

In the federal courts, the U.S. Supreme Court's 1973 decision in the *Keyes* case still prohibits school officials from intentionally segregative actions. Common activities, including school site selection, faculty promotion and assignment, student transfer and transportation policies, and redrawing school attendance and district boundaries, should not knowingly divide students or teachers on the basis of race.[67] Though intentional segregation is admittedly difficult to prove, showing that school officials chose the most segregating option among multiple proposals for school building sites, boundary line configurations, faculty promotion and assignment, transportation or transfer policies offers one way to do so.[68] Procedural or timeline abnormalities during related decision-making processes also raise suspicions, as, of course, would any overtly discriminatory statements made by public officials in meetings or via e-mail or social media. Contemporary *Keyes* violations are likely numerous, particularly in racially changing urban and suburban school systems.[69]

A federal leverage point for pursuing school desegregation more generally involves judicial along with administrative action. Though not widely known, a few hundred federal desegregation cases remain under the purview of either the Civil Rights Division in the Department of Justice or the Office for Civil Rights (OCR) in the Department of Education.[70] The Civil Rights Division's involvement stems from the 1964 Civil Rights Act, which gave the U.S. attorney general the power to intervene in school desegregation litigation. OCR has broad enforcement authority through Title VI of the same act, which prohibits discrimination on the basis of race, sex, or national origin in any institution receiving federal funding. Failure to comply with OCR guidelines, regulations, reviews, or enforcement actions can result in the loss of federal funds. Though the priorities of both of these federal arms change according to the political inclinations of the administration in power, they offer important possibilities for advancing school equity and diversity. An administration committed to civil rights might consider issuing guidelines clarifying what desegregation and unitary status look like in a changing society, providing much-needed technical assistance in these areas, and reviewing and reopening as needed the roughly 200 active desegregation cases remaining on the federal government's docket, among other things.[71] It might also tackle civil rights failures in the fast-growing charter sector. After decades of neglect, progress on a number of these fronts has occurred under Obama.[72] But much work remains and sustained attention to these issues should be a priority for future administrations.

With the addition of the Department of Housing and Urban Development, the same two federal agencies involved in school desegregation might also take up the intersection of school and housing issues. With all three at the table, formalized perhaps with an interagency task force like President Clinton's Fair Housing Council or an interagency partnership like President Obama's Partnership for Sustainable Communities, the prospect of holistic planning and guidelines—as well as enforcement—to help foster stable, desegregated regional communities would greatly increase. Nearly three decades ago, the Carter administration combined the education and housing sections in the Department of Justice, opening up a new path for pursuing broad-based injunctive relief—likely through interdistrict remedies.[73] Though the partnership did not last, it offers a reminder of what is possible in the future.

Another dimension of the school-housing segregation relationship involves enforcement of the Fair Housing Act of 1968. While the *Milliken* decision presents a difficult legal barrier to crossing school district lines, fair housing law, if proactively enforced, might advance regional housing opportunities (which in turn would positively influence school diversity efforts). In June 2015, the Supreme Court issued a strong and sweeping endorsement of both the goal of a racially integrated society and a legal standard that allows plaintiffs to bring suit against policies that may appear nondiscriminatory at first glance but that in practice have a negative impact on minority groups (e.g., exclusionary zoning laws, unfair lending practices, or steering[74]). That victory, in a fair housing case known as *Texas Department of Housing and Community Affairs v. The Inclusive Communities Project*, was quickly followed by the Obama administration's announcement of a new Affirmatively Furthering Fair Housing rule. The rules, which include substantial technical assistance—including mapping data showing patterns of racial and economic segregation, otherwise known as existing impediments to fair housing—also come with a critical threat: Failure to comply means a loss of federal funding.[75] Moreover, they encourage regional cooperation and expressly lay out the importance of combating racial isolation and promoting integration in housing. It remains to be seen, of course, if the updated rules and reaffirmation of disparate impact will be acted upon and enforced. As law professor and regional expert Myron Orfield said, "We have been given lightning bolts. Now we have to use them."[76]

Despite recent signs of hope, it may seem as though these different legal and administrative avenues toward educational regionalism face long odds at present. Also fresh in the nation's memory are a string of damaging Supreme Court decisions rolling back civil rights gains that cast fresh doubt on the possibility of constructive change emanating from the judicial system.[77] After nearly forty years, however, the political composition of the lower courts has slowly been shifting.[78] For example, two of the three judges presiding over the Fourth Circuit Court of Appeals, long a conservative stronghold, were appointed by a Democratic president. And the 2016 presidential election could deliver the first liberal majority on the highest court in the land since the judicial retrenchment on school desegregation began.

If—when—the courts shift direction again, we should be ready with sound legal theories about how the school-housing relationship works across metropolitan areas in the twenty-first century. We will also need to be able to point to the scope of the necessary remedies in light of demographic and geographic changes over the past four decades. It is worth remembering that in 1931, more than twenty years before the Warren Court heard *Brown v. Board of Education*, the NAACP began a study of funding disparities in separate and unequal schools, known as the Marigold Report. It was substantially augmented by pictures and data collected on Charles Hamilton Houston and Thurgood Marshall's journey to segregated schools throughout the South.[79] We need a similar strategy to ensure that contemporary legal theories and remedies are backed by the best available evidence research evidence.

RESEARCH

We already have a strong base of knowledge—much of it outlined and expanded upon in this book—indicating that educational regionalism is a deeply worthwhile endeavor. As always, though, we must seek to know more.

For many years now, scholars from a range of disciplines have documented educational disparities related to first- and second-generation school segregation, as well as the myriad benefits that flow from carefully designed desegregation. They have carefully examined related issues like the impact of school-related boundary lines, housing segregation, unitary status, and the school-to-prison pipeline. The research has not always been heeded—or funded in ways that produce the resources needed to carry out large-scale or longitudinal studies—but it has persisted. Moving forward, this body of work must be supported and extended.

The federal government, along with major foundations, should help fund research examining what desegregation looks like in a racially and socioeconomically changing society. What are the dynamics of educating three or more different racial or ethnic groups in the same schools? What are the impacts of widening inequality and triple segregation by race, class, and language? What are best practices for training teachers and leaders to build on the strengths of diverse student bodies? How can demographically transitioning cities and suburbs capitalize on those shifts to make regions work better for all students? We also need to know more about the effectiveness of post–*Parents Involved* desegregation efforts. How many districts are pursuing integration and what kinds of plans are they using? Do race-neutral plans work as well as race-conscious plans to desegregate students across various contexts? What about geography-based plans, which represent a middle ground of sorts?

Research, as noted above, has a significant role to play in future efforts to push educational regionalism through the courts. New studies emerging from the urban history field have begun to carefully document actions that cemented the close relationship between school and housing segregation.[80] That kind of research, especially involving the collusion of multiple jurisdictions, would be beneficial to civil rights organizations seeking to build the massive evidence trail required to win interdistrict relief. It should be encouraged and funded, if not by the government then by private foundations.

Government at all levels should support and sustain data collection on issues related to civil rights and education. Research is only as good as the data upon which it is based. The federal government has been an important source of information for scholars and advocates concerned with equity and access in education (see, e.g., the Civil Rights Data Collection and the National Center for Education Statistics). With the advent of No Child Left Behind, states began collecting important annual data, broken out into student subgroups like race and ethnicity. Such data should be augmented, not decimated, as it is important for raising awareness about inequities through research and advocacy.[81]

State and local governments, along with community foundations, should support studies of demographic change across major metropolitan areas. Advances in mapping technology provide locales with in-depth, visceral portraits of major shifts occurring—a first step toward understanding how to move forward with policy or legislation in service of educational regionalism.[82] Those same maps are also a critical tool for advocates looking to build the will to push for changes in law and policy.

Advocacy

Urging and undergirding positive shifts in law and policy are the actions of citizens concerned about the moral and economic wellbeing of their communities—quite simply: you. As an advocate, you will play a central role in pushing educational regionalism forward.

You will be the ones closely observing and commenting on processes involving school boundary lines, school and public housing site selection, regional fair-share housing and land use, and zoning ordinances. You will help call for more data and maps to better understand the impact of such processes. You will dig deeply into local histories and policies to understand how contemporary patterns of segregation and inequality took root. You will volunteer to be the testers for fair housing groups to help guard against discriminatory real estate practices. You will shore up and celebrate diverse schools and communities as good places to learn and live. You will use your voice to confront injustice and separation with a vision for equality and inclusion in countless conversations with family members, friends, and neighbors. You will seek out natural allies like religious groups, local universities, civic and teacher associations, citizens' committees, and civil rights organizations to begin the difficult but rewarding process of coalition building for positive change. And together, you will be the ones to press political candidates and elected officials to support efforts to advance educational regionalism.

How will you do these things? Overcoming entrenched structures and patterns that contribute to regional inequalities may seem overwhelming at first. But there are many available tools for interested individuals.

The first step usually involves gathering relevant information. Publicly available data sources can help provide information about classroom, school, district, and regional trends. The federal government's Civil Rights Data Collection, mentioned above, regularly collects information on a variety of key educational dimensions relating to civil rights. It also houses the National Center for Education Statistics, which collects annual enrollment data for nearly every district and school in the country. Again, state departments of education now have numerous data points disaggregated by subgroups like race, economic disadvantage, and student disability (though the data provided by different states varies substantially in quality and ease of use). Research offices within local districts may also be able to provide important data.

Partnering with local universities and colleges of education may prove fruitful, especially when it comes to higher-level analysis of the data. A number of higher education institutions have policies promoting school-community collaborations and are looking for ways to assist in these kinds of efforts. Even without explicit partnerships, though, reports and research documenting broader trends that are playing out in local communities can be helpful. Some universities and media outlets also have interactive tools that allow you to zoom in on trends in local communities. The *New York Times* maintains an extensive mapping project related to the 2010 census.[83] Similarly, the University of Virginia's Weldon Cooper Center for Public Service created a well-publicized "racial dot map" for the U.S. (each dot represents a person) based on the same data.[84] Finally, gaining a specific understanding of the different local and state laws and policies that relate to educational regionalism—many of which are outlined more generally above—is important.

All of this information can help identify key points of leverage. You will need to be on the lookout for upcoming policy decisions involving the structures that contribute to educational inequality. These are the processes mentioned earlier—things like where new schools are built or where older buildings are closed, how new school boundaries are drawn and which communities they include or exclude, various ways in which students are assigned to schools and classrooms, changes to or expansion

Education and the Regional Agenda 155

of school choice policies, where to build and how to distribute low-income housing throughout a region, and how to zone land (e.g., multi-family housing units versus single-family housing units) in existing and developing communities. All such decisions should be closely monitored for their impact on racial and economic stratification. Most involve some period of public comment or input where community members can make their voice and position heard.

These public comments can have a real impact on the outcome of a process. For instance, regional expert David Rusk tells the story of Ms. Smith, a young schoolteacher in Montgomery County, Maryland, whose testimony helped persuade the county to adopt its groundbreaking inclusionary zoning policy over the vocal objections of wealthy residents in the community of Potomac. Her simple statement, "I teach third grade at Potomac Elementary School. What I would like the county council to understand is that these previous speakers entrust me with the education of their children ... but they don't want me living in the neighborhood," ultimately helped swing the vote.[85] Even if your words go unattended to at the time, they become part of a public record that can be expanded upon. And they may inspire others to action.

Thinking carefully about how to articulate the vision for educational regionalism is critical. A message that draws diverse constituencies in by illuminating the common interest in promoting economic development, civic capacity, and democratic vitality, among other attributes of a more regional pursuit of educational equity, can build broad-based support for such efforts. Campaigns that utilize slogans like, "If every child were my child ... what would I do differently?"—an actual message guiding a three-year campaign conducted by a Richmond-based nonprofit called Hope in the Cities—can be persuasive.[86] These messages will of course vary according to local history and context, but they are important.

Developing close relationships with sympathetic media outlets or reporters will help spread the message. Stakeholders in Charlotte, for instance, pointed to the support of the local media as key to building support for consolidation and school desegregation.[87] Crafting talking points based on relevant information can help guide conversations with local media outlets.[88] Timely opinion pieces or messages from the editorial board (see, e.g., a string of *New York Times* editorial board statements in January 2015 regarding the importance of school integration in New York[89]) can help spur public dialogue around these issues.

You can and should turn to civil rights organizations like the NAACP's Legal Defense and Educational Fund, the Mexican American Legal Defense and Educational Fund, the American Civil Liberties Union, the Poverty and Race Research Action Council, the National Coalition on School Diversity, Building One America or local fair housing coalitions for guidance and support. These groups can provide assistance in understanding the historical and legal context, as well as ongoing or related efforts in a local area. They are especially useful when a pattern of discrimination in schools or housing is observed and legal action may be required. In turn, local chapters of well-established civil rights organizations can look to their state and national counterparts for help in understanding how a situation in their own community might speak to similar developments around the country. All can assess the circumstances and craft legal and advocacy strategies accordingly. They might also assist concerned citizens in filing administrative complaints with the Office for Civil Rights in the U.S. Department of Education or the Department of Housing and Urban Development (note, however, that individuals are free to file such complaints on their own).

For those of you already aligned with organizations, reaching out and across to natural allies can help promote educational regionalism. One of the major advantages of inserting education onto the regional agenda is the wide variety of possible stakeholders. These include environmental groups concerned about sprawl and smart growth; transit groups advocating for more extensive public transportation across regions; fair housing organizations bent on eliminating housing discrimination and increasing access to affordable housing in high-opportunity communities; members of national, state, and local teachers' associations who have firsthand knowledge of the harms of school segregation; state and local universities with a vested interest in the next generation of students and scholars; and religious groups closely connected to the morality embedded in efforts to promote social justice—just to name a few. Forming coalitions based on these different but related interests is a powerful mechanism for societal change. As Sheryll Chashin, law professor and former clerk for Justice Thurgood Marshall, points out, "Only by forming grassroots coalitions—by doing the hard work of building relationships across the boundaries of difference—will we jettison the existing institutional tendencies that pull us apart."[90]

All of which brings us to a final, important factor in the quest for educational regionalism: getting the politics right. We saw at the outset of this book that the legacy of bruising, and often failed, battles to expand school desegregation efforts beyond central cities may account for the failure to place education squarely on the contemporary regional agenda. But are there ways to overcome the wounds of the past? If so, what are they?

The Politics of Educational Regionalism

School district or municipal fragmentation has a way of shrinking the concerns of the residents divided among smaller communities. They become conditioned to view problems in the context of the narrow boundaries of their jurisdiction—and then either commit to trying to solve them within that jurisdiction or prevent them from coming inside it altogether. In the case of the latter, the popular refrain "Not in my backyard" becomes "Not in my school district or locality." Getting people to understand the interconnectedness of regional issues, as the ecological definition of community reminds us we must do, becomes the challenge.

The racial, ethnic, and socioeconomic changes sweeping through our major metropolitan areas offer some promise for changing the politics of educational regionalism. As populations within cities and inner suburbs begin to diversify, former divisions between the two may grow less distinct.[91] The evolving face of Henrico County—one of Richmond's adjacent suburbs—highlights how quickly suburban communities can take on the racial and economic patterns long associated with cities. Drawing on experiences in a number of American communities, regional authority Myron Orfield contends that helping residents of these close-in suburban areas find common ground with cities can help build the powerful political coalitions necessary to withstand the interests of wealthy and increasingly far-flung suburban and exurban areas.[92] These dynamics were largely nonexistent during previous skirmishes involving metropolitan desegregation and present important openings for changing the political calculus of present-day efforts to promote educational regionalism.

To be sure, swift changes may also present political challenges. Instability and fear of the unknown can make residents more willing to throw up fences than to tear them down. The idea of "seceding" from broader educational communities has cropped up in more than a few U.S. metropolitan areas, as we saw in Memphis, but it is an impulse that goes back to the founding of our country. Secession was at the heart of two bitter and defining American wars, the Revolutionary War and the Civil War. It emerged again as a theme after the landmark *Brown* ruling, when scholars observed a "retreat from the public sphere" made possible by state-sponsored vouchers for white children to attend private schools.[93] And it could be said that the same kind of retreat is occurring in public education today, as extensive efforts to privatize what has long been public overlap with growing diversity in school enrollments.

Interestingly, though, communities that actually engaged meaningfully with city-suburban school desegregation tended to be very happy with the result. What often began as a hostile, sometimes violent, upheaval profoundly lacking in political support usually gave way in a few short years not only to white and black satisfaction with the metro-wide plan, but to it being a point of civic pride and collaboration.[94] That such marked political and societal recalibration can occur over a brief period of time—given the opportunity—showcases the importance of strong and visionary leadership around educational regionalism. Leadership that can articulate the urgent need to broaden our parochial definitions of community and membership. Leadership that makes the case that educational regionalism is not just the right thing but also the only thing for a future that heavily depends on whether we can provide a world-class education for all of our children.

W. E. B. DuBois's famous quote, "the problem of the twentieth century is the problem of the color line," obviously applies to this book about the relationship between school district boundary lines, segregation, and equal educational opportunity. As we draw to a close, however, a lesser-known quote from the same brilliant scholar and tireless advocate for civil rights is also apt. DuBois, in 1915, wrote, "The theory of democratic government is not that the will of the people is always right, but rather that normal human beings of average intelligence will, if given a chance, learn the right and best course by bitter experience."[95] After *Milliken*, most American metropolitan areas allowed the racialized fences between urban and suburban children to stand—and we continue to pay the price for those divisions. *When the Fences Come Down* asks us to take a closer look at communities that took a different course of action and reaped the benefits accordingly. It is incumbent upon all of us to heed these lessons as we move forward into the twenty-first century.

Afterword with Dr. Gary Orfield

One Friday in late January 2015, I sat down to interview my advisor and mentor, Dr. Gary Orfield, over the phone. Two decades earlier, Gary wrote an article that my eyes and soul took in as a crucial explanation for why schools in my hometown of Richmond were so divided and unequal. In it, he also laid out a clear vision for how to fix them. That article, called "Metropolitan School Desegregation: Impacts on a Metropolitan Society," was foundational to this book on educational regionalism.

Gary, codirector of the Civil Rights Project, as well as professor of education, law, political science and urban planning at UCLA, remains the leading national expert on regional school desegregation—and desegregation more generally. He has been closely involved in many of the developments that unfolded in Louisville, Chattanooga, Charlotte, and Richmond. But Gary's reach has extended far beyond those four communities, touching the lives of countless schoolchildren across the country.

Gary helped negotiate the groundbreaking interdistrict transfer plan in St. Louis that gave thousands of students in one of the nation's most segregated cities the opportunity to transfer into higher-opportunity suburban schools. He was also involved in the successful metropolitan school desegregation litigation in Wilmington, Delaware. Over the years, Gary was a part of negotiations in school and/or housing segregation cases in Los Angeles, San Francisco, Little Rock, Chicago, Denver, Atlanta, Miami, Hartford, Kansas City, Houston, Rochester, Buffalo, Memphis, Milwaukee, Omaha, Austin, and Cleveland—just to name a few. Gary's involvement in these issues is so deep and so extensive that his students sometimes affectionately think of him as the desegregation equivalent of Tom Hanks's title character in *Forrest Gump*.

As part of his commitment to influencing government policy in service of civil rights ideals, in 1996 Gary cofounded the Civil Rights Project (CRP) at Harvard (now at UCLA). The CRP was established to connect the world of ideas with the world of action and has lived up to that goal in countless ways. Over the years, the project has commissioned over 400 studies, published roughly fifteen books, held many briefings on Capitol

Hill, and issued numerous reports authored by professors and students at universities and research centers around the country. CRP research was cited in the Supreme Court's 2003 affirmative action case and in Justice Breyer's strongly worded dissenting opinion in the 2007 voluntary K–12 school integration case.

But back to the present and our interview on a chilly, damp January afternoon—well, chilly for me at least. Despite the 3,000 miles that separated us, I could clearly picture Gary sitting in his bright Los Angeles office, surrounded by teetering towers of books and papers. After a decidedly off-topic conversation marveling at the technological advances enabling me to record our phone conversation with the option of sharing it via text, e-mail, Facebook, or Twitter (which we both agreed was a dangerous tool now in the hands of adolescents near you), we got down to business.

SIEGEL-HAWLEY: You wrote a piece in the 1990s called, "Metropolitan School Desegregation: Impacts on Metropolitan Society." I think it confirmed a lot of my own personal experiences growing up in Richmond, so that's why I was so drawn to it, but I wondered what motivated you to research and write the article.

ORFIELD: Well, like everybody who thinks about these issues in the long term, I was very deeply frustrated by the *Milliken* decision. We knew from the beginning that sealing off the suburbs from the city was going to create the disaster for the country that Thurgood Marshall predicted. I was also very well aware of what a different ruling in *Milliken* could have produced, because I'd been involved in Louisville and Charlotte and other places with countywide desegregation where there were really much better outcomes. It got me thinking about what it's like when you have the entire society needing to make a school system work, rather than certain, more advantaged people being able to access alternatives, which concentrates the problem somewhere else. The individual city school district that doesn't have the power to exclude people either through zoning or by rejecting affordable housing then gets blamed and basically becomes responsible for everything that goes wrong. People in other parts of the metro feel absolutely no concern or responsibility for the urban district's segregation—and the inequality that comes with it—and will punish that district in

Afterword 161

one way or another or just try to forget it and say, "Thank God we don't live there." So metropolitan school desegregation was a preoccupation of mine and I was thinking about it frequently. I was also thinking about the whole issue of how you create a larger community. That led me to the theory in James Madison's classic tenth *Federalist Paper*, written during the debate over the Constitution, as a way for people to understand this who really wouldn't understand metropolitan dynamics but who might understand something about American history or American political thought.

SIEGEL-HAWLEY: It's been twenty years since you first wrote the article, and the legal and political climate today arguably makes these kinds of efforts even more difficult than in 1995. Do you still think regional school desegregation is something that we should keep at the forefront of our minds?

ORFIELD: I think we have to. We're a metropolitan society. We think about it in everything else except our schools. We realize we can't solve an environmental problem if we treat each suburban line like it's something we can't cross. The same goes for supporting the arts in our area, or for making transportation work. We certainly would never think of creating lines that we couldn't cross for buying or selling things or for going back and forth to work. But for schools we create these barriers that guarantee there will be unequal opportunity. And because those boundaries interact with residential segregation, they guarantee that the poorest kids and the nonwhite kids automatically get an inferior education. The boundaries basically guarantee that the city school districts and resegregated suburban ones will be viewed as failures and that the rest of society, including employers, will have very negative stereotypes about the education that those students get. So, yes, we have to face this issue. We have to face it not just because of the city-suburban thing, but because the suburbs themselves face even more rapid racial changes than our cities do.

SIEGEL-HAWLEY: So what about the places that did consolidate their city and suburban school systems, like Charlotte? There's been some research suggesting that racial and demographic changes have gone past the scope of that original consolidation, with whiter exurban rings surrounding diversifying inner suburban rings. How should we think about educational regionalism as the geographic scale gets bigger?

ORFIELD: We really need to think about the whole metropolitan complex as it expands, because any solution to any problem will become less and less applicable and effective if we don't follow the actual dynamics of the metropolitan area. Distance becomes more of a problem when you have lower and lower density development further out, but we need to think about subregions within metropolitan areas, not just about each individual school district. It's just an unworkable model.

SIEGEL-HAWLEY: Subregions meaning smaller parts of a consolidated district or metro?

ORFIELD: Yes, because we have all this racial change going on in the suburbs. There's a lot more chance for district collaboration along the boundaries of those changes, the frontiers of those changes. We should be thinking about that constructively right now.

SIEGEL-HAWLEY: So how could we improve on the past versions of metropolitan school desegregation?

ORFIELD: It seems to me for many reasons, not just for schools, we need to revisit the metropolitan discussions, because our metropolitan areas are becoming more fragmented and low density and ineffectively developed. You know, the course of metropolitan reform in the United States in general has been so slow and so ineffective. It's really unlike almost every other modern nation that has realized you have to have more planning across metropolitan areas. We kind of assume we have this special dispensation and we can just let this completely fragmented and totally illogical development continue, which makes our society more and more segmented and builds in more and more intergenerational inequality. Right now nobody wants to think about this at all, but it seems to me that those of us who actually study urban space and urban inequality and recognize the fact that we are a metropolitan society where 80 percent of people live in metropolitan areas.... We have to keep mentioning the obvious even if nobody wants to hear it. I think it's ironic that the state of North Carolina is such a pioneer in metropolitan planning as far as schools go. They certainly didn't do it for any liberal reason, but they did the right thing.

SIEGEL-HAWLEY: Speaking of North Carolina and recent developments in Wake County schools, once you get the regional cooperation, how do you sustain it over time?

ORFIELD: Well, you know in most of the places that had metropolitan desegregation, it was sustainable. It wasn't really controversial politically and the community tended to elect people who tried to make it work. In our experiences in Louisville, they've been able to have enough political force to sustain it. I think that a lot of places would have just kept it if it hadn't been for the Supreme Court dissolving desegregation orders and really making it possible to end the plans. And not just possible—there were judges who went so far as to order communities to dissolve their plans and abandon metropolitan efforts even when nobody asked them to. This is going to be seen as one of the most shortsighted legal developments in American history: that we took successful models and required that they be dissolved. It's just crazy in a society that is so polarized by race and class that our courts actually did that to places that had viable answers and that were becoming more residentially integrated and so forth. Wake County's problems were the product of a dangerous political game of racial polarization played by conservatives that divided the community. And that strategy ultimately produced their defeat.

SIEGEL-HAWLEY: Given the current state of our judiciary, what will it take to shift things in the direction of positive change?

ORFIELD: It would take one vote on the Supreme Court and we will have a different set of possibilities. We're in a very rare period right now because for forty-two consecutive years we've had a Supreme Court with a majority of justices appointed by presidents who got virtually no black votes and who favored rolling back civil rights. You know, I think this will eventually end and we'll have a different court who will listen to civil rights issues in a different way. It really might not be far into the future. It depends on the presidential election of 2016.

SIEGEL-HAWLEY: Do you think the courts have a role to play in advancing educational regionalism? Some would argue that they are done with the business of desegregation.

ORFIELD: I think they have a huge role to play. I happen to know the whole story of Louisville. I was there at the beginning when they merged the city and suburban school districts and desegregated the schools. People thought it was crazy, but it created a new set of possibilities and within a very short period of time people realized it was a good idea. I think that if people are put in the middle of a different situation with new possibilities, even ones that they were once afraid of, lots of times people change their ideas. But you know, the basic problem is that there are so many vested interests in preserving all of the individual municipalities and school districts—and so much fear of any change—that something has to be done to precipitate it, either major incentives or just an order to do it. I think the courts can put people in a different situation, and if it happens to be a really good idea eventually it becomes manifest.

SIEGEL-HAWLEY: Let's go back to some of the underlying relationships that create the need for metropolitan desegregation, especially the relationship between school and housing segregation. I actually open the chapter dealing with this using a question from one of your classes: What should we think about first, remedying school segregation or remedying housing segregation? So . . . what's the answer? How should we be thinking about this relationship in terms of policy and law?

ORFIELD: It's like saying, should we have air or should we have water? You know, it's a silly question. I guess housing is a policy area where you can only move gradually. It's a private market; it's very dispersed; we have a limited enforcement power and very small provisions for creating new housing that's affordable. So unless we have something like incentives for regionalism in housing, and real sanctions and resources attached to them, housing is going to be something that has to be worked on in the long run. Still, it's very important we don't make decisions that make things worse . . . which we've often done with our major subsidy housing program. We really need to work on both. We can work on schools faster, but the only really intelligent thing to do is to think about places where things are hanging in the balance or where change is beginning and think about school and housing policies coherently. We need to have a central goal and idea about how school and housing integration can work positively together. We also need to know the consequences of not doing anything about it.

Afterword 165

SIEGEL-HAWLEY: Well, fortunately, that's where the chapter falls—that we need to think about school and housing policies together. You know, I was looking at your Ford Foundation study, the one that involved you interviewing school and housing officials in ten different metro areas, from a long time ago. Even then, there were just so few places that actually did think about school and housing together.

ORFIELD: It was astonishing. I had this grad student at the University of Illinois at the time that helped with that study. She was wonderful; she was one of these mothers returning to graduate school. And I asked her to help me plan to go to these ten cities and meet all the key housing and school people. I wanted to make sure that I had eight interviews a day and could see everybody who's important. In every place I went I would say, "What happens if there is a new housing project? How are the schools involved in it?" And they would say, "Well, the kids show up in September and we have to educate them." That was the answer. There was nobody in the school system who even knew what the basic housing programs were, and there was nobody in housing who thought about the schools. Right this week we're involved in a controversy over a housing project in Los Angeles. Professor Deirdre Pfeiffer and I wrote a letter to Los Angeles officials saying they shouldn't build another 400-unit all-black segregated housing unit down south of USC in a neighborhood that has some of the worst schools in Los Angeles. The city got together five or six professors, prominent professors, who said, "Oh this will be okay because it's near a major transit route and maybe middle-class people will move in as the subway system grows." And they've approved it. Can you imagine anything more stupid than that? Imagine thinking that the solution is high-density concentration of very poor families in already weak schools and envisioning it will be okay because people with choices will move there and use the schools. It's just so stupid, but it goes on and on. I mean, if I were to go to the same ten cities now, I'd find the same thing except there's less urban planning money than there used to be. In the Carter administration there was actually some urban planning money and there were some incentives for communities to do regional collaboration ... but those types of things have been gone since the early 1980s.

SIEGEL-HAWLEY: In Richmond, even though it's not yet a regional conversation per se, we have a suburban school board chair who's also a developer. She's been intent on bringing the school and housing people together. So say you've got a situation like that: What should they be talking about? What should they be thinking about today?

ORFIELD: You know, I had a housing developer from Texas in one of my classes at Harvard, a very dedicated guy who was coming back to school midcareer for a program at the Kennedy School. He was so proud of himself because he moved into poor neighborhoods and developed affordable housing. The problem was, he did it without thinking about schooling. After the class he said, "I will never develop another affordable housing project that doesn't have a good high school attached to it." That's a good test. If you have a high school where kids graduate and go to college, that's a reasonable place where families can actually develop a future for their kids. And of course most of those would be diverse at least by social class and often by race. If you don't have that, then developing in those locations should be an absolute no. At the end of the seventies, Carter was going to adopt a policy not to develop housing in places with bad, segregated schools. It was, of course, dropped immediately when President Reagan was elected, even though it was a totally rational policy.

The positive thing is that we have plenty of places where we have mixed-site housing and it works fine. In one of my classes I had a lawyer from Concord and he actually went around the neighborhood and surveyed everybody in a place where scattered-site housing had been put in. They were all horribly upset when it came in and pretty soon everybody said it was fine. Of course I lived on a block in Cambridge that had a house where one of George Washington's generals had lived a couple of hundred years earlier, but there was also scattered-site housing and zero problems. It just takes some courage to get it started.

SIEGEL-HAWLEY: What about families moving into gentrifying cities or moving out to diversifying suburbs—do you have any words of wisdom for them?

ORFIELD: In terms of gentrifying neighborhoods, people are moving in with lots of skills to help change some of the schools, and we need the school district to reach out to them and incorporate them because what they will want and what they will demand is exactly what every child should have: a school that will prepare their kid for college. So, we should enable them and we should put administrators in those schools that can deal with both the gentrifiers and the existing families. We should also have housing policy or housing subsidy money to capture some units in the neighborhood early in the gentrification process, so that people who have lived there for a long time can stay there and go to the diversifying school. We should be thinking consciously and ahead of the game in terms of using what's going to be a tide of rising wealth and value coming into a neighborhood and channeling it in a way so that you get a situation where families can have their kids grow up there and where the families that would be pushed out by market forces—at least a significant number of them—can stay. That's what our plan should be for gentrifying neighborhoods. There aren't very many cities that are really dramatically affected yet, but there are a lot of possibilities that aren't being realized. In terms of suburban change, we really have to give people in the suburbs that are going through this experience some assistance and a language to understand it and to talk about it publicly. One of the things happening in suburbs is that everybody notices when racial changes are happening. They see it on their playgrounds or when they see who's being shown houses and so forth, but nobody speaks the words. Everybody's afraid of the changes and nobody has a plan to incorporate them into the community. Nobody has a vision and, you know, they just hope the changes will stop. They don't, though, and there are very systematic things that occur with really negative consequences for most of suburban neighborhoods that go through resegregation. So we need to have a language that says if you become stably integrated, you have a situation that's good for everybody and good for the community. There are places that have done it, but it doesn't happen by accident. We have to work on it; at least we have to work on it through one generation until it becomes stable. Then we need to have government—county government, state government, and so forth, along with federal agencies, that recognizes and supports communities that are trying to achieve stable integration. We should give them planning money, give them resources and help them create regional magnet schools, and so on. You know, it's really pathetic how little has been done to stabilize these communities. It's not an impossible situation to change. It's a matter of changing flows, keeping a flow of whites and Asians coming into a community, making sure that all of the housing demands by African Americans and Latinos aren't channeled into one single community.

SIEGEL-HAWLEY: Let's talk about school choice for a minute. I can't remember what poll—it might have been for School Choice Week, so that tells you something—but it found that 70 percent of Americans support the idea of school choice. So, how can you leverage that kind of support for educational regionalism and school desegregation?

DR. ORFIELD: The basic problem with school choice is that it can mean a thousand things. So it can mean that you have a choice between one segregated low-quality school and one segregated low-quality charter school. That's not much of a choice. It could mean that you have a choice like they have had in Boston for the last almost fifty years now of going to one of the most elite suburban schools in the country instead of one of the poorest ones in the city. That's a life-transforming choice. Choice can really mean anything. There are also various dimensions of school choice that matter a lot. Do you choose or does the school choose? Is there information you can get about the school choices and can you understand it? Is there human outreach to help groups who don't understand the complexities of the different types of choices? Is there a system that only rewards the most connected people with the best choices? Are there screening mechanisms for admission to the school of choice? Is there transportation so that people can actually get to their school of choice? Those describe about a million different combinations of what a choice of schools could mean. Just talking about expanding school choice tends to be something everyone will agree with in one way or another but it doesn't have any actual content that helps you understand what kind of choice it is, whether it is equitable, and so forth. So we have to be much more specific about choice. The whole point of our book *Educational Delusions?* is that we learned a lot about the civil

Afterword 169

rights dimensions of fair school choice programs way back in the 1960s and then we forgot them in the 1990s as charter schools developed. We're paying for that, because choice that is unregulated and does not address any of those civil rights dimensions will almost always increase educational inequality.

SIEGEL-HAWLEY: Do you think we need new evidence, new political actors or coalitions, new legal strategies as we try to push for educational regionalism today?

ORFIELD: I think we need comparisons that are very clear. Show people what happens if you address this issue and what happens if you don't by comparing over time what's happened to communities that have actually approached these issues regionally and those that haven't. We have a lot of bits and pieces of that, but it needs to be presented very dramatically. I was involved in the early stages of the Chattanooga consolidation with local leaders and experts from Atlanta. In Chattanooga it was begun by the Chamber of Commerce looking at the problems of the central city and saying, "That's just not going to be viable in the long run." As I presented all the demographics to them they said, "We've got to do something," and it set in motion a process that eventually led to the consolidation of Chattanooga and Hamilton County. I think educational regionalism is really not a liberal or conservative issue if you look at the dynamics of it. It is often thought about in terms of politics, but it shouldn't be put in ideological terms. Anybody who has resources and who is spatially attached to parts of the metropolitan space is going to benefit from having some solutions. Existing patterns of continuous resegregation in most places have been very destructive for almost a century. We know that the spread of segregation doesn't work well for anybody. We know there are consequences. We know that there's been a systematic deterioration of school districts and schools that have been associated with resegregation. And we know that there are alternatives. It seems to me that discussion has got to be consistent and clear and persistent and hopefully—eventually—it will make some kind of impact on people. Maybe not for the reason that those of us who are concerned about racial equity would like, but maybe for reasons that those who are just concerned about the security of business and markets would care about.

A long time ago I coled a delegation of about twenty experts from around the South to look at the Little Rock school district. One of the guys on the committee was the head of the Chamber of Commerce in Shreveport, Louisiana. Not a liberal by any means. He went around talking to many local businessmen and reported that they were saying, "They are going to have to bail on our city if the schools become all black and poor." So we documented the inequalities in the segregated schools. The report helped stimulate the lawsuit that produced a settlement plan between Little Rock and Pulaski County that lasted for thirty years. It's a very imperfect plan, partly because it was negotiated into a temporary and limited plan through the Governor Clinton mediation, but it was much better than doing nothing at all. It reflected not just a liberal desire, but also the desire of people who owned land and property in Little Rock. They wanted to have viable real estate markets, people moving in, people with money, all kinds of things. People in the city wanted better schools with more secure resources. We really need to have those basic understandings. So much of this discussion is about race, you know, but we need to broaden the base by having people understand the economics of regionalism. The economics are pretty devastating.

And the alternatives are so hopeful. I'm very happy when I hear the head of the Chamber of Commerce in Louisville say that we can hire people from any high school in Louisville. They all understand each other; they work together; and they are trained adequately. We can't do that in the other cities where we work.

SIEGEL-HAWLEY: That's powerful testimony. All right, let's end on these hopeful notes. What gives you the most hope as you think about the future of regional school desegregation?

ORFIELD: Well, I think we're beginning to see some of the political effects of the demographic transition around the country.

Those of us who live in California can see it much more easily. After a decade of intentional politics playing on racial fears, the people who did that lost everything—all the statewide offices here—and now we have a government that's much more open to reconsidering some of these civil rights issues. We are thinking about reversing some of the mistakes that were done and written into the state constitution back in the 1990s. That will happen with the country as a whole eventually and then there will be real possibilities for positive change. There are better paths that actually work. We've put our chips down on segregation, which always fails, for far too long.

Notes

Introduction

1. Elizabeth Anderson, *The Integration Imperative* (Princeton, N.J.: Princeton University Press, 2011); Carl Nightingale, *Segregation: A Global History of Divided Cities* (Chicago: University of Chicago Press, 2012).

2. According to the National Center for Education Statistics, in 2011–12, 10 percent of U.S. schoolchildren in enrolled in private schools (National Center for Education Statistics, "Private School Enrollment" [Washington, D.C.: U.S. Department of Education, 2014]). That figure has remained largely consistent over time, with slight decreases in the past fifteen years; National Center for Education Statistics, "Private School Enrollment" (Sean Reardon and John Yun, "Private School Racial Enrollments and Segregation" [Cambridge, Mass.: Harvard Civil Rights Project, 2002]).

3. Jomills Braddock, "The Perpetuation of Segregation across Levels of Education: A Behavioral Assessment of the Contact Hypothesis," *Sociology of Education* 55, no. 3 (1980): 178–86; Jomills Braddock and James McPartland, "Social-Psychological Processes That Perpetuate Segregation: The Relationship between School and Employment Desegregation," *Journal of Black Studies* 19, no. 3 (1989): 267–89; Roslyn Mickelson, "The Reciprocal Relationship between Housing and School Integration," Research Brief No. 7 (Washington, D.C.: National Coalition on School Diversity, 2011); Amy Stuart Wells and Robert Crain, "Perpetuation Theory and the Long-Term Effects of School Desegregation," *Review of Educational Research* 6 (1994): 531 55.

4. Gary Orfield, *Must We Bus? Segregated Schools and National Policy* (Washington, D.C.: Brookings Institution Press, 1978); Erin Nave, "Getting to the Roots of School Segregation: The Challenges of Housing Remedies in Northern School Desegregation Litigation," *National Black Law Journal* 21, no. 2 (2008–9).

5. Chinh Le, "Racially Integrated Education and the Role of the Federal Government," *North Carolina Law Review* 88 (2010): 725–86; Orfield, *Must We Bus?*

6. Erica Frankenberg, "The Impact of School Segregation on Residential Housing Patterns: Mobile, Alabama and Charlotte, North Carolina," in *School Resegregation: Must the South Turn Back?*, ed. J. Boger and G. Orfield (Chapel Hill: University of North Carolina Press, 2005), 165–84; Gary Orfield, "Metropolitan School Desegregation: Impacts on Metropolitan Society," in *In Pursuit of a Dream Deferred: Linking Housing and Education Policy*, ed. john a. powell, Gavin Kearney, and Vina Kay (New York: Peter Lang, 2001); Myron Orfield, "*Milliken, Meredith* and Metropolitan Segregation," *UCLA Law Review* 62 (2015): 367–438; Genevieve Siegel-Hawley, "City Lines, Color Lines: An Analysis of School and Housing Segregation in Four Southern Metros, 1990–2010," *Teachers College Record* 115 (2013): 1–45.

7. Jennifer Jellison Holme, "Buying Homes, Buying Schools," *Harvard Educational Review* 72, no. 2 (2002): 177–206; Heather Beth Johnson, *The American Dream and the Power of Wealth: Choosing Schools and Inheriting Inequality in the Land of Opportunity* (New York: Routledge, 2006); Annette Lareau and Kimberly Goyette, *Choosing Homes, Choosing Schools* (New York: Russell Sage, 2014).

8. Orfield, "Metropolitan School Desegregation"; Frankenberg, "The Impact of School Segregation on Residential Housing Patterns."

9. For instance, a national poll of education leaders in 2014 found that just over half of respondents believed that merging high- and low-poverty districts would reduce racial and economic segregation and less than one-third thought such a merger would help close the achievement gap; Education Week Research Center, "Views of a Changing School District Landscape," *Education Week*, January 3, 2014, http://www.edweek.org/ew/qc/2014/complex-school-district-environment.html (June 30, 2015).

10. U.S. Census Bureau, *2010 Census of Population and Housing: Population and Housing Unit Counts* (Washington, D.C.: U.S. Government Printing Office, 2012), http://www.census.gov/prod/cen2010/cph-2-1.pdf (March 15, 2014). See also David Rusk, Building Sustainable Inclusive Communities (Washington, D.C.: Poverty and Race Research Action Council/Building One America, 2010), http://www.prrac.org/pdf/SustainableInclusiveCommunities.pdf.

11. john a. powell, "Reinterpreting Metropolitan Space as a Strategy for Social Justice," in *Breakthrough Communities: Sustainability and Justice in the Next American Metropolis*, ed. Paloma Pavel (Cambridge, Mass.: MIT Press, 2009), 23–32; David Rusk, *Inside Game, Outside Game: Winning Strategies for Saving Urban America* (Washington, D.C.: Brookings Press, 2012).

12. James Ryan, *Five Miles Away, a World Apart: One City, Two Schools and the Story of Modern Educational Inequality* (New York: Oxford University Press, 2010).

13. Kendra Bischoff, "School District Fragmentation and Racial Residential Segregation: How Do Boundaries Matter?," *Urban Affairs Review* 44 (2008): 182–217; Charles Clotfelter, *After Brown: The Rise and Retreat of School Desegregation* (Princeton, N.J.: Princeton University Press, 2004); Jeremy Fiel, "Decomposing School Resegregation: Social Closure, Racial Imbalance, and Racial Isolation," *American Sociological Review* 78 (2013): 828–48; Jeremy Fiel, "Closing Ranks: Closure, Status Competition, and School Segregation," *American Journal of Sociology* 121 (2015): 126–70; Kori Stroub and Meredith Phillips, "From Resegregation to Reintegration: Trends in Metropolitan School Segregation, 1993–2010," *American Educational Research Journal* 50 (2013); Sean Reardon and John Yun, "Suburban Racial Change and Suburban School Segregation, 1987–1995," *Sociology of Education* 74 (2002): 79–101.

14. Some estimates indicate that about 80 percent of all school segregation can be attributed to between-district segregation (Clotfelter, *After Brown*; Bischoff, "School District Fragmentation"; Reardon and Yun, "Suburban Racial Change"). A 2013 estimate put that figure at slightly less than 60 percent (Richards and Stroub, "From Resegregation to Reintegration").

15. Gary Orfield and Erica Frankenberg, "Increasingly Segregated and Unequal Schools as Courts Reverse Policy," *Educational Administration Quarterly* 50 (2014): 718–34.

16. Ibid.; Ann Owens and Sean Reardon, "Sixty Years after Brown: Trends and Consequences of School Segregation," *Annual Review of Sociology* 40 (2014): 199–218.

17. William Frey, *Diversity Explosion: How New Racial Demographics Are Remaking America* (Washington, D.C.: Brookings Institution, 2014).

18. Ibid.; Gary Orfield, Genevieve Siegel-Hawley, and John Kucsera, *E Pluribus... Separation: Deepening Double Segregation for More Students* (Los Angeles: UCLA Civil Rights Project, 2012); Orfield and Frankenberg, "Increasingly Segregated and Unequal Schools."

19. As Justice Thurgood Marshall elegantly pointed out in his dissenting opinion in *Milliken v. Bradley*, 1974.

20. Greg Duncan and Richard Murname, eds., *Whither Opportunity? Rising Inequality, Schools, and Children's Life Chances* (New York: Russell Sage, 2011).

21. Prudence Carter and Kevin Welner, eds., *Closing the Opportunity Gap: What America Must Do to Give Every Child an Even Chance* (New York: Oxford University Press, 2013); Robert Putnam, *Our Kids: The American Dream in Crisis* (New York: Simon and Schuster, 2015).

22. Jane Petrovich and Amy Stuart Wells, eds., *Bringing Equity Back: Research from a New Era in American Educational Policy* (New York: Teachers College Press, 2005).

23. Carter and Welner, *Closing the Opportunity Gap*.

24. Petrovich and Wells, *Bringing Equity Back*.

25. Ibid.; Carter and Welner, *Closing the Opportunity Gap*; Katherine Magnuson and Jane Waldfogel, eds., *Steady Gains and Stalled Progress: Inequality and the Black-White Test Score Gap* (New York: Russell Sage, 2008).

26. Bruce Katz, *Reflections on Regionalism* (Washington, D.C.: Brookings Institution, 2001).

27. Jennifer Holme and Kara Finnegan, "School Diversity, School District Fragmentation and Metropolitan Policy," *Teachers College Record* 115 (2013): 1–29; Myron Orfield and Thomas Luce, *Region: Planning the Future of the Twin Cities* (Minneapolis: University of Minnesota Press, 2010).

28. Gregory Weiher, *The Fractured Metropolis: Political Fragmentation and Metropolitan Segregation* (Albany: State University of New York Press, 1992).

29. Though high-profile regionalists have advocated intensely for inclusive housing policies that would help promote diverse schools. See, e.g., David Rusk, *Building Sustainable, Inclusive Communities: How America Can Pursue Smart Growth and Reunite Our Metropolitan Communities* (Washington, D.C.: Poverty and Race Research Action Council and Building One America, 2010).

30. Frankenberg, "The Impact of School Segregation," 165–84; Michael B. de Leeuw et al., *Brief of* Amicus Curiae *Housing Scholars and Research & Advocacy Organizations in Support of Respondents*, nos. 05-908 and 05-915, U.S. Supreme Court Brief (October 10, 2006); Orfield, "Milliken, Meredith and Metropolitan Segregation";

Diana Pearce, *Breaking Down the Barriers: New Evidence on the Impact of Metropolitan School Desegregation on Housing Patterns* (Washington, D.C.: National Institute of Education, 1980); Siegel-Hawley, "City Lines, Color Lines," 1–45.

31. See, e.g., Gary Orfield and Erica Frankenberg, *Educational Delusions: Why Choice Can Deepen Inequality and How to Make Schools Fair* (Berkeley: University of California Press, 2013).

Chapter One

1. David Rusk, email correspondence with author, October 11, 2015.

2. Sarah Diem, Genevieve Siegel-Hawley, Erica Frankenberg, and Colleen Cleary, "Consolidation vs. Fragmentation: The Relationship between School District Boundaries and Segregation in Three Southern Metropolitan Areas," *Penn State Law Review* 119, no. 3 (2015): 687–746; Sam Dillon, "Merger of Memphis and County School Districts Revives Race and Class Challenges," *New York Times*, November 5, 2011, http://www.nytimes.com/2011/11/06/education/merger-of-memphis-and-county-school-districts-revives-challenges.html (July 6, 2015).

3. Dillon, "Merger of Memphis and County School Districts."

4. Sainz, "Memphis City Schools Merger Ignites Racial Tensions."

5. Associated Press, "Judge Dismisses Lawsuit over Suburban Schools in Memphis Area," *Chattanooga Times Free Press*, March 11, 2014, http://www.timesfreepress.com/news/local/story/2014/mar/11/judge-dismissed-lawsuit-over-suburban-schools-memp/133961/ (July 6, 2015).

6. Jaclyn Zubrzycki and Tajuana Cheshier, "One County, Seven Districts: Vying for Students as Shelby County Schools De-merges," *Chalkbeat Tennessee*, March 7, 2014, http://tn.chalkbeat.org/2014/03/07/one-county-seven-districts-vying-for-students-as-shelby-county-schools-de-mergers/ (July 6, 2015).

7. Gregory Weiher, *The Fractured Metropolis: Political Fragmentation and Metropolitan Segregation* (Albany: State University of New York Press, 1992).

8. Jennifer Jellison Holme, "Buying Homes, Buying Schools," *Harvard Educational Review* 72, no. 2 (2002): 177–206; Heather Beth Johnson, *The American Dream and the Power of Wealth: Choosing Schools and Inheriting Inequality in the Land of Opportunity* (New York: Routledge, 2006); Annette Lareau and Kimberly Goyette, *Choosing Homes, Choosing Schools* (New York: Russell Sage, 2014).

9. James Ryan, *Five Miles Away, a World Apart: One City, Two Schools and the Story of Modern Educational Inequality* (New York: Oxford University Press, 2010); Gerald Grant, *Hope and Despair in the American City: Where There Are No Bad Schools in Raleigh* (Cambridge, Mass.: Harvard University Press, 2009); Jonathan Kozol, *Savage Inequalities: Children in America's Schools* (New York: HarperPerennial, 1992).

10. Weiher, *Fractured Metropolis*, xi.

11. Gary Orfield and Chungmei Lee, *Why Segregation Matters: Poverty and Educational Inequality* (Cambridge, Mass.: Civil Rights Project, 2005).

12. James S. Coleman, *Equality of Educational Opportunity Study* (Washington, D.C.: U.S. Department of Health, Education and Welfare, 1966).

13. Geoffrey Borman and Maritza Dowling, "Schools and Inequality: A Multi-level Analysis of Coleman's Equality of Educational Opportunity Data," *Teachers College Record* 112 (2010): 1201–46. See also, National Center for Education Statistics, *School Composition and the Black-White Achievement Gap* (Washington, D.C.: U.S. Department of Education, 2015).

14. Richard Kahlenberg, *All Together Now* (Washington, D.C.: Brookings Institution, 2001).

15. Gregory Palardy, "High School Socioeconomic Segregation and Student Attainment," *American Educational Research Journal* 50 (2013): 714–54.

16. Russell Rumberger and Gregory Palardy, "Test Scores, Dropout Rates and Transfer Rates as Alternative Indicators of School Performance," *American Education Research Journal* 41 (2005): 3–42; Christopher Jencks and Susan Mayer, "The Social Consequences of Growing Up in a Poor Neighborhood," in *Inner City Poverty in the United States*, ed. L. E. Lynn Jr. and M. G. H. McGeary (Washington, D.C.: National Academy Press, 1990).

17. Steven Rivkin, Eric Hanushek, and John Kain, "Teachers, Schools, and Academic Achievement," *Econometrica* 73 (2005): 417–58.

18. On experience, Hamilton Lankford, Susanna Loeb, and James Wycoff, "Teacher Sorting and the Plight of Urban Schools: A Descriptive Analysis," *Educational Evaluation and Policy Analysis* 24 (2002): 37–62; Charles T. Clotfelter, Helen F. Ladd, and Jacob Vigdor, "Who Teaches Whom? Race and the Distribution of Novice Teachers," *Economics of Education Review* 24 (2005): 377–92. On qualifications, Richard Ingersoll, "The Problem of Underqualified Teachers in American Secondary Schools," *Educational Researcher* 28 (1999): 26–37.

19. Robert Hanna, Max Marchitello, and Catherine Brown, "Comparable but Unequal: School Funding Disparities" (Washington, D.C.: Center for American Progress, 2015), https://cdn.americanprogress.org/wp-content/uploads/2015/03/ESEAComparability-brief2.pdf (July 6, 2015); Frank Adamson and Linda Darling Hammond, "Addressing the Inequitable Distribution of Teachers: What It Will Take to Get Qualified, Effective Teachers in All Communities" (Palo Alto, Calif.: Stanford Center for Opportunity Policy in Education, 2011), http://www.boldapproach.org/uploads/db_files/SCOPE%20teacher%20salary%20brief.pdf (July 6, 2015).

20. Kacey Guin, "Chronic Teacher Turnover in Urban Elementary Schools," *Education Policy Analysis Archives* 12 (2004): 42.

21. Charles T. Clotfelter, Helen F. Ladd, and Jacob L. Vigdor, "Are Teacher Absences Worth Worrying about in the U.S.?," *Education Finance and Policy* 4 (Spring 2009): 115–49; UCLA/IDEA, "Separate and Unequal 50 Years after Brown: Racial Opportunity Gaps in California's Schools" (Los Angeles: UCLA/IDEA, 2004), http://idea.gseis.ucla.edu/publications/files/brownsu2.pdf (February 10, 2015).

22. Jean Anyon, *Ghetto Schooling: A Political Economy of Urban Education Reform* (New York: Teachers College Press, 1997); Kozol, *Savage Inequalities*.

23. Gail Sunderman, James Kim, and Gary Orfield, *NCLB Meets School Realities: Lessons from the Field* (Thousand Oaks, Calif.: Corwin, 2005); Jennifer Jennings and Jonathan Bearak, "'Teaching to the Test' in the NCLB Era: How Test Predictability

Affects Our Understanding of Student Performance," *Educational Researcher* 43 (2008): 381–89.

24. Jeannie Oakes, Adam Gamoran, and Reba Page, "Curriculum Differentiation: Opportunities, Outcomes and Meanings," in *Handbook of Research on Curriculum*, ed. Peter Jackson (New York: Macmillan, 1992), 570–608.

25. Meredith Phillips and Tiffani Chin, "School Inequality: What Do We Know?," in *Social Inequality*, ed. Kathryn Neckerman (New York: Russell Sage, 2004), 467–519.

26. Jonathan Kozol, *The Shame of the Nation: The Restoration of Apartheid Schooling in America* (New York: Random House, 2005), 41.

27. "Critical Needs of RPS Buildings Dominate New School Year," *RVANews*, August 25, 2014, http://rvanews.com/news/critical-needs-of-rps-buildings-dominate-new-school-year/116198?east-end-daily (February 9, 2015).

28. Rumberger and Palardy, "Test Scores, Dropout Rates"; Robert Ketner Ream, *Uprooting Children: Mobility, Social Capital, and Mexican American Underachievement* (New York: LFB, 2005).

29. Richard Verdugo, "Race-Ethnicity, Social Class and Zero Tolerance Policies," *Education and Urban Society* 35 (2002): 50–75; Tammy Johnson, Jennifer Emiko Boyden, and William J. Pitz, "Racial Profiling and Punishment in U.S. Schools: How Zero Tolerance Policies and High Stakes Testing Subvert Academic Excellence and Racial Equity" (Oakland, Calif.: Applied Research Center, 2001).

30. Paul Jargowsky, *Poverty and Place: Ghettos, Barrios, and the American City* (New York: Russell Sage, 1997); Douglas Massey and Nancy Denton, *American Apartheid: Segregation and the Making of the Underclass* (Cambridge, Mass.: Harvard University Press, 1993); Patrick Sharkey, *Stuck in Place: Urban Neighborhoods and the End of Progress toward Racial Equality* (Chicago: University of Chicago Press, 2013).

31. Paul Jargowsky and Mohamed El Komi, "Before or after the Bell? School Context and Neighborhood Effects on Student Achievement," in *Neighborhood and Life Chances: How Place Matters in Modern America*, ed. H. Newburger, E. Birch, and S. Wachter (Philadelphia: University of Pennsylvania Press, 2011), 50–75; Richard Rothstein, *Class and Schools: Using Social, Economic, and Educational Reform to Close the Black-White Achievement Gap* (New York: Teachers College Press, 2004).

32. Martin Luther King, "Letter from Birmingham Jail," in *A Testament of Hope*, ed. James Washington (New York: HarperCollins, 1986), 293.

33. Roslyn Mickelson and Mokubung Nkomo, "Integrated Schooling, Life-Course Outcomes, and Social Cohesion in Multiethnic Democratic Societies," *Review of Research in Education* 36 (2012): 197–238.

34. Kathryn Borman et al., "Accountability in a Postdesegregation Era: The Continuing Significance of Segregation in Florida's Schools," *American Educational Research Journal* 41 (2004): 605–31; Robert Balfanz and Nettie E. Legters, "NCLB and Reforming the Nation's Lowest-Performing High Schools," in *Holding NCLB Accountable: Achieving Accountability, Equity, and School Reform*, ed. G. L. Sunderman (Thousand Oaks, Calif.: Corwin, 2008), 191–207.

35. Although, as of this writing, popular media outlets like *NPR*, the *New York Times*, the *Huffington Post* and the *Washington Post* are increasingly running stories and op-eds about school segregation and desegregation.

36. Charles Tilly, *Durable Inequality* (Berkeley: University of California Press, 1999).

37. In fact, a national campaign has sprung up around this very idea, calling for a "Broader, Bolder Approach to Education." It underscores the multifaceted challenges surrounding high-poverty schools and students and highlights policies that would address the needs of children both in and outside of schools. See Broader, Bolder Approach to Education, http://www.boldapproach.org/.

38. Roslyn Mickelson, "Subverting Swann: First and Second Generation Segregation in the Charlotte-Mecklenburg Schools," *American Educational Research Journal* 38 (2001): 215–52.

39. Jeannie Oakes, *Keeping Track: How Schools Structure Inequality* (New Haven, Conn.: Yale University, 2010).

40. Scott Page, *The Difference: How the Power of Diversity Creates Better Groups, Firms, Schools and Societies* (Princeton, N.J.: Princeton University Press, 2007).

41. Shelley Brown-Jeffy, "The Race Gap in High School Reading Achievement: Why School Racial Composition Still Matters," *Race, Gender and Class* 13 (2006): 268–94; Xiaoxia Newton, "End of High School Mathematics Attainment: How Did Students Get There?," *Teachers College Record* 112 (2010); Douglas Harris, *Lost Learning, Forgotten Promises: A National Analysis of School Racial Segregation, Student Achievement, and "Controlled Choice Plans"* (Washington, D.C.: Center for American Progress, 2006); Eric Hanushek, John Kain, and Steven Rivkin, "New Evidence about *Brown v. Board of Education*: The Complex Effects of School Racial Composition on Achievement," *Journal of Labor Economics* 29 (2009): 349–83; Robert Linn and Kevin Welner, eds., *Race-Conscious Policies for Assigning Students to Schools: Social Science Research and the Supreme Court Cases* (Washington, D.C.: National Academy of Education, 2007); Mickelson and Nkomo, "Integrated Schooling, Life-Course Outcomes;" National Center for Education Statistics, *School Composition and the Black-White Achievement Gap*.

42. Roslyn Mickelson and Martha Bottia, "Integrated Education and Mathematics Outcomes: A Synthesis of Social Science Research," *North Carolina Law Review* 88 (2010): 993.

43. Jomills Braddock and Tamela Eitle, "The Effects of School Desegregation," in *Handbook of Research on Multicultural Education*, ed. James Banks and Cherry Banks (New York: John Wiley, 2004), 828–46; Maureen Hallinan, "Diversity Effects on Student Outcomes: Social Science Evidence," *Ohio State Law Journal* 59 (1998): 733–54; Linn and Welner, *Race-Conscious Policies for Assigning Students to Schools*; Roslyn Mickelson, "Twenty-First Century Social Science on School Racial Diversity and Educational Outcomes," *Ohio State Law Journal* 69 (2008): 1173–1228; Jacob Vigdor and Jens Ludwig, "Segregation and the Black-White Test Score Gap," Working Paper no. 12988 (New York: National Bureau of Economic Research, 2007); Amy Stuart Wells and Robert Crain, "Perpetuation Theory and the Long-Term Effects of School Desegregation," *Review of Educational Research* 6 (1994): 531–55.

44. Willis Hawley, "Designing Schools That Use Student Diversity to Enhance Learning of All Students," in *Lessons in Integration: Realizing the Promise of Racial Diversity in American Schools*, ed. Gary Orfield and Erica Frankenberg (Charlottesville: University of Virginia Press, 2007), 31–56; Mickelson and Bottia, "Integrated Education and Mathematics Outcomes"; Thomas Pettigrew and Linda Tropp, "A Meta-Analytic Test of Intergroup Contact Theory," *Journal of Personality and Social Psychology* 90 (2006): 751; Douglas Ready and Megan Silander, "School Racial and Ethnic Composition and Young Children's Cognitive Development: Isolating Family, Neighborhood and School Influences," in *Integrating Schools in a Changing Society: New Policies and Legal Options for a Multiracial Generation*, ed. Erica Frankenberg and Elizabeth DeBray (Chapel Hill: University of North Carolina Press, 2011), 91–113; Janet Schofield, "Review of Research on School Desegregation's Impact on Elementary and Secondary Students," in *Handbook of Multicultural Education*, ed. J. A. Banks and Cherry Banks (New York: Macmillan), 597–617.

45. Jonathan Guryan, "Desegregation and Black Dropout Rates," *American Economic Review* 94 (2004): 919–43; Schofield, "Review of Research on School Desegregation's Impact"; Jencks and Mayer, "The Social Consequences of Growing Up in a Poor Neighborhood"; Robert Teranishi, Walter Allen, and Daniel Solorzano, "Opportunities at the Crossroads: Racial Inequality, School Segregation, and Higher Education in California," *Teachers College Record* 106 (2004); Robert Teranishi and Tara Parker, "Social Reproduction of Inequality: Racial Segregation, Secondary Schools, and Postsecondary Opportunities," *Teachers College Record* 112 (2010); William Trent, "Outcomes of School Desegregation: Findings from Longitudinal Research," *Journal of Negro Education* 66 (1997): 255–57; Marvin Dawkins, "Black Students' Occupational Expectations: A National Study of the Impact of School Desegregation," *Urban Education* 18 (1983): 98–113; Mark Granovetter, "The Idea of 'Advancement' in Theories of Social Evolution and Development," *American Journal of Sociology* 85 (1979): 489–515; James McPartland and Jomills Braddock, "The Impact of School Desegregation on Going to College and Getting a Good Job," in *Effective School Desegregation*, ed. Willis Hawley (New York: Sage, 1981), 141–54; Trent, "Outcomes of School Desegregation."

46. Mickelson and Nkomo, "Integrated Schooling, Life Course Outcomes and Social Cohesion."

47. Jomills Braddock, "The Perpetuation of Segregation across Levels of Education: A Behavioral Assessment of the Contact-Hypothesis," *Sociology of Education* 53 (1980): 187; Jomills Braddock, "Looking Back: The Effects of Court-Ordered Desegregation," in *From the Courtroom to the Classroom: The Shifting Landscape of School Desegregation*, ed. Claire Smrekar and Ellen Goldring (Cambridge, Mass.: Harvard Education Press, 2009), 3–18; Donnell Butler, "Ethnic Racial Composition and College Preference: Revisiting the Perpetuation of Segregation Hypothesis," *Annals of the American Academy of Political and Social Science* 26 (2010); Elizabeth Stearns, "Long-Term Correlates of High School Racial Composition: Perpetuation Theory Reexamined," *Teachers College Record* 112 (2010); Wells and Crain, "Perpetuation Theory."

48. Charles Clotfelter, *After Brown: The Rise and Retreat of School Desegregation* (Princeton, N.J.: Princeton University Press, 2004).

49. Ibid.; Sean Reardon, John Yun, and Tamela Eitle, "The Changing Structure of School Segregation: Measurement and Evidence of Multiracial Metropolitan-Area School Segregation, 1989–1995," *Demography* 37 (2000): 351–64; Kori Stroub and Meredith Richards, "From Resegregation to Reintegration: Trends in Metropolitan School Segregation, 1993–2010," *American Educational Research Journal* 50 (2013): 497–531.

50. Reardon et al., "The Changing Structure of School Segregation."

51. Jennifer Jellison Holme and Kara Finnegan, "School Diversity, School District Fragmentation and Metropolitan Policy," *Teachers College Record* 115 (2013): 1–29; Weiher, *Fractured Metropolis*; Erica Frankenberg, "Splintering School Districts: Understanding the Link between Segregation and Fragmentation," *Law and Social Inquiry* 34 (2009).

52. Frankenberg, "Splintering School Districts."

53. Kendra Bischoff, "School District Fragmentation and Racial Residential Segregation: How Do Boundaries Matter?," *Urban Affairs Review* 44 (2008): 182–217.

54. Holme and Finnegan, "School Diversity, School District Fragmentation and Metropolitan Policy."

55. William Fischel, "The Congruence of American School Districts with Other Local Government Boundaries: A Google Earth Exploration" (Hanover, N.H.: Dartmouth College of Economics Department Working Paper, 2007).

56. Ibid.

57. Myron Orfield, "*Milliken, Meredith* and Metropolitan Segregation," *UCLA Law Review* 62 (2015): 367–438; David Hackett Fisher, *Albion's Seed: Four British Folkways in America* (Oxford: Oxford University, 1989), 181–90.

58. Ibid.

59. Jon Teaford, *City and Suburb: The Political Fragmentation of Metropolitan America, 1850–1970* (Baltimore, Md.: Johns Hopkins University Press, 1979).

60. Douglas Massey and Nancy Denton, *American Apartheid: Segregation and the Making of the Underclass* (Cambridge, Mass.: Harvard University Press, 1993).

61. Ibid.

62. Douglas Massey, "Origins of Economic Disparities: The Historical Role of Housing Segregation," in *Segregation: The Rising Costs for America*, ed. James Carr and Nandinee Kutty (New York: Routledge, 2008).

63. Bruce Haynes, *Red Lines, Black Spaces: The Politics of Race and Space in a Black Middle-Class Suburb* (New Haven, Conn.: Yale University Press, 2001).

64. Massey and Denton, *American Apartheid*.

65. Orfield, "*Milliken, Meredith* and Metropolitan Segregation."

66. David Freund, *Colored Property: State Policy and White Racial Politics in Suburban America* (Chicago: University of Chicago Press, 2007); Grant, *Hope and Despair in the American City*; Haynes, *Red Lines, Black Spaces*; Massey and Denton, *American Apartheid*; Elizabeth Banks, *A History of Black-White Residential Segregation in America* (Nashville: Fiske University, Race Relations Institute, 2006).

67. Susan Glassberg, "Legal Control of Blockbusting," *Urban Law Annual* 145 (1972): 145.

68. Grant, *Hope and Despair in the American City*.

69. john a. powell, "Reinterpreting Metropolitan Space as a Strategy for Social Justice," in *Breakthrough Communities: Sustainability and Justice in the Next American Metropolis*, ed. Paloma Pavel (Cambridge, Mass.: MIT Press, 2009), 23-32.

70. Freund, *Colored Property*; Massey, "Origins of Economic Disparities."

71. Gary Orfield, *Housing Segregation: Causes, Effects, Possible Cures* (Cambridge, Mass.: Harvard Civil Rights Project, 2001).

72. Mindy Fullilove, Lourdes Hernandez-Cordero, and Robert Fullilove, "The Ghetto Game: Apartheid and the Developer's Imperative in Postindustrial American Cities," in *The Integration Debate: Competing Futures for American Cities*, ed. C. Hartman and G. Squires (New York: Routledge, 2010), 199-212.

73. William Taylor, "Mounting a Concerted Federal Attack on Urban School Segregation: A Preliminary Exploration," in *Racial Segregation: Two Policy Views*, ed. Ford Foundation (New York: Ford Foundation, 1979).

74. U.S. Senate, Select Committee on Equal Educational Opportunity, *Toward Equal Educational Opportunity: The Report of the Select Committee on Equal Educational Opportunity* (Washington, D.C.: U.S. Government Printing Office, 1972), 249.

75. Harold Howe II, "Foreword," in *Law and School Reform*, ed. Jay Heubert (New Haven, Conn.: Yale University Press, 1998), vii.

76. Robert Pratt, *The Color of Their Skin: Education and Race in Richmond, Virginia, 1954-89* (Charlottesville: University of Virginia Press, 1991).

77. "A Bumpy Road in Richmond," *Time*, February 28, 1972, http://www.time.com/time/magazine/article/0,9171,905831,00.html (July 7, 2015).

78. Robert Green, ed., *Metropolitan Desegregation* (New York: Plenum, 1985), 19.

79. William Taylor, "Metropolitan Remedies for Public School Discrimination: The Neglected Option," *Urban Review* 10 (1979): 184.

80. *Milliken v. Bradley*, 418 U.S. 717, 732-33 (1974) (quoting Pet. App. at 57a) (internal quotation marks omitted).

81. *Bradley v. Sch. Bd of Richmond Va.*, 338 F. Supp. 67, 84 (E.D. Va. 1972).

82. Orfield, "*Milliken, Meredith* and Metropolitan School Segregation."

83. Ibid.

84. Grant, *Hope and Despair in the American City*, 144; Orfield, "*Milliken, Meredith* and Metropolitan School Segregation."

85. *Milliken v. Bradley*, 743.

86. Joyce Baugh, *The Detroit Busing Case: Milliken v. Bradley and the Controversy of Desegregation* (Lawrence: University Press of Kansas, 2011).

87. *Milliken v. Bradley*, Marshall dissenting, 783.

88. Green, *Metropolitan Desegregation*.

89. *Keyes v. School District No. 1*, Denver, 413 U.S. 189 (1973); Orfield, "*Milliken, Meredith* and Metropolitan School Segregation."

90. Grant, *Hope and Despair in the American City*, 150.

91. U.S. Commission on Civil Rights, *Statement on Metropolitan School Desegregation* (Washington, D.C.: U.S. Commission on Civil Rights, February 1977), 92–93.

92. Green, *Metropolitan Desegregation*, 24.

93. These included Charlotte, North Carolina; Daytona Beach, Florida; Greensboro, North Carolina; Indianapolis, Indiana; Lakeland, Florida; Las Vegas, Nevada; Louisville, Kentucky; Nashville, Tennessee; Orlando, Florida; Pensacola, Florida; Wilmington, Delaware; Raleigh, North Carolina; Durham, North Carolina; Sarasota, Florida; Tampa, Florida; St. Petersburg, Florida; and West Palm Beach, Florida. See Orfield, "*Milliken, Meredith* and Metropolitan School Segregation."

94. Ibid.

95. Amy Stuart Wells, Bianca J. Baldridge, Jacquelyn Duran, Courtney Grzesikowski, Richard Lofton, Allison Roda, Miya Warner and Terrenda White, *Boundary Crossing for Diversity, Equity and Achievement: Inter-district Desegregation and Equal Educational Opportunity* (Cambridge, Mass.: Charles Hamilton Houston Institute for Race and Justice, 2009); One Nation Indivisible, *Inter-district Transfer Programs: A (Brief) National Overview* (Cambridge, Mass.: One Nation Indivisible, n.d.), http://www.onenationindivisible.org/wp-content/uploads/2012/09/ONI_Interdistrict_Overview.PPT.pdf (October 28, 2015); Susan Eaton, *The Children in Room E4: American Education on Trial* (Chapel Hill: Alonquin Books, 2006).

96. Taylor, "Metropolitan Remedies for Public School Discrimination"; Sheneka Williams, "Micropolitics and Rural School Consolidation: The Quest for Equal Educational Opportunity in Webster Parish," *Peabody Journal of Education* 88 (2013).

97. Taylor, "Metropolitan Remedies for Public School Discrimination," 188.

98. David Armor, "White Flight, Demographic Transition and the Future of School Desegregation" (Santa Monica, Calif.: Rand, 1978); James Coleman, Sarah Kelley, and John More, "Trends in School Segregation, 1968–1973" (Washington, D.C.: Urban Institute, 1975); Charles Clotfelter, "School Desegregation, 'Tipping' and Private School Enrollment," *Journal of Human Resources* 11 (1976): 28–49.

99. Thomas Pettigrew and Robert Green, "School Desegregation in Large Cities: A Critique of Coleman's 'White Flight' Thesis," *Harvard Educational Review* 4 (1976): 1–53.

100. U.S. Commission on Civil Rights, "Statement on Metropolitan School Desegregation" (Washington, D.C.: U.S. Commission on Civil Rights, 1977); Gary Orfield, "Metropolitan School Desegregation: Impacts on Metropolitan Society," in *In Pursuit of a Dream Deferred: Linking Housing and Education Policy*, ed. john a. powell, Gavin Kearney, and Vina Kay (New York: Peter Lang, 2001); Taylor, "Metropolitan Remedies for Public School Discrimination."

101. Erica Frankenberg, "The Impact of School Segregation on Residential Housing Patterns: Mobile, Alabama and Charlotte, North Carolina," in *School Resegregation: Must the South Turn Back?*, ed. J. Boger and G. Orfield (Chapel Hill: University of North Carolina Press, 2005), 165–84; Orfield, "Metropolitan School Desegregation"; Orfield, "*Milliken, Meredith* and Metropolitan Segregation."

102. National Commission on Excellence in Education, *A Nation at Risk: The Imperative for Educational Reform* (Washington, D.C.: U.S. Department of Education, 1983), 1.

103. Gary Orfield and Erica Frankenberg, *Educational Delusions? Why Choice Can Deepen Inequality and How to Make Schools Fair* (Berkeley: University of California Press, 2013).

104. "Charter Schools," National Center for Education Statistics, http://nces.ed.gov/fastfacts/display.asp?id=30 (February 9, 2015).

105. Jal Mehta, "How Paradigms Create Politics: The Transformation of American Educational Policy, 1980–2001," *American Educational Research Journal* 50 (2013): 285–325.

106. Jaekyung Lee and Kenneth Wong, "The Impact of Accountability on Racial and Socioeconomic Equity: Considering Both School Resources and Achievement Outcomes," *American Educational Research Journal* 41 (2004): 797–832; Sam Dillon, "'No Child' Law Is Not Closing a Racial Gap," *New York Times*, April 28, 2009, http://www.nytimes.com/2009/04/29/education/29scores.html (July 7, 2015).

107. Katherine Magnuson and Jane Walfogel, *Steady Gains and Stalled Progress: Inequality and the Black-White Test Score Gap* (New York: Russell Sage, 2008).

108. Prudence Carter and Kevin Welner, eds., *Closing the Opportunity Gap: What America Must Do to Give Every Child an Even Chance* (Cambridge: Oxford University Press, 2013), 2.

109. Greg Duncan and Richard Murnane, eds., *Whither Opportunity* (New York: Russell Sage, 2011).

110. Gary Orfield, "Policy and Equity: A Third of a Century of Educational Reforms in the United States," *Quarterly Review of Education* 29 (1999): 579–94.

111. For a summary, see Carter and Welner, *Closing the Opportunity Gap*.

112. Ibid. See also David Berliner, "Effects of Inequality and Poverty vs. Teachers and Schooling on America's Youth," *Teachers College Record* 115 (2013).

113. "When Outsiders Take Over Schools: Lessons from Memphis," *The Atlantic*, http://www.theatlantic.com/education/archive/2013/10/when-outsiders-take-over-schools-lessons-from-memphis/280919/ (February 10, 2015); Baris Dawes, Thomas Luce, and Myron Orfield, "Examining the Rapid Growth of the Charter Sector in New Orleans," in *Educational Delusions?*, ed. Gary Orfield and Erica Frankenberg (Berkeley: University of California Press, 2013).

114. Sainz, "Memphis City Schools System Merger Ignites Racial Tensions."

115. Excellence in Education National, "Excel National Applauds Tennessee Senate for Passage of A–F School Grading," April 8, 2015, http://excelnational.org/excel-national-applauds-tennessee-senate-passage-f-school-grading/ (July 7, 2015).

116. Gary Orfield and Chungmei Lee, *Brown at 50: King's Dream or Plessy's Nightmare?* (Cambridge, Mass.: Harvard Civil Rights Project, 2004).

117. *Newsweek* magazine began publishing a list of "schools that beat the odds" or performed better than expected given the level of student poverty in the schools. See, e.g., "Beating the Odds 2014: Top Schools for Low-Income Students," *Newsweek*, September 9, 2014, http://www.newsweek.com/high-schools/beating-odds-2014;

Richard Rothstein, *Class and Schools* (New York: Teachers College Press/Economic Policy Institute, 2004).

118. Bruce Katz, ed., *Reflections on Regionalism* (Washington, D.C.: Brookings Institution, 2001); Bruce Katz and Jennifer Bradley, *The Metropolitan Revolution: How Cities and Metros Are Fixing Our Broken Politics and Fragile Economy* (Washington, D.C.: Brookings Institution, 2013).

119. Katz, *Reflections on Regionalism*.

120. Nate Berg, "The Emerging and Interconnected 'Megapolitan' Regions," *The Atlantic*, January 3, 2012, http://www.citylab.com/work/2012/01/emerging-and-interconnected-megapolitan-regions/847/ (July 6, 2015).

121. David Troutt, *The Price of Paradise: The Costs of Inequality and a Vision for a More Equitable America* (New York: New York University Press, 2013).

122. Myron Orfield, *Metropolitics* (Washington, D.C.: Brookings Institution, 2002), 1.

123. john a. powell, "Addressing Regional Dilemmas for Minority Communities," in *Reflections on Regionalism*, ed. Bruce Katz (Washington, D.C.: Brookings Institution, 2001), 239.

124. Trimet, "Livable Portland: Land Use and Transportation Initiatives," November 2010, http://trimet.org/pdfs/publications/Livable-Portland.pdf (July 6, 2015).

125. powell, "Addressing Regional Dilemmas for Minority Communities."

126. Metropolitan Council, "Who We Are," http://www.metrocouncil.org/About-Us/The-Council-Who-We-Are.aspx (July 6, 2015).

127. Charles Tiebout, "A Pure Theory of Local Expenditures," *Journal of Political Economy* 64 (1956): 416–24.

128. Katz and Bradley, *The Metropolitan Revolution*.

129. Ibid., 41–63.

Chapter Two

1. Gary Orfield, *Toward a Strategy for Urban Integration: Lessons in School and Housing Policy from Twelve Cities* (New York: Ford Foundation, 1981).

2. Jack Dougherty and contributors, *On the Line: How Schooling, Housing and Civil Rights Shaped Hartford and Its Suburbs* (Hartford, Conn.: Trinity College, 2015), http://epress.trincoll.edu/ontheline2015/ (July 9, 2015); Richard Rothstein, *The Making of Ferguson: Public Policies at the Root of Its Troubles* (Washington, D.C.: Economic Policy Institute, 2014); Amy Stuart Wells et al., "Why Boundaries Matter: A Study of Five Separate and Unequal Long Island School Districts" (New York: Teachers College/Long Island Index, 2009).

3. Edward Glaeser and Jacob Vigdor, *The End of the Segregated Century: Racial Separation in America's Neighborhoods, 1890–2010* (New York: Manhattan Institute, 2012); William Frey, *Diversity Explosion: How New Racial Demographics Are Remaking America* (Washington, D.C.: Brookings Institution, 2014).

4. John R. Logan and Charles Zhang, "Global Neighborhoods: New Pathways to Diversity and Separation," *American Journal of Sociology* 115 (2010): 1069–1109;

Daniel Kay Hertz, "The New Asymmetry of Segregation," *City Notes*, January 5, 2015, http://danielkayhertz.com/2015/01/05/the-new-asymmetry-of-segregation/ (July 9, 2015); Dan Keating, "Why Whites Don't Understand Black Segregation," *Washington Post Wonkblog*, November 21, 2014, http://www.washingtonpost.com/blogs/wonkblog/wp/2014/11/21/why-whites-dont-understand-black-segregation/ (July 9, 2015).

5. Patrick Sharkey, *Stuck in Place: Urban Neighborhoods and the End of Progress toward Racial Equality* (Chicago: University of Chicago Press, 2013).

6. Kendra Bischoff and Sean Reardon, "Growth in the Residential Segregation of Families by Income, 1970–2009," US2010 Project (Providence, R.I.: Brown University, 2011).

7. Paul Jargowsky, "Segregation, Neighborhoods and Schools," in *Choosing Homes and Schools*, ed. Annette Lareau and Kimberly Goyette (New York: Russell Sage, 2014), 97–136.

8. Sean Reardon, Lindsay Fox, and Joseph Townsend, "Neighborhood Income Composition by Household Race and Income, 1990–2009," *Annals of the American Academy of Political and Social Science* 660 (2015): 78–97; David Rusk, *Inside Game/Outside Game* (Washington, D.C.: Brookings Institution, 1999): Table A-5

9. Richard Alba and Steven Romalewski, "The End of Segregation? Hardly" (New York: Center for Urban Research, 2012), http://www.gc.cuny.edu/Page-Elements/Academics-Research-Centers-Initiatives/Centers-and-Institutes/Center-for-Urban-Research/CUR-research-initiatives/The-End-of-Segregation-Hardly (February 10, 2015).

10. Ibid.

11. John Logan and Brian Stults, "The Persistence of Segregation in the Metropolis: New Findings from the 2010 Census," US2010 Project (Providence, R.I.: Brown University, 2011).

12. Sean Reardon and John Yun, "Integrating Neighborhoods, Segregating Schools: The Retreat from School Desegregation in the South, 1990–2000," in *School Resegregation: Must the South Turn Back?*, ed. Jack Boger and Gary Orfield (Chapel Hill: University of North Carolina Press, 2005), 51–69.

13. For a summary, see Gary Orfield, Genevieve Siegel-Hawley, and John Kucsera, *Sorting Out Deepening Confusion on Segregation Trends* (Los Angeles: UCLA Civil Rights Project, 2014). See also Sean Reardon and Ann Owens, "Sixty Years after *Brown*: Trends and Consequences of School Segregation," *Annual Review of Sociology* 40 (2014): 199–218.

14. Gary Orfield and Erica Frankenberg, "Increasingly Segregated and Unequal Schools as Courts Reverse Policy," *Educational Administration Quarterly* 50 (2014): 718–34.

15. Roslyn Mickelson, "Exploring the School-Housing Nexus: A Synthesis of Social Science Evidence," in *Finding Common Ground: Coordinating Housing and Education Policy to Promote Integration*, ed. P. Tegeler (Washington, D.C.: Poverty and Race Research Action Council, 2011), 5–8; Deneesh Sohoni and Sal Saporito, "Mapping School Segregation: Using GIS to Explore Racial Segregation between

Schools and Their Corresponding Attendance Areas," *American Journal of Education* 115 (2009): 569.

16. Jennifer Jellison Holme, "Buying Homes, Buying Schools," *Harvard Educational Review* 72, no. 2 (2002): 177–206; Heather Beth Johnson, *The American Dream and the Power of Wealth: Choosing Schools and Inheriting Inequality in the Land of Opportunity* (New York: Routledge, 2006); Annette Lareau and Kimberly Goyette, *Choosing Homes, Choosing Schools* (New York: Russell Sage, 2014); Thomas Shapiro, *The Hidden Cost of Being African American: How Wealth Perpetuates Inequality* (New York: Oxford University Press, 2004).

17. Jonathan Kozol, *Savage Inequalities: Children in America's Schools* (New York: HarperPerennial, 1992); James Ryan, *Five Miles Away, a World Apart: One City, Two Schools and the Story of Modern Educational Inequality* (New York: Oxford University Press, 2010); A. Chiodo, R. Hernández-Murillo, and M. Owyang, "Nonlinear Effects of School Quality on House Prices," *Federal Reserve Bank of St. Louis Review* 92 (2010): 185–204; T. Kane, S. Riegg, and D. Steger, "School Quality, Neighborhoods and Housing Prices: Effects of Free Choice among Public Schools," *Review of Economic Studies* 7 (2010).

18. Z. Di and X. Liu, *The Importance of Wealth and Income for Housing Studies at Harvard University* (Cambridge, Mass.: Joint Center for Housing Studies at Harvard University, 2005); G. Masnick, "Home Ownership Trends and Racial Inequality in the United States in the 20th Century," Working Paper W01-3 (Cambridge, Mass.: Joint Center for Housing Studies, 2001); M. Oliver and T. Shapiro, *Black Wealth, White Wealth: A New Perspective on Racial Inequality* (New York: Routledge, 1995).

19. Nicholas Kristof, "When Whites Just Don't Get It," *New York Times*, August 30, 2014, http://www.nytimes.com/2014/08/31/opinion/sunday/nicholas-kristof-after-ferguson-race-deserves-more-attention-not-less.html (February 10, 2015).

20. Shapiro, *The Hidden Cost of Being African American*.

21. Oliver and Shapiro, *Black Wealth, White Wealth*.

22. Ta-Nehisi Coates, "The Case for Reparations," *The Atlantic*, June 2014, http://www.theatlantic.com/features/archive/2014/05/the-case-for-reparations/361631/ (February 10, 2015).

23. Stephen L. Ross and John Yinger, *The Color of Credit: Mortgage Discrimination, Research Methodology, and Fair-Lending Enforcement* (Boston: MIT Press, 2002).

24. Myron Orfield and Thomas Luce, *Region: Planning the Future of the Twin Cities* (Minneapolis: University of Minnesota, 2010).

25. Johnson, *The American Dream and the Power of Wealth*.

26. Ibid.

27. Camille Charles, "The Dynamics of Racial Residential Segregation," *Annual Review of Sociology* 29 (2003); Lawrence Bobo et al., *Prismatic Metropolis: Inequality in Los Angeles* (New York: Russell Sage, 2002); Thomas C. Schelling, "Dynamic Models of Segregation," *Journal of Mathematical Sociology* 143 (1971): 154–59.

28. Anthony Downs, "Policy Directions Concerning Racial Discrimination in U.S. Housing Markets," *Housing Policy Debate* 3 (1992): 708–10; Reynolds Farley

et al., "Stereotypes and Segregation: Neighborhoods in the Detroit Area," *American Journal of Sociology* 100 (1994): 754-55; Orfield and Luce, *Region*, 117

29. Camille Zubrinsky Charles, "Can We Live Together? Racial Preferences and Neighborhood Outcomes," in *The Geography of Opportunity: Race and Housing Choice in Metropolitan America*, ed. Xavier de Souza Briggs (Washington, D.C.: Brookings Institution, 2005).

30. Reynolds Farley et al., *"Chocolate City, Vanilla Suburbs": Will the Trend toward Racially Separate Communities Continue?,"* Social Science Research 7 (1978): 319-22; Charles, *Can We Live Together?*, 45, 56.

31. Mickelson, "Exploring the School-Housing Nexus," 5-8; Amy Stuart Wells and Robert Crain, "Perpetuation Theory and the Long-Term Effects of School Desegregation," *Review of Educational Research* 6 (1994): 531-55.

32. Holme, "Buying Homes, Buying Schools"; David Liebowitz and Lindsay Page, "Does School Policy Affect Housing Choices? Evidence from the End of Desegregation in Charlotte-Mecklenburg," *American Educational Research Journal* 51 (2014): 671-703.

33. Holme, "Buying Homes, Buying Schools"; Shapiro, *The Hidden Cost of Being African American*.

34. Holme, "Buying Homes, Buying Schools."

35. Though the year 2014-15 brought a renewed sense of urgency to issues of racial hostility and inequality with events in Ferguson, Baltimore, and Charleston.

36. David Freund, *Colored Property: State Policy and White Racial Politics in Suburban America* (Chicago: University of Chicago Press, 2007).

37. Ibid., 10; Ian Haney Lopez, *Dog Whistle Politics: How Coded Racial Appeals Have Reinvented Racism and Wrecked the Middle Class* (New York: Oxford University Press, 2014); Eduardo Bonilla Silva, *Racism without Racists: Colorblind Racism and the Persistence of Racial Inequality* (Lanham, Md.: Rowman and Littlefield, 2009).

38. David Rusk, *The "Segregation Tax": The Cost of Racial Segregation to Black Homeowners* (Washington, D.C.: Brookings Institution, 2001), http://www.brookings.edu/~/media/research/files/reports/2001/10/metropolitanpolicy-rusk/rusk.pdf (October 30, 2015).

39. John Clapp, Anupam Nanda, and Stephen Ross, "Which School Attributes Matter? The Influence of School District Performance and Demographic Composition on Property Values," *Journal of Urban Economics* 63 (2008): 451-66.

40. Jack Dougherty et al., "School Choice in Suburbia: Test Scores, Race, and Housing Markets," *American Journal of Education* 115 (2009): 523-48.

41. Kane, Riegg, and Steger, "School Quality, Neighborhoods and Housing Prices."

42. Clapp, Nanda, and Stephen, "Which School Attributes Matter?"

43. Jonathan Rothwell, *Housing Costs, Zoning, and Access to High-Scoring Schools* (Washington, D.C.: Brookings Institution, 2012).

44. "Unequal Opportunity: Perpetuating Housing Segregation in America," (Washington, D.C.: National Fair Housing Alliance, 2006), http://www.mvfair

housing.com/pdfs/2006%20Fair%20Housing%20Trends%20Report.PDF (February 10, 2015).

45. Fair Housing Act, 42 U.S.C. §§ 3601-19; Vivian Toy, "Questions Your Broker Can't Answer," *New York Times*, June 24, 2007, http://www.nytimes.com/2007/06/24/realestate/24cov.html (July 9, 2015).

46. Dougherty et al., *On the Line*.

47. Ibid.

48. Ibid.

49. Bruce Haynes, *Red Lines, Black Spaces: The Politics of Race and Space in a Black Middle-Class Suburb* (New Haven, Conn.: Yale University Press, 2001); Dougherty et al., *On the Line*.

50. Wells et al., "Why Boundaries Matter."

51. Karen Benjamin, "Suburbanizing Jim Crow: The Impact of School Policy on Residential Segregation in Raleigh," *Journal of Urban History* 30 (March 2012): 225-46.

52. Ansley Erickson, "Building Inequality: The Spatial Organization of Schooling in Nashville, Tennessee after *Brown*," *Journal of Urban History* 38 (2012): 241-70.

53. Ansley Erickson and Andrew Highsmith, "Segregation as Splitting, Segregation as Joining: Schools, Housing and the Many Modes of Jim Crow," *American Journal of Education* 121, no. 4 (2015): 563-95.

54. Mathew Lassiter, "De Jure/De Facto: The Long Shadow of a National Myth," in *The Myth of Southern Exceptionalism*, ed. Mathew Lassiter (New York: Oxford University Press, 2010), 25-48.

55. *Swann v. Charlotte-Mecklenburg Board of Education*, 402 U.S. 1 (1971), 20.

56. Roslyn Mickelson, Stephen Smith, and Amy Hawn, *Yesterday, Today and Tomorrow* (Cambridge, Mass.: Harvard Education Press, 2015); Mathew Lassiter, *The Silent Majority: Suburban Politics in the Sunbelt South* (Princeton, N.J.: Princeton University Press, 2007).

57. *Keyes v. School District No. 1, Denver*, 413 U.S. 189 (1973), 203.

58. Ibid.

59. Ibid.

60. Myron Orfield, "*Milliken, Meredith* and Metropolitan Segregation," *UCLA Law Review* 62 (2015): 367-438.

61. *Milliken v. Bradley*, 418 U.S. 717 (1974), 756, note 2.

62. Gary Orfield, "Metropolitan School Desegregation: Impacts on Metropolitan Society," in *In Pursuit of a Dream Deferred: Linking Housing and Education Policy*, ed. john a. powell, Gavin Kearney, and Vina Kay (New York: Peter Lang, 2001); Charles Clotfelter, *After Brown: The Rise and Retreat of School Desegregation* (Princeton, N.J.: Princeton University Press, 2004); Sean Reardon and John Yun, "Suburban Racial Change and Suburban School Segregation, 1987-1995," *Sociology of Education* 74 (2002): 79-101.

63. Gary Orfield, "Segregated Housing and School Resegregation," in *Dismantling Desegregation: The Quiet Reversal of Brown v. Board of Education*, ed. G. Orfield and S. Eaton (New York: New Press, 1996), 302.

64. *Armour v. Nix*, 522 F.2d 717 (1979).

65. Ibid.

66. J. L. Hochschild and M. Danielson, "Can We Desegregate Public Schools and Subsidized Housing? Lessons from the Sorry History of Yonkers, New York," in *Changing Urban Education*, ed. Clarence Stone (Lawrence: University Press of Kansas, 1998), 23–44.

67. *Board of Education of Oklahoma v. Dowell*, 416 U.S. 696, 1991; *Freeman v. Pitts*, 503 U.S. 467 (1992); *Missouri v. Jenkins*, 515 U.S. 70 (1995).

68. *Freeman v. Pitts*.

69. Ibid.

70. Orfield, "Segregated Housing and School Resegregation."

71. David Armor, *White Flight: Demographic Transition and the Future of School Desegregation* (Santa Monica, Calif.: Rand, 1978).

72. Erica Frankenberg and Genevieve Siegel-Hawley, "Reassessing the School-Housing Segregation Link in the Post-Parents Involved Era," *Wake Forest Law Review* 48 (2013).

73. *Freeman v. Pitts*, 513.

74. *Parents Involved in Community Schools v. Seattle School District No. 1*, 551 U.S. 701 (2007), 2738.

75. Ibid., Kennedy concurring in part and Breyer dissenting.

76. National Center for Education Statistics, *The Condition of Education* (Washington, D.C.: U.S. Department of Education, 2009).

77. Heather Schwartz, *Housing Policy Is School Policy: Economically Integrative Housing Promotes Academic Success in Montgomery County, Maryland* (New York: Century Foundation, 2010), 1–57.

78. Erica Frankenberg, "The Impact of School Segregation on Residential Housing Patterns: Mobile, Alabama and Charlotte, North Carolina," in *School Resegregation: Must the South Turn Back?*, ed. J. Boger and G. Orfield (Chapel Hill: University of North Carolina Press, 2005), 165–84; Orfield, "*Milliken, Meredith* and Metropolitan Segregation."

79. Liebowitz and Page, "Does School Policy Affect Housing Choices?"

80. James Madison, "The Same Subject Continued: The Union as a Safeguard against Domestic Faction and Insurrection," in *The Federalist Papers* (1787), 5, http://www.let.rug.nl/usa/documents/1786-1800/the-federalist-papers/the-federalist-10.php (July 9, 2015).

81. Ibid.

82. Orfield, *Metropolitan School Desegregation*.

83. Diana Pearce, *Breaking Down the Barriers: New Evidence on the Impact of Metropolitan School Desegregation on Housing Patterns* (Washington, D.C.: National Institute of Education, 1980).

84. Jomills Braddock, "The Perpetuation of Segregation across Levels of Education: A Behavioral Assessment of the Contact-Hypothesis," *Sociology of Education* 53 (1980): 187; Jomills Braddock, "Looking Back: The Effects of Court-Ordered Desegregation," in *From the Courtroom to the Classroom: The Shifting Landscape of School Desegregation*, ed. Claire Smrekar and Ellen Goldring (Cambridge, Mass.:

Harvard Education Press, 2009), 3–18; Donnell Butler, "Ethnic Racial Composition and College Preference: Revisiting the Perpetuation of Segregation Hypothesis," *Annals of the American Academy of Political and Social Science* 26 (2010); Elizabeth Stearns, "Long-Term Correlates of High School Racial Composition: Perpetuation Theory Reexamined," *Teachers College Record* 112 (2010); Wells and Crain, "Perpetuation Theory."

Chapter Three

1. In Virginia, school district consolidation was particularly relevant given the structure of local government. The state's system of independent cities, coupled with a 1979 ban in the state legislature on annexation, meant that school system consolidation represented one of the few avenues for meaningful regionalism. As expert David Rusk has pointed out, however, Virginia cities could revert to "town" status, folding into their surrounding counties and regaining annexation powers (David Rusk, email correspondence with author, October 11, 2015).

2. Handwritten notes, Virginia Crockford Papers, Special Collections at the James Branch Cabell Library, Virginia Commonwealth University, circa 1970.

3. Robert Pratt, *The Color of Their Skin: Education and Race in Richmond Virginia, 1954–89* (Charlottesville: University of Virginia Press, 1989).

4. *Bradley v. Sch. Bd. of Richmond Va.*, 338 F. Supp. 67, 84 (E.D. Va. 1972).

5. William Schneider, "The Suburban Century Begins," *The Atlantic*, July 1992, http://www.theatlantic.com/past/politics/ecbig/schnsub.htm (July 14, 2015).

6. S. Jones, "Consolidation of City-County Schools in Area Rejected by High Court, 4-4," *Richmond News-Leader*, May 21, 1973, 1.

7. "Timeline: Desegregation in Jefferson County Public Schools," *Louisville Courier-Journal*, September 4, 2005, http://www.courier-journal.com/apps/pbcs.dll/article?AID=2005509040428 (February 12, 2015).

8. Betsy Levin and Willis D. Hawley, eds., *The Courts, Social Science and School Desegregation* (New Brunswick, N.J.: Transaction, 1977), 360.

9. *Haywood v. Board of Education of Louisville*, 510 F. F2d 1358, 1361 (6th Circuit, 1974).

10. Davison Douglas, *Reading, Writing and Race: The Desegregation of the Charlotte Schools* (Chapel Hill: University of North Carolina Press, 1995).

11. Ibid., 76–77.

12. Stephen Smith, *Boom for Whom? Education, Desegregation and Development in Charlotte* (Albany: State University of New York Press, 2004).

13. Ibid.

14. An Office for Civil Rights complaint related to the crossing of the city-county boundary lines was active during the consolidation discussions.

15. Former school leader (name withheld), personal communication with author, March 2014.

16. Ruth Holmberg, "Milestones in Chattanooga's History," Chattanooga Area Chamber of Commerce, Spring 2004, http://www.chattanoogachamber.com/news

-media/news/unsorted-news/commitees/chattanooga-area-business-trend/the-renaissance-remembered- (July 13, 2015).

17. Former school leader, personal communication.

18. Pratt, *The Color of Their Skin*.

19. Ibid.

20. Christopher Silver and John Moeser, *The Separate City: Black Communities in the Urban South, 1940–1968* (Lexington: University of Kentucky Press, 1995), 83.

21. "New Kent School and George W. Watkins School," National Park Service, http://www.nps.gov/nr/travel/civilrights/va2.htm (February 12, 2015).

22. *Green v. County School Board of New Kent County*, 391 U.S. 430 (1968).

23. K. Phillips, R. Rodosky, M. Munoz, and E. Larsen, "Integrated Schools, Integrated Futures? A Case Study of School Desegregation in Jefferson County, Kentucky," in *From the Courtroom to the Classroom: The Shifting Landscape of School Desegregation*, ed. C. Smrekar and E. Goldring (Cambridge, Mass.: Harvard Education Press, 2009); Smith, *Boom for Whom?*

24. See, e.g., Richard Pride and J. David Woodward, *The Burden of Busing: The Politics of Desegregation in Nashville, Tennessee* (Nashville: University of Tennessee Press, 1995).

25. "Timeline"; Sarah Garland, *Divided We Fail: The Story of an African American Community That Ended the Era of School Desegregation* (Boston: Beacon, 2012).

26. Garland, *Divided We Fail*; Otto Kerner, *Report of the National Advisory Commission on Civil Disorders* (Washington, D.C.: U.S. Government Printing Office, 1966).

27. Phillips et al., "Integrated Schools, Integrated Futures?"

28. "Timeline."

29. Mathew Lassiter, *The Silent Majority: Suburban Politics in the Sunbelt South* (Princeton, N.J.: Princeton University Press, 2007).

30. Douglas, *Reading, Writing and Race*; R. Mickelson, S. Smith, and S. Southworth, "Resegregation, Achievement and the Chimera of Choice in Post-Unitary Charlotte-Mecklenburg Schools," in *From the Courtroom to the Classroom: The Shifting Landscape of School Desegregation*, ed. C. Smrekar and E. Goldring (Cambridge, Mass.: Harvard Education Press, 2009).

31. Mickelson, Smith, and Southworth, "Resegregation, Achievement and the Chimera of Choice."

32. Richmond School Board minutes, April 15, 1971.

33. Pratt, *The Color of Their Skin*.

34. Daniel Duke, *The School That Refused to Die: Continuity and Change at Thomas Jefferson High School* (Albany: State University of New York Press, 1995).

35. *Bradley v. Baliles*, 639 F. Supp. 680 (E.D.Va.1986).

36. C. Mauney, "An Analysis of Court-Ordered Desegregation in Tennessee: Facts and Opinions," *American Journal of Education* 90 (1982): 227–57.

37. *Freeman v. Pitts*, 498 U.S. 1081 (1992); *Board of Education of Oklahoma City v. Dowell*, 498 U.S. 237 (1991); *Missouri v. Jenkins* 515 U.S. 70 (1995).

38. Gary Orfield, *Toward a Strategy for Urban Integration: Lessons in School and Housing Policy from Twelve Cities* (New York: Ford Foundation, 1981).

39. Ibid.

40. K. Briley, "School Desegregation Spurs First Housing Desegregation Gain in Forty Years in Louisville and Jefferson County: Three Decades of Increased Segregation Erased between 1970 and 1980," (Staff Report, 1980), 85–88.

41. Orfield, *Toward a Strategy for Urban Integration*, 21.

42. Smith, *Boom for Whom?*

43. Ibid.; Orfield, *Toward a Strategy for Urban Integration*.

44. Orfield, *Toward a Strategy for Urban Integration*, 67.

45. Smith, *Boom for Whom?*, 224.

46. Ibid.

47. Mickelson, Smith, and Southworth, "Resegregation, Achievement and the Chimera of Choice."

48. Janelle Scott and Rand Quinn, "The Politics of Education in the Post-*Brown* Era," *Educational Administration Quarterly* 50 (2014): 749–63; J. Petrovich and A. Wells, eds., *Bringing Equity Back: Research from a New Era in American Educational Policy* (New York: Teachers College Press, 2005).

49. C. Smrekar and E. Goldring, "Magnet Schools and the Pursuit of Racial Balance," *Education and Urban Society* 33 (2000).

50. Duke, *The School That Refused to Die*.

51. Ibid., 160.

52. Ibid., 161.

53. Genevieve Siegel-Hawley, "Race, Choice and Richmond Public Schools: New Possibilities and Ongoing Challenges for Diversity in Urban Districts," *Urban Review* 46, no. 4 (2014): 507–34, DOI 10.1007/s11256-014-0277-6 (July 13, 2015).

54. Pratt, *The Color of Their Skin*; B. Keller, "Charging the Gap," *Education Week*, March 1, 2006, http://www.edweek.org/ew/articles/2006/03/01/25chattanooga.h25.html (February 12, 2015).

55. O. Johnson, "Integration, Reconstructed," *Duke Forum for Law and Social Change* 1 (2009): 19–46.

56. "Ky. District 'Keeps Faith' on School Desegregation," *Education Week*, May 13, 2014, http://www.edweek.org/ew/articles/2014/05/14/31brown_louisville.h33.html (February 12, 2015).

57. A. Bhargava, E. Frankenberg, and C. Le, *Still Looking to the Future: Voluntary K–12 School Integration* (New York: NACCP Legal and Defense Fund/Civil Rights Project, 2008).

58. Smith, *Boom for Whom?*

59. Wendy Parker, "Desegregating Teachers," *Washington University Law Review* 86 (2009); Erica Frankenberg, "The Segregation of American Teachers," *Education Policy Analysis Archives* 17 (2009).

60. Roslyn Mickelson, Stephen Smith, and Amy Hawn Nelson, *Yesterday, Tomorrow and Tomorrow: School Desegregation and Resegregation in Charlotte* (Cambridge, Mass.: Harvard Education Press, 2015).

61. Mickelson, Smith, and Southworth, "Resegregation, Achievement and the Chimera of Choice."

62. Lassiter, *The Silent Majority*.

63. Smith, *Boom for Whom?*

64. Mickelson, Smith, and Southworth, "Resegregation, Achievement and the Chimera of Choice."

65. R. Fausset, "In North Carolina, a Racial Uproar over Schools Stirs Old Echoes," *Los Angeles Times*, December 19, 2010, http://articles.latimes.com/2010/dec/19/nation/la-na-charlotte-schools-20101219 (February 12, 2015).

66. James Ryan, *Five Miles Away, a World Apart: One City, Two Schools and the Story of Modern Educational Inequality* (New York: Oxford University Press, 2010).

67. "Open Enrollment," Richmond Public Schools, http://web.richmond.k12.va.us/Departments/PupilPersonnelServices/OpenEnrollment.aspx (July 13, 2015).

68. Office of Innovation and Improvement, "Creating Successful Magnet Schools Programs" (Washington, D.C.: U.S. Department of Education, 2004); Register, personal communication.

69. Karla Riddle (former director of magnet schools), personal communication, March 2008. This applies to the years under study; when MSAP support ended, the district dropped its emphasis on magnet diversity goals.

70. Former school leader, personal communication.

71. Y. Putman, "School Improvements Follow NAACP Complaint," *Chattanooga Times Free Press*, February 20, 2011, http://www.timesfreepress.com/news/2011/feb/20/school-improvements-follow-naacp-complaint/ (February 12, 2015).

72. *Parents Involved in Community Schools v. Seattle School District No. 1*, 551 U.S. 701 (2007).

73. U.S. Departments of Education and Justice, "Guidance on the Voluntary Use of Race to Achieve Diversity and Avoid Racial Isolation in Elementary and Secondary Schools" (2004), http://www2.ed.gov/about/offices/list/ocr/docs/guidance-ese-201111.html (February 12, 2015).

74. G. Orfield and E. Frankenberg, *Experiencing Integration in Louisville: How Parents and Students See the Gains and Challenges* (Los Angeles: UCLA, Civil Rights Project, 2011); Phillips et al., "Integrated Schools, Integrated Futures."

Chapter Four

1. Gary Orfield, *Reviving the Goal of an Integrated Society: A 21st Century Challenge* (Los Angeles: UCLA Civil Rights Project/Proyecto Derechos Civiles, 2009).

2. U.S. Commission on Civil Rights, "Statement on Metropolitan School Desegregation" (Washington, D.C.: U.S. Commission on Civil Rights, 1977); Gary Orfield, "Metropolitan School Desegregation: Impacts on Metropolitan Society," in *In Pursuit of a Dream Deferred: Linking Housing and Education Policy*, ed. john a. powell, Gavin Kearney, and Vina Kay (New York: Peter Lang, 2001); Erica Frankenberg, "The Impact of School Segregation on Residential Housing Patterns: Mobile, Alabama and Charlotte, North Carolina," in *School Resegregation: Must the South Turn Back?*, ed. J. Boger and G. Orfield (Chapel Hill: University of North Carolina Press, 2005), 165–84; Myron Orfield, "*Milliken, Meredith* and Metropolitan Segregation," *UCLA Law Review* 62 (2015): 367–438; Diana Pearce, "Breaking

Down the Barriers: New Evidence on the Impact of Metropolitan School Desegregation on Housing Patterns" (Washington, D.C.: National Institute of Education, 1980).

3. School enrollment data are from 1992, the earliest year for which the federal government collected statistics from all four metros.

4. For example, the Charlotte Metropolitan Statistical Area includes five North Carolina counties and one county in South Carolina. For the purposes of this study, though, the Charlotte area refers to Charlotte city and Mecklenburg County (which encircles the city).

5. Richmond, of course, is a special case, since the metro area did not experience consolidation. This analysis defines the Richmond metro as the city and two surrounding counties that were targeted under the original consolidation proposal.

6. Gary Orfield, *Must We Bus? Segregated Schools and National Policy* (Washington, D.C.: Brookings Institution, 1978).

7. Also referred to as Free and Reduced Priced Meals (FARM).

8. Southern Education Foundation, *A New Diverse Majority: Students of Color In the South's Public Schools* (Atlanta, Ga.: Southern Education Foundation, 2010); Gary Orfield and Erica Frankenberg, "Increasingly Segregated and Unequal Schools as Courts Reverse Policy," *Educational Administration Quarterly* 50 (2014): 718–34; William Frey, *Diversity Explosion: How New Racial Demographics are Remaking America* (Washington, D.C.: Brookings Institution, 2014).

9. Robert Pratt, *The Color of Their Skin: Education and Race in Richmond, Virginia: 1954–89* (Charlottesville: University of Virginia Press, 1991).

10. Richmond city schools—a separate jurisdiction within the Richmond metro—reported the highest poverty levels.

11. Though Charlotte-Mecklenburg was the only district with data on free and reduced-price lunch eligible students for all three time periods.

12. Orfield, *Reviving the Goal of an Integrated Society.*

13. Patricia Gandara and Gary Orfield, *A Return to the "Mexican Room": The Segregation of Arizona's English Learners* (Los Angeles: UCLA Civil Rights Project, 2010); Gary Orfield, *Historic Reversals: Accelerating Resegregation and the Need for New Integration Strategies* (Los Angeles: UCLA Civil Rights Project, 2007).

14. Roslyn Mickelson, Stephen Smith, and Amy Hawn Nelson, *Yesterday, Tomorrow and Tomorrow: School Desegregation and Resegregation in Charlotte* (Cambridge, Mass.: Harvard Education Press, 2015).

15. Jacob Vigdor, "School Desegregation and the Black White Test Score Gap," in *Whither Opportunity? Rising Inequality, Schools, and Children's Life Chances*, ed. G. J. Duncan and R. J. Murnane (New York: Russell Sage, 2011), 443–64.

16. R. A. Mickelson, "The Academic Consequences of Desegregation and Segregation: Evidence from the Charlotte–Mecklenburg Schools," *North Carolina Law Review* 81 (2003): 1513–62.

17. S. Billings, D. Deming, and J. Rockoff, "School Segregation, Educational Attainment and Crime: Evidence from the End of Busing in Charlotte-Mecklenburg," *Quarterly Journal of Economics* 129 (2014): 435–76.

18. Kirabo Jackson, "Student Demographics, Teacher Sorting, and Teacher Quality: Evidence from the End of School Desegregation," *Journal of Labor Economics* 27 (2009): 213–56.

19. Billings, Deming, and Rockoff, "School Segregation, Educational Attainment and Crime."

20. Roslyn Mickelson, "Subverting *Swann*: First and Second Generation Segregation in the Charlotte-Mecklenburg Schools," *American Educational Research Journal* 38 (2001): 215–52.

21. The number for 1992 reflects a combined city and suburban district for comparison's sake (though the two systems remained separate at the time).

22. Gary Orfield and Erica Frankenberg, *Experiencing Integration in Louisville: How Parents and Students See the Gains and Challenges* (Los Angeles: UCLA Civil Rights Project, 2011).

23. Ibid.

24. Ibid.

25. Annette Lareau and Kimberly Goyette, *Choosing Homes, Choosing Schools* (New York: Russell Sage, 2014).

26. Sean Reardon and John Yun, "Integrating Neighborhoods, Segregating Schools: The Retreat from School Desegregation in the South, 1990–2000," in *School Resegregation: Must the South Turn Back?*, ed. Jack Boger and Gary Orfield (Chapel Hill: University of North Carolina Press, 2005), 51–69; Erica Frankenberg, "The Role of Residential Segregation in Contemporary School Segregation," *Education and Urban Society* 45 (2013): 548–70, doi:10.1177/0013124513486288 (July 22, 2015).

27. Frankenberg, "The Impact of School Segregation on Residential Housing Patterns."

28. J. Madison, "The Same Subject Continued: The Union as a Safeguard against Domestic Faction and Insurrection," in *The Federalist Papers* (1787), 5, http://www.montpelier.org/explore/james_madison/media/pdf/jm_federalist_10.pdf (July 9, 2015); Orfield, "Metropolitan School Desegregation."

29. Orfield, "Metropolitan School Desegregation."

30. Jomills Braddock, "The Perpetuation of Segregation across Levels of Education: A Behavioral Assessment of the Contact-Hypothesis," *Sociology of Education* 53 (1980): 187; Amy Stuart Wells and Robert Crain, "Perpetuation Theory and the Long-Term Effects of School Desegregation," *Review of Educational Research* 6 (1994): 531–55.

31. Donnell Butler, "Ethnic Racial Composition and College Preference: Revisiting the Perpetuation of Segregation Hypothesis," *Annals of the American Academy of Political and Social Science* 26 (2010); Elizabeth Stearns, "Long-Term Correlates of High School Racial Composition: Perpetuation Theory Reexamined," *Teachers College Record* 112 (2010); Kristie J. R. Phillips, Robert J. Rodosky, Marco A. Munoz, and Elizabeth S. Larsen, "Integrated Schools, Integrated Futures? A Case Study of School Desegregation in Jefferson County, Kentucky," in *From the Courtroom to the Classroom: The Shifting Landscape of School Desegregation*, ed. Claire E. Smrekar and Ellen B. Goldring, (Cambridge, MA: Harvard Education Press, 2009), 239–70.

32. Roslyn Mickelson, "Exploring the School-Housing Nexus: A Synthesis of Social Science Evidence," in *Finding Common Ground: Coordinating Housing and Education Policy to Promote Integration*, ed. P. Tegeler (Washington, D.C.: Poverty and Race Research Action Council, 2011), 5–8.

33. The slow decline in black-white housing segregation in the four metros mirrors national trends over the same time period. W. Frey "Census Data: Blacks and Hispanics Take Different Segregation Paths" (Washington, D.C.: Brookings Institution, 2010).

34. Myron Orfield and Thomas Luce, "America's Racially Diverse Suburbs: Opportunities and Challenges," *Housing Policy Debates* 23 (2013): 395–430.

35. Ibid.

36. Gary Orfield, "Metropolitan School Desegregation: Impacts on a Metropolitan Society," *Minnesota Law Review* 80 (1995): 849.

37. Frey, *Diversity Explosion*; Gary Orfield, Genevieve Siegel-Hawley, and John Kucsera, *E Pluribus ... Separation: Deepening Double Segregation for More Students* (Los Angeles: UCLA Civil Rights Project, 2012); Orfield and Frankenberg, "Increasingly Segregated and Unequal Schools as Courts Reverse Policy."

38. Orfield and Frankenberg, "Increasingly Segregated and Unequal Schools as Courts Reverse Policy."

39. Southern Education Foundation, *A New Diverse Majority*.

40. Southern Education Foundation, "A New Majority Research Bulletin: Low Income Students Now a Majority in the Nation's Public Schools," 2015, http://www.southerneducation.org/Our-Strategies/Research-and-Publications/New-Majority-Diverse-Majority-Report-Series/A-New-Majority-2015-Update-Low-Income-Students-Now (July 22, 2015).

41. Gary Orfield and Jongyeon Lee, *Segregating California's Future: Inequality and Its Alternative 60 Years after* Brown v. Board of Education (Los Angeles: Civil Rights Project, 2014); Ruben Donato, *Segregation, Desegregation, and Integration of Chicano Students: Problems and Prospects* (Washington, D.C.: U.S. Department of Education, 1993).

42. Robert Putnam, *Our Kids: American Dream in Crisis* (New York: Simon and Schuster, 2015).

43. Kevin Welner, "K–12 Race-Conscious Student Assignment Policies: Law, Social Science, and Diversity," *Review of Educational Research* 76 (2006): 349–82. Similar understanding holds true in the higher education context. See Liliana Garces and Uma M. Jayakumar, "Dynamic Diversity toward a Contextual Understanding of Critical Mass," *Educational Researcher* 43 (2014): 115–24.

44. See, e.g., *Parents Involved in Community Schools v. Seattle School District No. 1*, 551 U.S. 701 (2007).

45. See, e.g., Erica Frankenberg and Gary Orfield, *The Resegregation of Suburban Schools* (Cambridge, Mass.: Harvard Education Press, 2012); Orfield and Luce, "America's Racially Diverse Suburbs"; Jennifer Holme, Angele Welton, and Sarah Diem, "Suburban Schools and Demographic Change," *Educational Administration Quarterly* 50 (2014): 34–66.

46. Orfield, "*Milliken, Meredith* and Metropolitan Segregation."

47. William Taylor, "Metropolitan Remedies for Public School Discrimination: The Neglected Option," *Urban Review* 10 (1979).

48. William Frey, "Will This Be the Decade of Big City Growth?" (Washington, D.C.: Brookings Institution, May 23, 2014), http://www.brookings.edu/research/opinions/2014/05/23-decade-of-big-city-growth-frey (July 24, 2015).

49. William Frey, "Melting Pot Cities and Suburbs: Racial and Ethnic Change in Metro America in the 2000s" (Washington, D.C.: Brookings Institution, 2011), http://www.brookings.edu/~/media/research/files/papers/2011/5/04%20census%20ethnicity%20frey/0504_census_ethnicity_frey.pdf (November 6, 2015).

50. Jennifer Holme and Kara Finnegan, "School District Fragmentation and Metropolitan Policy," *Teachers College Record* 115 (2013); Kendra Bischoff, "School District Fragmentation and Racial Residential Segregation: How Do Boundaries Matter?," *Urban Affairs Review* 44 (2008): 182–217.

Chapter Five

1. Janelle Scott, "School Choice as a Civil Right: The Political Construction of a Claim and Its Implications for School Desegregation," in *Integrating Schools in a Changing Society*, ed. Erica Frankenberg and Elizabeth Debray (Chapel Hill: University of North Carolina Press).

2. Lisa Stulberg, *Race, Schools, and Hope: African Americans School Choice after Brown* (New York: Teachers College Press, 2008).

3. Ibid.

4. Gary Orfield, "Choice and Civil Rights: Forgetting History, Facing Consequences," in *Educational Delusions?*, ed. Gary Orfield and Erica Frankenberg (Los Angeles: University of California Press, 2013).

5. Susan Eaton, "A Stolen Nation," *The Nation*, March 26, 2009, http://sheffmovement.org/the-nation-a-stolen-education/ (July 29, 2015).

6. American Federation for Children, "New National Poll Shows Growing Momentum for School Choice as 2016 Race Kicks Off," January 22, 2015, http://www.federationforchildren.org/new-national-poll-shows-growing-momentum-school-choice-2016-race-kicks-off/ (July 29, 2015).

7. U.S. Department of Education, *Condition of Education 2009* (Washington, D.C.: National Center for Education Statistics, 2009).

8. Edwin Dolan, *Economics: Economies in Transition: Understanding the Movement Towards Markets*, 7th ed. (Oak Brook, IL: Dryden Press, 1994).

9. One America with Justice for All, "An Age of Migration: Globalization and the Root Causes of Migration" (Seattle, WA: One America with Justice for All, 2015), https://www.weareoneamerica.org/root-causes-migration-fact-sheet (July 29, 2015).

10. Example is based on a fictional family but inspired by research conducted in Chicago by Mary Patillo, Lori Delale-O'Connor, and Felicia Butts, "High Stakes Choosing," in *Choosing Homes, Choosing Schools*, ed. Annette Lareau and Kimberly Goyette (New York: Russell Sage, 2014).

11. Milton Friedman, "The Role of Government in Education," in *Economics and the Public Interest*, ed. R. A. Solo (New Brunswick, N.J.: Rutgers University Press, 1955), 123–44; J. Chubb and T. Moe, *Politics, Markets, and America's Schools* (Washington, D.C.: Brookings Institution, 1990).

12. Charles Tiebout, "A Pure Theory of Local Expenditures," *Journal of Political Economy* 64 (1956): 416–24.

13. Orfield, "Choice and Civil Rights," 55.

14. Gary Orfield and Erica Frankenberg, eds., *Educational Delusions?* (Los Angeles: University of California Press, 2013).

15. Ibid.; J. Petrovich and A. S. Wells, eds., *Bringing Equity Back: Research from a New Era in American Educational Policy* (New York: Teachers College Press, 2005).

16. B. Fuller, R. F. Elmore, and G. Orfield, eds., *Who Chooses? Who Loses? Culture, Institutions, and the Unequal Effects of School Choice* (New York: Teachers College Press, 1996), 25–49; S. Gewirtz, S. J. Ball, and R. Bowe, *Markets, Choice and Equity in Education* (Buckingham: Open University Press, 1995); P. McEwan, "Evaluating Multigrade School Reform in Latin America," *Comparative Education* 44 (November 2008): 465–83; E. A. Morphis, "The Shift to School Choice in New Zealand," National Center for the Study of Privatization, no. 179, http://www.ncspe.org/publications_files/OP179.pdf (July 29, 2015).

17. Note that considerable variation exists within the different categories of school choice, and the information reviewed here does not necessarily apply to every open enrollment or controlled choice plan, or each magnet and charter school, around the country.

18. Orfield and Frankenberg, *Educational Delusions?*

19. Daniel Duke, *The School That Refused to Die: Continuity and Change at Thomas Jefferson High School* (Albany: State University of New York Press, 1995).

20. Corey Koedel et al., "The Integrating and Segregating Effects of School Choice," *Peabody Journal of Education* 84 (2009): 110–29.

21. James Ryan, *Five Miles Away, a World Apart* (New York: Oxford University Press, 2010); Genevieve Siegel-Hawley, "Race, Choice and Richmond Public Schools," *Urban Review* 46 (2014).

22. Siegel-Hawley, "Race, Choice and Richmond Public Schools."

23. No Child Left Behind (NCLB) Act of 2001, Pub. L. No. 107-110, § 115, Stat. 1425 (2002).

24. Jennifer Holme and Amy Stuart Wells, "School Choice beyond District Borders," in *Improving on No Child Left Behind: Getting Education Reform Back on Track*, ed. Richard Kahlenberg (New York: Century Foundation Press, 2009), 139–216.

25. Georges Vernez et al., "State and Local Implementation of the No Child Left Behind Act Volume IV—School Choice and Supplemental Educational Services—Final Report" (Washington, D.C.: U.S. Department of Education, 2009).

26. Holme and Wells, "School Choice beyond District Borders."

27. Michele McNeil and Alyson Klein, "Obama Offers Waivers from Key Provisions of NCLB," *Education Week*, September 27, 2008, http://www.edweek.org/ew/articles/2011/09/28/05waiver_ep.h31.html (July 29, 2015).

28. Laura Resnick, Mary Stein, and Sarah Coon, "Standards Based Reform: A Powerful Idea, Unmoored" (Washington, D.C.: National Press Club, 2008).

29. Jennifer Jellison Holme and Meredith Richards, "School Choice and Stratification in a Regional Context: Examining the Role of Inter-District Choice," *Peabody Journal of Education* 84 (2009): 150–71.

30. Education Commission of the States, "Does the State Have a Voluntary Interdistrict Open Enrollment Program?" (Denver: Education Commission of the States, June 2013), http://ecs.force.com/mbdata/mbquestU?SID=a0i70000006fu14&rep=OE13203&Q=Q3650 (July 30, 2015).

31. Ibid.

32. John Witte, Deven Carlson, and Lesley Lavery, "The Determinants of Interdistrict Open Enrollment Flows: Evidence from Two States," *Educational Evaluation and Policy Analysis* 33 (2011): 76–94.

33. Joshua Cowen, Benjamin Creed, and Venessa A. Keesler, "Dynamic Participation in Inter-District Open Enrollment: Evidence from Michigan 2005–2013" (Lansing: Education Policy Center at Michigan State, 2015), http://education.msu.edu/epc/library/papers/WP-49-Dynamic-Participation-in-Open-Enrollment-Cowen.asp (July 30, 2015).

34. Institute on Metropolitan Opportunity, "Open Enrollment and Racial Segregation in the Twin Cities" (Minneapolis: Institute on Metropolitan Opportunity, 2013).

35. Robert Bifulco, Casey Cobb, and Courtney Bell, "Can Interdistrict Choice Boost Student Achievement? The Case of Connecticut's Interdistrict Magnet School Program," *Educational Evaluation and Policy Analysis* 31 (2009): 323–45.

36. Lauri Steele and Robert Levine, "Educational Innovations in Multiracial Contexts: The Growth of Magnet Schools in American Education" (Washington, D.C.: U.S. Department of Education, 1994); Lauri Steele and Marian Eaton, "Reducing, Eliminating, and Preventing Minority Isolation in American Schools: The Impact of the Magnet Schools Assistance Program" (Washington, D.C.: U.S. Department of Education, 1996); B. Christenson, M. Eaton, M. Garet, L. Miller, H. Hikowa, and P. DuBois, "Evaluation of the Magnet Schools Assistance Program" (Washington, D.C.: U.S. Department of Education, 2003); Erica Frankenberg and Chinh Le, "The Post-Seattle/Louisville Challenge: Extra-Legal Obstacles to Integration," *Ohio State Law Journal* 69 (2009): 1015–72.

37. James Anderson, "Race-Conscious Educational Policies versus a 'Colorblind Constitution': A Historical Perspective," *Education Researcher* 36 (2007): 249–57.

38. *Eisenberg v. Montgomery County Public Schools*, 197 F.3d 123 (4th Cir. 1999).

39. *Wessman v. Gittens*, 160 F.3d 790 (1st Cir. 1998).

40. Mira Debs, "Parent Choice and Involvement on the Ground: A Qualitative Study of Families at Two Hartford Magnet Schools," presentation, Common Hour event, Trinity College, Hartford, Conn., February 6, 2015, https://www.dropbox.com/s/vpgo8lcs59ez7zu/TrinityPresentationONLINEVERSION.pptx (July 31, 2015).

41. Sarah Garland, *Divided We Fail: The Story of an African American Community That Ended the Era of School Desegregation* (Boston: Beacon, 2013), 169.

42. Ibid.

43. K. Phillips, R. Rodosky, M. Munoz, and E. Larsen, "Integrated Schools, Integrated Futures? A Case Study of School Desegregation in Jefferson County, Kentucky," in *From the Courtroom to the Classroom: The Shifting Landscape of School Desegregation*, ed. C. Smrekar and E. Goldring (Cambridge, Mass.: Harvard Education Press, 2009).

44. U.S. Department of Education, "Creating and Sustaining Successful K–8 Magnet Schools" (Washington, DC: U.S. Department of Education Office of Innovation and Improvement, 2008), http://www2.ed.gov/admins/comm/choice/magnet-k8/report_pg6.html (July 31, 2015).

45. Genevieve Siegel-Hawley and Erica Frankenberg, *Reviving Magnet Schools: Strengthening a Successful Choice Option. A Research Brief* (Los Angeles: UCLA Civil Rights Project, 2012).

46. U.S. Department of Education, "Creating and Sustaining Successful K–8 Magnet Schools," 29.

47. Karla Riddle (director of Magnet Schools and Fine Arts, Hamilton County Department of Education), phone interview with author, July 16, 2008.

48. Hamilton County Department of Education, "Application, Selection and Admissions Processes for Lottery Magnet Schools," http://images.pcmac.org/Uploads/HamiltonCountyDE/HamiltonCountyDE/Departments/DocumentsCategories/Documents/Applying%20for%20Lottery%20Magnet%20School.pdf (July 31, 2015).

49. Genevieve Siegel-Hawley and Erica Frankenberg, "Designing Choice: Magnet School Structures and Racial Diversity," in *Educational Delusions?*, ed. Gary Orfield and Erica Frankenberg (Berkeley: University of California Press, 2013); Steele and Levine, "Educational Innovations in Multiracial Contexts"; Steele and Eaton, "Reducing, Eliminating, and Preventing Minority Isolation in American Schools"; Christensen et al., "Evaluation of the Magnet Schools Assistance Program."

50. Department of Education and Department of Justice, "Guidance on the Voluntary Use of Race to Achieve Diversity and Avoid Racial Isolation in Elementary and Secondary Schools" (Washington, D.C.: Departments of Education and Justice, 2011), http://www2.ed.gov/about/offices/list/ocr/docs/guidance-ese-201111.pdf (July 31, 2015).

51. Ibid.

52. Frankenberg and Le, "The Post-Seattle/Louisville Challenge"; Christensen et al., "Evaluation of the Magnet Schools Assistance Program."

53. Siegel-Hawley and Frankenberg, "Designing Choice."

54. Ibid.

55. Ibid.; Siegel-Hawley and Frankenberg, "Reviving Magnet Schools."

56. Ibid.; Jack Dougherty et al., "School Information, Parental Decisions and the Digital Divide: The SmartChoices Project in Hartford," in *Educational Delusions?*, ed. Gary Orfield and Erica Frankenberg (Berkeley: University of California Press, 2013).

57. Bill Bosher (retired superintendent of Henrico and Chesterfield County Schools), personal communication, March 2014.

58. Adam Gamoran, "Student Achievement in Public Magnet, Public Comprehensive, and Private City High Schools," *Evaluation and Policy Analysis* 19 (1996); Julie Cullen, Brian Jacob, and Steven Levitt, "The Impact of School Choice on Student Outcomes: An Analysis of the Chicago Public Schools," *Journal of Public Economics* 89 (2005): 729–60; Dale Ballou, Ellen Goldring, and Keke Liu, "Magnet Schools and Student Achievement" (New York: National Center for the Study of Privatization in Education at Teachers College, 2006), http://vvvvw.ncspe.org/publications_files/OP123.pdf (July 31, 2015); Rolf Blank, "Educational Effects of Magnet High Schools" (Madison, Wis.: National Center on Effective Secondary Schools, 1989); Julian Betts, Andrew Zau, and Lorien Rice, "Determinants of Student Achievement: New Evidence from San Diego" (San Francisco: Public Policy Institute of California, 2003); Steele and Levine, "Educational Innovations in Multiracial Contexts"; Steele and Eaton, "Reducing, Eliminating, and Preventing Minority Isolation in American Schools"; Christensen et al., "Evaluation of the Magnet Schools Assistance Program."

59. Siegel-Hawley and Frankenberg, "Reviving Magnet Schools."

60. Sarah Garland, *Divided We Fail: The Story of an African American Community That Ended the Era of School Desegregation* (Boston: Beacon, 2012).

61. *Parents Involved in Community Schools v. Seattle School District No. 1*, 551 U.S. 701 (2007).

62. Ibid., at 2768 (opinion of J. Roberts).

63. In fact, Justice Sotomayor offered a pointed rebuttal of Chief Justice Roberts's reasoning in a later case. Dissenting in *Schuette v. Coalition to Defend Affirmative Action, Integration and Immigrant Rights and Fight for Equality by Any Means Necessary (BAMN)*, she wrote, "The way to stop discrimination on the basis of race is to speak openly and candidly on the subject of race, and to apply the Constitution with eyes open to the unfortunate effects of centuries of racial discrimination" (134 S. Ct. 1623 (2014)).

64. Genevieve Siegel-Hawley, "The Integration Report, Issue 3" (Los Angeles: UCLA Civil Rights Project, February 11, 2008), https://theintegrationreport.wordpress.com/2008/02/11/issue-03/ (July 31, 2015).

65. Ibid.; john a. powell and Stephen Menendian, "*Fisher v. Texas*: The Limits of Exhaustion and the Future of Race-Conscious University Admissions," *University of Michigan Journal of Law Reform* 47 (2014): 899–933.

66. Ibid.

67. Rosalyn Mickelson, Stephen Smith, and Stephanie Southworth, "Resegregation, Achievement and the Chimera of Choice in Post-Unitary Charlotte-Mecklenburg Schools," in *From the Courtroom to the Classroom*, ed. C. Goldring and E. Smrekar (Cambridge, Mass.: Harvard Education Press, 2009), 130.

68. Roslyn Mickelson, Stephen Smith, and Amy Hawn Nelson, *Yesterday, Tomorrow and Tomorrow: School Desegregation and Resegregation in Charlotte* (Cambridge, Mass.: Harvard Education Press, 2015).

69. Charlotte was not the only community to do so in the aftermath of unitary status. See, e.g., Hillsborough County (Tampa), Florida. Kathryn Wiley, Barbara Shircliffe, and Jennifer Morley, "Conflicting Mandates amid Suburban Change,"

in *The Resegregation of Suburban Schools: A Hidden Crisis in Education*, ed. Erica Frankenberg and Gary Orfield (Cambridge, Mass.: Harvard Education Press, 2012).

70. Michael Alves and Charles Willie, "Controlled Choice Assignments: A New Approach to Desegregation," *Urban Review* 19 (1987): 67–86; Christine Rossell, "Controlled-Choice Desegregation Plans: Not Enough Choice, Too Much Control?," *Urban Affairs Review* 31 (1995): 43–76; Richard Kahlenberg, "Socioeconomic School Integration: Preliminary Lessons from More Than 80 Districts," in *Integrating Schools in a Changing Society: New Policies and Legal Options for a Multiracial Generation*, ed. Erica Frankenberg and Elizabeth DeBray (Chapel Hill: University of North Carolina Press, 2011), 167–86; Lisa Chavez and Erica Frankenberg, *Integration Defended* (Los Angeles: UCLA Civil Rights Project, 2009).

71. Meredith Richards, Kori Stroub, Julian Vasquez Heilig, and Michale Voloninno, "Achieving Diversity in the *Parents Involved* Era: Evidence for Geographic Plans in Metropolitan Areas," *Berkeley Journal of African American Law and Policy* 14 (2012): 65–94.

72. John Chubb and Terry Moe, *Politics, Markets and America's Schools* (Washington, D.C.: Brookings Institution, 1991).

73. Erica Frankenberg and Genevieve Siegel-Hawley, *Equity Overlooked: Charter Schools and Civil Rights Policy* (Los Angeles: UCLA Civil Rights Project, 2009).

74. National Center for Education Statistics, "The Condition of Education 2014 (NCES 2014-083), Charter School Enrollment" (Washington, D.C.: U.S. Department of Education, 2014).

75. 21st Century School Fund, "Policy Brief #3: The Landscape for Student Assignment and School Choice in D.C." (Washington, D.C.: Office for the Deputy Mayor for Education, 2014), http://dme.dc.gov/publication/policy-brief-3-landscape-student-assignment-and-school-choice (July 31, 2015).

76. Janelle Scott and Rand Quinn, "The Politics of Education in the Post-Brown Era: Race, Markets, and the Struggle for Equitable Schooling," *Educational Administration Quarterly* 50 (2014): 749–63.

77. Richard Mora and Mary Christianakis, "Charter Schools, Market Capitalism, and Obama's Neo-liberal Agenda," *Journal of Inquiry and Action in Education* 4 (2011).

78. Halley Potter, "Charter Schools Take a Stand on Integration," Century Foundation, July 1, 2014, http://tcf.org/work/education/detail/charter-schools-take-a-stand-on-integration (July 31, 2015).

79. Richard Kahlenberg and Halley Potter, "Diverse Charter Schools: Can Racial and Socioeconomic Integration Promote Better Outcomes for Students?" (Washington, D.C.: Century Foundation, 2012), http://tcf.org/assets/downloads/Diverse_Charter_Schools.pdf (July 31, 2015).

80. Kahlenberg and Potter, "Diverse Charter Schools," 23. See also Richard Kahlenberg and Halley Potter, *A Smarter Charter? Finding What Works for Charter Schools and Public Education* (New York: Teachers College Press, 2014).

81. Erica Frankenberg, Genevieve Siegel-Hawley, and Jia Wang, "Choice without Equity: Charter School Segregation," *Education Policy Analysis Archives* 19 (2011), http://epaa.asu.edu/ojs/article/view/779 (July 31, 2015).

82. M. Carnoy, R. Jacobsen, L. Mishel, and R. Rothstein, *The Charter School Dust-Up: Examining the Evidence on Enrollment and Achievement* (New York: Teachers College Press, 2005); K. Finnegan, N. Adelman, L. Anderson, L. Cotton, M.B. Donnelly, and T. Price, *Evaluation of Charter Schools Program: 2004 Final Report* (Washington, D.C.: U.S. Department of Education, 2004), https://www2.ed.gov/rschstat/eval/choice/pcsp-final/finalreport.pdf (July 31, 2015); J. Heubert, "Schools without Rules? Charter Schools, Federal Disability Law and the Paradoxes of Deregulation," *Harvard Civil Rights-Civil Liberties Law Review* 32 (1997): 301–35.

83. Jennifer Ayscue, John Kucsera, Genevieve Siegel-Hawley, and Brian Woodward, "Three Distinct Histories with One Common Future? School Segregation in Charlotte, Raleigh and Richmond, 1989–2010," *Educational Policy* (accepted for publication).

84. Ibid.

85. Other research has corroborated these findings. See, for example, Institute on Metropolitan Opportunity, "Charter Schools in the Twin Cities, 2013 Update" (Minneapolis: Institute on Metropolitan Opportunity, 2013).

86. See, e.g., Kevin Welner, "The Dirty Dozen: How Charter Schools Influence Enrollment," *Teachers College Record*, April 22, 2013; Gary Miron, Jessica Urschel, William J. Mathis, and Elana Tornquist, *Schools without Diversity: Education Management Organizations, Charter Schools, and the Demographic Stratification of the American School System* (Boulder, Col.: NEPC, 2010); J. Vasquez Heilig, A. Williams, L. McNeil, and C. Lee, "Is Choice a Panacea? An Analysis of Black Secondary Student Attrition from KIPP, Other Private Charters and Urban Districts," *Berkeley Review of Education* 2 (2011): 153–78; Hilary Hammel, *Charging for Access: How California Charter Schools Exclude Vulnerable Students by Imposing Illegal Family Work Quotas* (San Francisco: Public Advocates, 2014), http://www.publicadvocates.org/sites/default/files/library/charging_for_access_how_california_charter_schools_exclude_vulnerable_students_by_imposing_illegal_family_work_quotas.pdf (July 31, 2015); Kate Taylor, "At a Success Academy Charter School, Singling Out Pupils who Have 'Got to Go'" *New York Times*, October 29, 2015, http://www.nytimes.com/2015/10/30/nyregion/at-a-success-academy-charter-school-singling-out-pupils-who-have-got-to-go.html?_r=0 (November 11, 2015).

87. Welner, "The Dirty Dozen."

88. G. Siegel-Hawley and E. Frankenberg, "Does Law Influence Charter School Diversity? An Analysis of Federal and State Legislation," *Michigan Journal of Race and Law* 16 (2011): 321–76.

89. Siegel-Hawley and Frankenberg, "Reviving Magnet Schools."

90. Kahlenberg and Potter, "Diverse Charter Schools." http://www2.ed.gov/programs/charter/legislation.html (November 9, 2015).

91. U.S. Department of Education, "Charter Schools Program Title V, Part B of the ESEA," (Washington, D.C., U.S. Department of Education, 2014); Richard Kahlenberg, conversation with author, November 10, 2015.

92. Kahlenberg and Potter, "Diverse Charter Schools."

93. U.S. Department of Education, "Charter Schools Program (CSP) Grants to State Educational Agencies," 80 *Fed. Reg.* 34202 (June 15, 2015).

94. Frankenberg and Siegel-Hawley, "Does Law Influence Charter School Diversity?"

95. Education Commission of the States, "School or Student Preference," database, 2010, http://mb2.ecs.org/reports/Report.aspx?id=79.

96. See, e.g., Robert Linn and Kevin Welner, eds., *Race-Conscious Policies for Assigning Students to Schools: Social Science Research and the Supreme Court Cases* (Washington, D.C.: National Academy of Education, 2007).

97. Julian Betts and Y. Emily Tang, *The Effect of Charter Schools on Student Achievement: A Meta-Analysis of the Literature* (Seattle, Wash.: Center on Reinventing Public Education, 2011); Robert Bifulco and Helen Ladd, "The Impacts of Charter Schools on Student Achievement: Evidence from North Carolina," *Education Finance and Policy* 1 (2006), 50–90. Iris Rotberg, "Charter Schools and the Risk of Increased Segregation," *Phi Delta Kappan* 95 (2014): 26–31, http://pdk.sagepub.com/content/95/5/26.abstract (July 31, 2015).

98. In particular, private school vouchers were excluded from this discussion given the chapter's emphasis on the importance of civil rights protections for regional schools of choice. Such protections are difficult to implement and regulate in the private school sector. Further, though some experts have suggested that vouchers might be used as regional policy tools for desegregation (see, e.g., James Ryan, *Five Miles Away, a World Apart: One City, Two Schools and the Story of Modern Educational Inequality* [New York: Oxford University Press, 2010]), evidence on their effectiveness as such tools is extremely limited. This is perhaps not surprising, given their historical roots in Massive Resistance.

99. Kara Finnigan, Jennifer Jellison Holme, Myron Orfield, Tom Luce, Sarah Diem, Allison Mattheis, and Nadine D. Hylton, "Regional Educational Policy Analysis: Rochester, Omaha and Minneapolis' Interdistrict Agreements," *Educational Policy* 29 (2014).

100. Stuart Wells, Bianca J. Baldridge, Jacquelyn Duran, Courtney Grzesikowski, Richard Lofton, Allison Roda, Miya Warner, and Terrenda White, *Boundary Crossing for Diversity, Equity and Achievement* (Cambridge, Mass.: CHHHRJ, 2009); Kara Finnigan and Jennifer Holme, "Learning from Inter-District School Integration Programs" (Washington, D.C.: Poverty and Race Research Action Council, 2015).

101. Ibid.
102. Ibid.
103. Ibid.
104. Ibid.
105. Ibid.
106. Susan Eaton, *The Other Boston Busing Story: What's Won and Lost across the Boundary Line* (Princeton, N.J.: Princeton University Press, 2002), 44.
107. Wells et al., *Boundary Crossing for Diversity*.
108. Eaton, *The Other Boston Busing Story*.
109. Finnigan et al., "Regional Educational Policy Analysis."
110. Ibid.
111. Ibid.
112. Wells et al., *Boundary Crossing for Diversity*.

113. For instance, 10,000 students are on Boston's METCO waiting list. Kate Apfelbaum and Ken Ardon, "Expanding METCO and Closing Achievement Gaps" (Boston: Pioneer Institute, 2015), http://pioneerinstitute.org/featured/new-report-closing-the-achievement-gap-through-metco/ (July 31, 2015).

114. Eaton, *The Other Boston Busing Story*; Amy Stuart Wells and Robert Crain, *Stepping over the Color Line: African American Students in White Suburban Schools* (New Haven, Conn.: Yale University Press, 1997).

115. Wells et al., *Boundary Crossing for Diversity*.

116. Ibid.

Chapter Six

1. Oxford Dictionaries, "community," http://www.oxforddictionaries.com/us/definition/american_english/community (August 1, 2015).

2. Jeannie Oakes, *Keeping Track: How Schools Structure Inequality*, 2nd ed. (New Haven, Conn.: Yale University Press, 2005); Jeffrey Brooks, *Black School/White School: Racism and Educational (Mis)Leadership* (New York: Teachers College Press, 2012).

3. John Hope Franklin, "Behind the *Brown* Decision: A Conversation with John Hope Franklin," *Stetson Law Review* 34 (April 20, 2005).

4. James Ryan, *Five Miles Away, a World Apart: One City, Two Schools and the Story of Modern Day Educational Inequality* (New York: Oxford University Press, 2010).

5. Jean Anyon, *Radical Possibilities: Public Policy, Urban Education, and a New Social Movement* (New York: Routledge, 2005).

6. Richard Rothstein, *Class and Schools: Using Social, Economic, and Educational Reform to Close the Black-White Achievement Gap* (New York: Teachers College Press, 2004); David Berliner, "Effects of Inequality and Poverty vs. Teachers and Schooling on America's Youth," *Teachers College Record* 115 (2013); Pedro Noguera, *City Schools and the American Dream: Reclaiming the Promise of Public Education* (New York: Teachers College Press, 2003); Broader, Bolder Approach, "A Broader, Bolder Approach to Education," http://www.boldapproach.org/bold_approach_full_statement.pdf (August 1, 2015).

7. Rosalyn Mickelson, Stephen Smith, and Amy Hawn Nelson, *Yesterday, Today and Tomorrow: School Desegregation and Resegregation in Charlotte* (Cambridge, Mass.: Harvard Education Press, 2015).

8. Andrew Dunn, "CMS Launching 18-Month Student Assignment Review," *Charlotte Observer*, March 12, 2015, http://www.charlotteobserver.com/news/local/education/your-schools-blog/article13858598.html (August 1, 2015).

9. Benjamin Campbell, *Richmond's Unhealed History* (Richmond: Brandylane, 2012); National Center for Education Statistics, Student Membership, 2011 (author's calculations); Virginia State Department of Education, Fall Membership, 2013 (author's calculations); William Frey, *Melting Pot Cities and Suburbs: Racial and Ethnic Change in Metro America in the 2000s* (Washington, D.C.: Brookings Institution, 2011), 12.

10. john a. powell, "A New Theory of Integrated Education: True Education," in *School Resegregation: Must the South Turn Back?*, ed. John Boger and Gary Orfield (Chapel Hill: University of North Carolina Press, 2005).

11. john a. powell, "Addressing Regional Dilemmas for Minority Communities," *Reflections on Regionalism*, ed. Bruce Katz (Washington, D.C.: Brookings Institution, 2000).

12. William Taylor, "Metropolitan Remedies for Public School Segregation: The Neglected Option," *Urban Review* 10 (1979).

13. Ibid.; Gary Orfield, "Metropolitan School Desegregation: Impacts on Metropolitan Society," in *In Pursuit of a Dream Deferred: Linking Housing and Education Policy*, ed. john a. powell, Gavin Kearney, and Vina Kay (New York: Peter Lang, 2001); Myron Orfield, "*Milliken, Meredith* and Metropolitan Segregation," *UCLA Law Review* 62 (2015): 367-438; Erica Frankenberg, "The Impact of School Segregation on Residential Housing Patterns: Mobile, Alabama and Charlotte, North Carolina," in *School Resegregation: Must the South Turn Back?*, ed. J. Boger and G. Orfield (Chapel Hill: University of North Carolina Press, 2005), 165-84.

14. Broader, Bolder Approach, "A Broader, Bolder Approach to Education"; Harvey Kantor and Robert Lowe, "Educationalizing the Welfare State, Privatizing Education: Educational Reform and the Evolution of Social Policy from the New Deal to the Era of No Child Left Behind," in *Closing the Opportunity Gap*, ed. Prudence Carter and Kevin Welner (New York: Oxford University Press, 2013).

15. Deborah McKoy and Jeffrey Vincent, "Framing the Connections: Integrating Housing, Transportation and Education in City and Regional Planning," in *Finding Common Ground: Coordinating Housing and Education Policy to Promote Integration*, ed. Phil Tegeler (Washington, D.C.: PRRAC, 2011).

16. Over 80 percent of U.S. society is urbanized (U.S. Census Bureau, *2010 Census of Population and Housing: Population and Housing Unit Counts* [Washington, D.C.: U.S. Government Printing Office, 2012], http://www.census.gov/prod/cen2010/cph-2-1.pdf [March 15, 2014]); 90 percent of U.S. schoolchildren attend public schools (National Center for Education Statistics, "Private School Enrollment" [Washington, D.C.: U.S. Department of Education, 2014]).

17. Raj Chetty et al., "Is the United States Still a Land of Opportunity? Recent Trends in Intergenerational Mobility," *American Economic Review* 104 (2014): 141-47.

18. John Moeser, "Unpacking the Census" (presented at Eyes on Richmond lunch series, St. Paul's Church, Richmond, Va., September 23, 2011).

19. David Rusk, *Cities without Suburbs*, 4th ed. (Washington, D.C.: Woodrow Wilson Center Press, 2013).

20. Taylor, "Metropolitan Remedies for Public School Discrimination."

21. NYSED, "Guide to the Reorganization of School Districts in New York State," May 27, 2015, http://www.p12.nysed.gov/mgtserv/sch_dist_org/GuideToReorganizationOfSchoolDistricts.htm#FormsofReorganization (August 1, 2015).

22. Len Stevens, "The Dilemma of Metropolitan School Desegregation," *Education and Urban Society* 23 (1990): 61-72.

23. Ibid.

24. Ibid.

25. Including, for instance, Catherine Lhamon, assistant secretary, Office for Civil Rights at the U.S. Department of Education, Vanita Gupta, acting assistant attorney general for the Civil Rights Division at the U.S. Department of Justice, and Anurima Bhargavara, chief of the Educational Opportunities Section of the Civil Rights Division at the U.S. Department of Justice.

26. ED/DOJ, "Guidance on the Voluntary Use of Race to Achieve Diversity and Avoid Racial Isolation in Elementary and Secondary Schools" (Washington, D.C.: Departments of Education and Justice, 2011), http://www2.ed.gov/about/offices/list/ocr/docs/guidance-ese-201111.pdf (July 31, 2015).

27. Arne Duncan, "Maintaining Racial Diversity in Schools," *Washington Post*, January 13, 2011, http://www.washingtonpost.com/wp-dyn/content/article/2011/01/13/AR2011011305529.html (August 1, 2015).

28. Erica Frankenberg, Kathryn McDermott, Elizabeth DeBray, and Ann Blankenship, "The New Politics of Diversity: Lessons from a Federal Technical Assistance Grant," *American Educational Research Journal* 52 (2015): 440–74.

29. U.S. Department of Education, "Magnet Schools Assistance: Program Description," June 11, 2015, http://www2.ed.gov/programs/magnet/index.html (July 31, 2015); see also Genevieve Siegel-Hawley and Erica Frankenberg, *Reviving Magnet Schools: Strengthening a Successful Choice Option. A Research Brief* (Los Angeles: UCLA Civil Rights Project); National Coalition on School Diversity, "Federal Support for School Integration: A Status Report" (Washington, D.C.: National Coalition on School Diversity, June 2012), http://www.school-diversity.org/pdf/DiversityIssueBriefNo4.pdf (July 30, 2015); Phil Tegeler, "The 'Compelling Government Interest' in School Diversity: Rebuilding the Case for an Affirmative Government Role," *University of Michigan Journal of Law Reform* 47 (2014), http://repository.law.umich.edu/mjlr/vol47/iss4/5/ (July 31, 2015).

30. Emma Brown, "Will the Obama administration now focus on desegregating schools?," *Washington Post*, October 11, 2015, https://www.washingtonpost.com/local/education/will-the-obama-administration-now-focus-on-desegregating-schools/2015/10/11/625a0f8a-6e27-11e5-9bfe-e59f5e244f92_story.html (November 9, 2015); Rebecca Klein, "Here Is What We Know About John King, The Next Secretary Of Education," *Huffington Post*, October 3, 2015, http://www.huffingtonpost.com/entry/john-king-education-secretary_560ea564e4b0dd85030baf66 (November 9, 2015).

31. Susan Flinspach and Karen Banks, "Moving beyond Race: Socioeconomic Diversity as a Race-Neutral Approach to Desegregation in the Wake County Schools," in *School Resegregation: Must the South Turn Back?*, ed. Jack Boger and Gary Orfield (Chapel Hill: University of North Carolina Press, 2005), 261–80.

32. Jennifer Ayscue and Brian Woodward, *Segregation Again: North Carolina's Transition from Leading Desegregation Then to Accepting Segregation Now* (Los Angeles: UCLA Civil Rights Project, 2014), http://civilrightsproject.ucla.edu/research/k-12-education/integration-and-diversity/segregation-again-north-carolina2019s-transition-from-leading-desegregation-then-to-accepting-segregation-now

/Ayscue-Woodward-Segregation-Again-2014.pdf (July 31, 2015); Orfield, "Metropolitan School Desegregation."

33. Michael Gormey, "Cuomo to Strapped NY Cities, Schools: Merge," *Yahoo News*, March 15, 2013, http://news.yahoo.com/cuomo-strapped-ny-cities-schools-182321047.html (August 1, 2015).

34. David Klepper, "Cuomo: Use State's Surplus to Spur Municipal Consolidation," WIVB.com, September 19, 2014, http://wivb.com/2014/09/19/cuomo-use-states-surplus-to-spur-municipal-consolidation/ (August 1, 2015).

35. Suzanne Leland and Kurt Thumaier, eds., *Case Studies of City-County Consolidation: Reshaping the Local Government Landscape* (New York: M. E. Sharpe, 2004).

36. Ibid.

37. Amy Stuart Wells et al., *Boundary Crossing for Diversity, Equity and Achievement* (Cambridge, Mass.: CHHHRJ, 2009).

38. UCLA Civil Rights Project/MALDEF, *Preserving Integration Options for Latino Children* (Los Angeles: UCLA Civil Rights Project/MALDEF, 2008); Patricia Gándara and Megan Hopkins, *Forbidden Language* (New York: Teachers College Press, 2009).

39. David Rusk, email correspondence with author, October 4, 2015.

40. Several basic principles should guide choice-based permeability policies. First, a range of districts—urban, suburban, and exurban—need to participate. Second, free transportation must be provided. Third, extensive outreach efforts should notify a community about the interdistrict options available to them. Fourth, diversity goals should govern the application process to ensure that all students have a fair shot at being incorporated into a program. And fifth, resources and support for students moving across the boundaries should be built into the programs.

41. Jennifer Holme, Sarah Diem, and Katherine Mansfield, "Regional Coalitions and Educational Policy: Lessons from the Nebraska Learning Community," in *Integrating Schools in a Changing Society: New Policies and Legal Options for a Multiracial Generation*, ed. Erica Frankenberg and Elizabeth DeBray (Chapel Hill: University of North Carolina Press, 2011), 153.

42. Ibid.

43. Jennifer Holme and Sarah Diem, "Regional Governance in Education: A Case Study of the Metro Area Learning Community in Omaha, Nebraska," *Peabody Journal of Education* 90 (2015), 156–77.

44. Tegeler, "The 'Compelling Government Interest' in School Diversity."

45. Jennifer Holme and Amy Stuart Wells, "School Choice beyond District Borders," in *Improving on No Child Left Behind: Getting Education Reform Back on Track*, ed. Richard Kahlenberg (New York: Century Foundation, 2009), 139–216. Emily Hodge, Kendra Taylor, and Erica Frankenberg, "Lessons from the Past, Model for the Future: A Return to Promoting Integration through a Reauthorized ESEA," *Education Law & Policy Review* (forthcoming, 2016).

46. Siegel-Hawley and Frankenberg, *Reviving Magnet Schools*.

47. New York State Department of Education, "NYS Schools to Receive Grants to Promote Socioeconomic Integration," December 30, 2014, http://www.nysed

.gov/news/2015/nys-schools-receive-grants-promote-socioeconomic-integration (July 31, 2015).

48. Stephen Menendian, "Promoting Racial Diversity and Reducing Racial Isolation in Ohio," *PRRAC* 21 (July/August 2012), http://prrac.org/newsletters/julaug2012.pdf (August 1, 2015).

49. David Rusk, *Inside Game, Outside Game: Winning Strategies for Saving Urban America* (Washington, D.C.: Brookings Institution, 1999).

50. Gary Orfield, *Toward a Strategy for Urban Integration: Lessons in School and Housing Policy from Twelve Cities. A Report to the Ford Foundation* (New York: Ford Foundation, 1981).

51. David Rusk, "Can We still Hope?," Building One America, July 23, 2015.

52. David Rusk, *Building Sustainable, Inclusive Communities: How America Can Pursue Smart Growth and Reunite our Metropolitan Communities* (Washington, D.C.: Poverty and Race Research Action Council, May 2010), http://www.prrac.org/pdf/SustainableInclusiveCommunities.pdf (November 11, 2015).

53. Erica Frankenberg and Elizabeth Debray, eds., *Integrating Schools in a Changing Society: New Policies and Legal Options for a Multiracial Generation* (Chapel Hill: University of North Carolina Press, 2011).

54. Ibid.; Lora Engdahl, "New Homes, New Neighborhoods, New Schools: A Progress Report on the Baltimore Housing Mobility Program" (Washington, D.C.: PRRAC and the Baltimore Regional Housing Campaign, October 2009).

55. Orfield, *Toward a Strategy for Urban Integration*; Phil Tegeler, ed., *Finding Common Ground: Coordinating Housing and Education Policy to Promote Integration* (Washington, D.C.: PRRAC, 2011).

56. Kyle Spencer, "Can Schools Integrate When Neighborhoods Do?," *The Atlantic*, July 29, 2015, http://www.theatlantic.com/education/archive/2015/07/can-schools-integrate-when-neighborhoods-do/399836/ (August 1, 2015).

57. Amy Davidson, "Southern Honeymoon," *New Yorker*, January 5, 2015, http://www.newyorker.com/magazine/2015/01/05/southern-honeymoon (August 1, 2015).

58. Gerald Rosenberg, *The Hollow Hope: Can Courts Bring About Social Change?* (Chicago: University of Chicago Press, 2008).

59. Jack Boger, "Introduction," in *School Resegregation: Must the South Turn Back?*, ed. Jack Boger and Gary Orfield (Chapel Hill: University of North Carolina Press, 2005); Erwin Chemerinsky, *The Case against the Supreme Court* (New York: Viking, 2014).

60. Erwin Chemerinsky, "The Segregation and Resegregation of American Public Education: The Courts' Role," in *School Resegregation: Must the South Turn Back?*, ed. Jack Boger and Gary Orfield (Chapel Hill: University of North Carolina Press, 2005); Gary Orfield and Susan Eaton, *Dismantling Desegregation: The Quiet Reversal of Brown v. Board of Education* (New York: New Press, 1996).

61. *San Antonio Independent School District v. Rodriguez*, 411 U.S. 1 (1973).

62. William Clune, "The Shift from Equity to Adequacy in School Finance," *Educational Policy* 8 (1994): 376–94; Committee on Education Finance, *Equity and Adequacy in Education Finance: Issues and Perspectives* (Washington, D.C.: National Academy of Education Press, 1999).

63. Ryan, *Five Miles Away*.

64. Robert Bifulco, Casey Cobb, and Courtney Bell, "Can Interdistrict Choice Boost Student Achievement? The Case of Connecticut's Interdistrict Magnet School Program," *Educational Evaluation and Policy Analysis* 31 (2009): 323–45.

65. Susan Eaton, *The Children in Room E4: American Education on Trial* (Chapel Hill, NC: Alonquin Press, 2007).

66. Ryan, *Five Miles Away*.

67. *Keyes v. School District No. 1*, 413 U.S. 189 (1973); Orfield, "*Milliken, Meredith* and Metropolitan Segregation."

68. Gary Orfield, *Must We Bus? Segregated Schools and National Policy* (Washington, D.C.: Brookings Institution, 1976).

69. Orfield, "*Milliken, Meredith* and Metropolitan Segregation."

70. Chinh Le, "The Federal Role in Education," in *Integrating Schools in a Changing Society: New Policies and Legal Options for a Multiracial Generation*, ed. Erica Frankenberg and Elizabeth DeBray (Chapel Hill: University of North Carolina Press, 2011).

71. Ibid.; Gary Orfield, *Reviving the Goal of Integrated Schools* (Los Angeles: UCLA Civil Rights Project, 2009).

72. U.S. Department of Education, Office of Civil Rights, "Dear Colleague Letter: Resource Comparability," October 1, 2014, http://www2.ed.gov/about/offices/list/ocr/letters/colleague-resourcecomp-201410.pdf (August 1, 2015); Kate Cerve, "Riverview Faces Stringent Orders to Boost Minority Enrollment," *Island Packet*, July 25, 2009, http://www.islandpacket.com/2009/07/25/915709/riverview-faces-stringent-orders.html (August 1, 2015). The Civil Rights Division at the U.S. Department of Justice has also attended to these issues. See, for instance, Allie Bidwell, "Justice Deparment Attempts to Block Louisiana School Voucher Program," *U.S. News and World Report*, August 26, 2013, http://www.usnews.com/news/articles/2013/08/26/justice-department-attempts-to-block-louisiana-school-voucher-program (August 1, 2015); Claire Aiello, "Huntsville City Schools, Department of Justice Announce Consent in Months-Long Mediation; Some Issues Remain," *WHNT News*, January 26, 2015, http://whnt.com/2015/01/26/huntsville-city-schools-department-of-justice-announce-consent-in-months-long-mediation-some-issues-remain/ (August 1, 2015).

73. Gary Orfield, "10th Annual Brown Lecture in Education: A New Civil Rights Agenda for American Education," *Educational Researcher* 43(2013): 273–92; Erin Nave, "Getting to the Roots of School Segregation: The Challenges of Housing Remedies in Northern School Desegregation Litigation," *National Black Law Journal* 21 (2009).

74. Emily Badger, "The Supreme Court May Soon Disarm the Single Best Weapon for Desegregating U.S. Housing," *Washington Post*, January 21, 2015, http://www.washingtonpost.com/blogs/wonkblog/wp/2015/01/21/the-supreme-court-may-soon-disarm-the-single-best-weapon-for-desegregating-u-s-housing/ (August 1, 2015).

75. U.S. Department of Housing and Urban Development, "An Overview of HUD's Proposed Affirmatively Furthering Fair Housing Rule," http://www.fhco.org/pdfs/AFFHJeffrey1.pdf (August 2015).

76. Myron Orfield, "Opening Remarks" (presentation), Building One America Conference, Washington, D.C., July 23, 2015.

77. *Parents Involved in Community Schools v. Seattle School District No. 1*, 551 U.S. 701 (2007); *Shelby County v. Holder*, 570 U.S. (2013).

78. James Oliphant, "Obama Losing Chance to Reshape Judiciary," *Los Angeles Times*, March 15, 2010, http://www.latimes.com/news/nation-and-world/la-na-obama-judges15-2010mar15,0,118526.story (August 1, 2015).

79. Garth Massey, *Ways of Social Change: Making Sense of Modern Times* (New York: Sage, 2011).

80. See, e.g., a special 2012 section of the *Journal of Urban History*; Mathew Lassiter, "Schools and Housing in Metropolitan History: An Introduction," *Journal of Urban History* 38 (2012): 195–204.

81. Note, for instance, growing challenges of accurately measuring student poverty; e.g., James Vaznis, "State Revises Count of Impoverished Students," *Boston Globe*, June 22, 2014, https://www.bostonglobe.com/metro/2015/06/21/mass-deems-fewer-students-poor-under-new-methodology/61zx5rGtwKmoCblQztqxGL/story.html (August 1, 2015).

82. Sheryll Cashin, *The Failures of Integration: How Race and Class Are Undermining the American Dream* (New York: Perseus, 2004).

83. Matthew Bloch, Shan Carter, and Alan Mclean, "Mapping the 2010 U.S. Census," *New York Times*, http://projects.nytimes.com/census/2010/map (August 1, 2015).

84. Dustin Cable, "The Racial Dot Map," Demographics Research Group, University of Virginia, Weldon Cooper Center for Public Service, 2013), http://demographics.coopercenter.org/DotMap/ (August 1, 2015).

85. David Rusk, "Inclusionary Zoning: Opening Up Opportunity-Based Housing," in *Fifty Years Later: Brown v. Board of Education and Housing Opportunity, the NIMBY Report* (Washington, D.C.: National Low Income Housing Coalition, 2004), 17, http://nhlp.org/files/greenbook4/Chapter2/FN%20680%20The%20NIMBY%20Report,%20Fifty%20Years%20Later%20(Sep.%202004).pdf (August 4, 2015).

86. Rob Corcoran, *Trustbuilding: An Honest Conversation on Race, Reconciliation and Responsibility* (Charlottesville: University of Virginia Press, 2010), 149.

87. Stephen Smith, *Boom for Whom? Education, Desegregation and Development in Charlotte* (Albany: State University of New York Press, 2004).

88. For an excellent and more detailed overview of possible ways to build both media and public support for voluntary integration, see Anurima Bhargava, Erica Frankenberg, and Chinh Le, *Still Looking to the Future: Voluntary K–12 School Integration* (New York: NAACP Legal and Defense Fund/Civil Rights Project at UCLA, 2008).

89. Editorial Board, "Racial Isolation in Public Schools," *New York Times*, January 9, 2015, http://www.nytimes.com/2015/01/10/opinion/racial-isolation-in-public-schools.html (August 3, 2015); Editorial Board, "The Central Crisis in New York Education," *New York Times*, January 4, 2015, http://www.nytimes.com/2015/01/05/opinion/the-central-crisis-in-new-york-education.html (August 3, 2015); Editorial Board, "Fighting Racial Isolation in Hartford," *New York Times*, Janu-

ary 31, 2015, http://www.nytimes.com/2015/02/01/opinion/sunday/fighting-racial-isolation-in-hartford.html (August 3, 2015).

90. Cashin, *Failures of Integration*, 290.

91. Ryan, *Five Miles Away*.

92. Myron Orfield, *American Metropolitics: The New Suburban Reality* (Washington, D.C.: Brookings Institution, 2002).

93. john a. powell and Stephen Menendian, "Little Rock and the Legacy of Dred Scott," *St. Louis University Law Journal* 52 (2007): 1153, http://scholarship.law.berkeley.edu/facpubs/1158 (August 3, 2015).

94. Willis Hawley and John McConhahy, *Attitudes of Louisville and Jefferson County Citizens toward Busing for Public School Desegregation: Preliminary Results* (Durham, N.C.: Duke University and Louis Harris and Associates, 1976); Smith, *Boom for Whom?*; Alena Samuels, "The City That Believed in Desegregation," *The Atlantic*, March 27, 2015, http://www.theatlantic.com/features/archive/2015/03/the-city-that-believed-in-desegregation/388532/ (August 3, 2015).

95. W. E. B. DuBois, *The Negro* (1915; repr., Radford, Va.: Wilder, 2008), 129.

Index

Achievement School Districts (Tennessee), 32
Affirmatively Furthering Fair Housing rule, 152
Affordable Housing Policy Task Force (Charlotte), 66
African Americans: charter schools and, 126; Great Migration and, 22–23, 40; magnet schools and, 119–20, 122; poverty and, 37–38, 39–40; school administration and, 28, 64. *See also* Housing segregation; School desegregation; School segregation
Albuquerque, 143
American Civil Liberties Union, 58, 157
Arkansas, 171
Asian students, 3, 38, 75, 76, 77, 102
Atlanta, 47
Atlantic, The, 40

Bilingual Education Act of 1968, 30
Blackstone Valley Mayoral Prep, 125, 128
Blockbusting, 22, 44
Boston, 119, 129, 130, 206 (n. 113)
Bradley v. Richmond, 57, 58
Brookings Institution, 43, 102, 106
Brown v. Board of Education, 3, 33, 57, 134, 136, 152; resistance to and, 7, 28, 30, 61, 111, 149, 159; school choice and, 111, 112, 114; school district boundaries and, 23, 25; token compliance with and, 59, 61
Building One America, 157
Burger, Warren E., 26, 46

Bush, George W., 31, 70, 103, 121
Busing, 25, 26, 28, 46, 48, 62–63, 64, 68, 69, 89, 120; "collaboratives" and, 130; exemptions and, 37, 65, 135, 140, 147. *See also* Free transportation

Carter, Jimmy, 151, 166, 167
Century Foundation, 125
Charlotte: charter schools and, 126, 127; Latino students and, 76, 77, 80, 98, 102, 103; magnet schools and, 56, 67–68; poverty and, 77, 94, 103, 195 (n. 11); school and housing desegregation and, 64, 65–66, 68–69, 71, 73, 89, 90–92, 93, 95, 97, 98, 100, 135–36, 147; school and housing segregation and, 42, 46, 87, 89, 93, 95, 96, 97, 98, 100, 123–24; school choice and, 67–68, 71, 96, 99–100, 123–24, 126; school desegregation and, 5–6, 46, 56, 57, 59, 62, 63, 64, 67–68, 80, 81, 87, 103, 107, 156; school enrollments and, 71, 75, 76, 93, 102; school segregation and, 69, 71, 80–82, 88, 93, 94, 95, 103, 126, 127, 136, 202–3 (n. 69); urban/suburban consolidation and, 56, 57, 59, 62, 64, 71, 87, 89, 95, 136, 195 (n. 4); voluntary efforts at desegregation and, 68–69, 73, 80, 82, 99–100, 136, 147. *See also* Unitary status
Charter School Program, 127
Charter schools, 30, 32, 143, 145, 146, 151; school choice and, 114, 124–29, 131, 170
Chashin, Sheryll, 157

215

Chattanooga: after urban/suburban consolidation and, 60–61, 67, 69, 70, 71, 73, 76, 77, 78, 82–84, 86–87, 93, 98, 100–101, 120; before urban/suburban consolidation and, 76, 77, 78, 82, 83, 87; busing and, 64, 69, 70; Latino students and, 76, 77; poverty and, 82, 94; school and housing desegregation and, 95–96, 135; school and housing segregation and, 89, 90–93, 95, 96–98, 100–101; school desegregation and, 56, 57, 60–61, 62, 64, 77, 78, 82–84, 89, 93, 103, 121, 191 (n. 14); school enrollments and, 64, 76, 77, 82, 89; school segregation and, 64, 78, 82, 83, 86, 87, 88, 89, 94; urban/suburban consolidation and, 5, 6, 56, 57, 62, 170, 191 (n. 14), 196 (n. 21); urban vs. suburban schools and, 64, 70, 78, 86; voluntary efforts at desegregation and, 6, 82, 84

Chattanooga magnet schools, 56, 66, 67; diversity and, 6, 60, 69, 71, 82, 103, 194 (n. 69); school choice and, 70, 71, 120–21, 128; school desegregation and, 73, 82, 84, 87, 100–101

Chicago, 40, 148
Civil Rights Act of 1964, 30, 140, 150–51; Title VI, 151
Civil Rights Data Collection, 155
Civil Rights Project (CRP), 160–61
Clark County, Nev., 28
Clinton, Bill, 151, 171
Coates, Ta-Nehisi, 40
Coleman Report of 1966, 13
"Collaboratives," 129–32, 206 (n. 113)
Community, 133, 134, 154, 155, 156
Congress for Racial Equality, 58
Connecticut, 27, 42, 44, 118, 143, 150
Crockford, Virginia, 57
Cruz, Ted, 111, 112
Cuomo, Andrew, 141
Curriculum, 14

Denver, 35, 117
Detroit, 2, 24–25, 26, 42, 47
Diversity: charter schools and, 125, 127–28, 143, 146; housing segregation and, 38, 41, 42, 99; magnet schools and, 6, 60, 67, 69, 71, 82, 103, 120–22, 194 (n. 69); school choice and, 7, 123; school district boundaries and, 60, 71, 75, 103; school enrollments and, 3, 6, 7, 73, 74–77, 102, 103, 115–16, 134. *See also* School desegregation
DuBois, W. E. B., 159
Duncan, Arne, 140, 141

Eaton, Susan, 130
Educational regionalism, 5, 35, 134, 156; courts and, 148–53, 164–65; elements of, 137–38; housing segregation and, 138, 146–48; policies and, 139–46, 157–59; research and, 153–54; school and housing desegregation and, 138–39. *See also* Regionalism
Eisenberg v. Montgomery County Public Schools, 119
Elementary and Secondary Education Act (ESEA) of 1966, 30, 143, 145
Emergency School Aid Act (ESAA), 120
Equity Assistance Centers, 140

Fair Housing Act of 1968, 151
Fair Housing Council, 151
Family Choice Plan (Charlotte), 123–24, 126
Federal Housing Administration, 22
Federalism, 50, 99, 162
Five Miles Away, a World Apart (Ryan), 16, 134
Florida school districts, 19, 20
Fourteenth Amendment, 24, 26, 129
Franklin, John Hope, 134
Freeman v. Pitts, 48

Free transportation: school choice and, 114, 116, 117, 118, 121, 126, 129–30; school desegregation and, 69, 70, 137, 143, 146, 147. *See also* Busing
Frey, William, 102

Gautraux Project (Chicago), 148
Gay rights, 149
Gordon, Teddy, 122
Great Recession, 32, 40
Green v. County School Board of New Kent County, 57, 61, 62

Hamilton County School System, 60. *See also* Chattanooga
Head Start, 30
Higher education, 18, 31, 155, 197 (n. 43)
Holmberg, Ruth, 60
Holme, Jennifer Jellison, 145
Home Owner's Loan Corporation (HOLC) of 1933, 22
Hope in the Cities (Richmond), 156
Housing segregation: courts and, 45–49; diversity and, 38, 41, 42, 99; federal government and, 151–52; inclusionary housing policies and, 49–50, 65–66, 138, 139, 175 (n. 29); poverty and, 37–38, 39–41; racial discrimination and, 21, 22–24, 40, 42, 157; real estate practices and, 43–44, 51; recent times and, 37–38, 99, 197 (n. 33); regionalism and, 138, 146–48, 175 (n. 29); school choice and, 41–42, 112; school district boundaries and, 12–13, 18, 26–27, 35, 42, 47, 99, 162. *See also* School and housing segregation, School desegregation and housing segregation
"Housing Strategies to Racially Integrate Schools" (Charlotte), 65
Houston, Charles Hamilton, 14, 152
Hurricane Katrina, 32

Immigration, 21
Indianapolis, 27

Individuals with Disabilities Act of 1974, 30

Kennedy, Anthony, 49, 190 (n. 75)
Kentucky Human Rights Commission, 58
Keyes v. School District No. 1 Denver, 26, 46, 48, 150
King, John, 141
King, Martin Luther, Jr., 3, 16
Kozol, Jonathan, 14–15

Latino population: housing desegregation and, 37, 41; housing segregation and, 38; school enrollments and, 74–77, 98, 102; school segregation and, 3, 38, 42, 80, 86, 93, 103, 104
Learning Community (Omaha), 144
Los Angeles, 166
Louisville: busing and, 63, 65, 120, 147; Latino students and, 74–75, 77, 78, 86, 93, 103; magnet schools and, 67, 84, 119–20, 122, 123, 128; poverty and, 78, 86, 93, 94; school and housing desegregation and, 64, 65, 66, 71, 90–93, 95, 97, 98, 100, 101, 107, 135, 147; school and housing segregation and, 73, 89, 96, 97; school choice and, 56, 67, 73, 84, 86, 87, 93, 96, 99–100, 119–20, 122, 123, 128; school desegregation and, 5, 6, 27, 56, 57, 58–59, 62–63, 64, 84–87, 89, 164–65, 171; school enrollments and, 67, 75, 76, 77, 78, 86; school segregation and, 59, 86, 87, 88, 93, 94; urban/suburban consolidation and, 5, 6, 56, 57, 58–59, 62, 64, 71, 84, 87, 89, 95, 101, 164–65; voluntary efforts at desegregation and, 63, 67, 70, 71, 84, 86, 93, 99–100, 103, 120, 122, 123, 147
Low Income Housing Tax Credit, 147
Luce, Thomas, 101

Index 217

Madison, James, 50, 51, 52, 99, 162
Magnet schools, 145, 150; Charlotte and, 56, 67–68; Louisville and, 67, 84, 119–20, 122, 123, 128; Richmond and, 56, 66–67, 70, 122, 128; school choice and, 30, 56, 66–68, 111, 113, 114, 118–22, 123; school desegregation and, 27, 30, 66–68, 121, 122, 141, 143. *See also* Chattanooga magnet schools
Magnet Schools Assistance Program (MSAP), 69, 70, 103, 120, 121, 122, 194 (n. 69)
Marigold Report, 152
Marshall, Thurgood, 25, 152, 157, 161, 175 (n. 19)
Massive Resistance, 30, 61, 205 (n. 98)
Memphis, 11–12, 18, 20, 27, 32–33, 35, 51, 60, 158
Meredith v. Jefferson County, 122. See also *Parents Involved in Community Schools v. Seattle School District No. 1*
Merhige, Robert, 24, 57, 64, 104
"Metropolitan School Desegregation: Impacts on Metropolitan Society" (Orfield), 160, 161
Metropolitan Statistical Area, 73–74, 195 (n. 4)
Mexican American Legal Defense and Educational Fund, 157
Michigan, 45, 117
Milliken v. Bradley: divided ruling and, 24–25, 26, 48, 58, 149, 175 (n. 19); school desegregation and, 27, 114; school district boundaries and, 2, 5, 23, 46–47, 58, 59, 111, 112, 134–35, 151, 159, 161; school segregation and, 29, 48, 55, 57, 134–35
Minneapolis, 34, 117, 129
Minnesota, 117, 124
Mondale, Walter, 23
Montgomery County, Md., 49–50, 119, 156
Moving to Opportunity, 148

NAACP (National Association for the Advancement of Colored People), 70, 152, 157
Nashville, 44, 45
National Assessment of Educational Progress (NAEP), 30–31
National Center for Education Statistics, 73, 155
National Coalition of Diverse Charter Schools, 125
National Coalition on School Diversity, 157
National Commission on Excellence in Education, 29
National Education Association, 58
Nation at Risk, A (National Commission on Excellence in Education), 29, 30, 32
New Deal, 22, 40
New Orleans, 32
Newsom, Gavin, 148
New York school districts, 129, 145, 146, 156; fragmentation and, 19, 20, 43, 139, 141–42; housing segregation and, 43–44, 47
New York Times, 155, 156, 179 (n. 35)
Nixon, Richard M., 26, 58, 140
No Child Left Behind (NCLB) Act of 2001, 30, 43, 116, 117, 154
Northwest Ordinance of 1787, 20

Obama, Barack, 32, 122, 127, 140–41, 145, 151, 152
Ohio, 146
Omaha, 130, 144
Orfield, Gary, 48, 50, 114, 160–61
Orfield, Myron, 33, 101, 152, 158

Parents Involved in Community Schools v. Seattle School District No. 1, 48, 70, 93, 122–23, 140–41, 153, 190 (n. 75), 202 (n. 63)
Partnership for Sustainable Communities, 151
Pfeiffer, Deirdre, 166

Plessy v. Ferguson, 14, 33
Portland, Ore., 33–34
Poverty, 33, 34, 134, 146, 184–85 (n. 117), 212 (n. 81); academic achievement and, 3–4, 13, 14, 32, 49–50; African Americans and, 37–38, 39–40; Charlotte and, 77, 94, 103, 195 (n. 11); Chattanooga and, 82, 94; housing segregation and, 37–38, 39–41; Louisville and, 78, 86, 93, 94; Richmond and, 75, 77, 78, 94, 136, 195 (n. 10); school choice and, 112, 145; school policies and, 30, 32, 50, 75, 102, 179 (n. 37); school segregation and, 13, 15, 74, 75, 93, 94, 95, 136, 171
Poverty and Race Research Action Council, 157
Powell, Lewis, 58
Private schools, 30, 159, 173 (n. 2); school choice and, 111, 112, 113, 114, 205 (n. 98)
Project Renaissance (Louisville), 67
Public school system: academic achievement and, 13–14, 30–32; charter schools and, 30, 125, 126; inequality and, 4–5, 30–32, 33, 184–85 (n. 117); metropolitan areas and, 135, 138, 207 (n. 16); policies and, 4, 16, 179 (n. 37); reform and, 29–30; school choice and, 30, 111, 113; standardized testing and, 14, 30, 31–32, 43; teachers and, 14, 32, 68
Pupil Placement Board (Richmond), 61

Race to the Top initiative, 32, 126, 141
Racial discrimination, 122–23, 202 (n. 63). *See also* Housing segregation; School segregation
Racial hostility, 42, 188 (n. 35)
Raleigh, N.C., 44, 140, 141, 164
Reagan, Ronald, 29, 68, 167
Redlining, 22, 40, 45

Regionalism: economic development and, 33–34; education and, 4–5, 7, 35, 175 (n. 29); housing segregation and, 138, 146–48, 175 (n. 29); inequality and, 12; metropolitan areas and, 33–35. *See also* Educational regionalism
Rhode Island, 125, 128
Richmond, Va.: busing and, 64, 69, 70; magnet schools and, 56, 66–67, 70, 122, 128; poverty and, 75, 77, 78, 94, 136, 195 (n. 10); racial diversity and, 75–77, 78, 102, 103, 104, 106, 115–16, 158; school and housing desegregation and, 106, 135, 158, 167; school and housing segregation and, 24, 89, 90–92, 94, 95, 96–98, 100, 101, 106; school choice and, 56, 61, 62, 69; school desegregation and, 1, 24, 25, 55–58, 61, 62, 63–64, 66, 67, 69, 71, 95, 129, 136, 156; school enrollments and, 61, 71, 75–77, 78, 89, 115–16, 128; school segregation and, 15, 61, 62, 64, 71, 75, 78, 79, 87, 88, 104–6, 136, 160, 161; urban/suburban consolidation and, 1–2, 6, 24, 25, 55–58, 59, 62, 71, 87, 104, 195 (n. 5); urban vs. suburban schools and, 1, 5, 24, 55, 57, 64, 75, 77, 78, 79, 95, 104, 106, 136
Richmond Newsleader, 61
Roberts, John, 123
Ross, Clyde, 40
Rusk, David, 42, 156
Ryan, James, 16, 134

San Francisco, 148
School and housing segregation, 5, 6, 35, 36–38; basic relationship between and, 39–44, 153; courts and, 24, 26–27, 45–49; new schools and, 44–45; poverty and, 37–38, 40–41; school desegregation and, 49–52, 73, 74, 87, 89, 95–101. *See also* Charlotte; Chattanooga; Louisville; Richmond, Va.

Index 219

School-busting, 44

School choice, 30, 198 (n. 10), 199 (n. 17), 206 (n. 113); academic achievement and, 116–17; Charlotte and, 67–68, 71, 96, 99–100, 123–24, 126; charter schools and, 114, 124–29, 131, 170; Chattanooga magnet schools and, 70, 71, 120–21, 128; controlled choice and, 67, 73, 84, 87, 96, 99–100, 118–24; courts and, 62, 107, 111; free transportation and, 114, 116, 117, 118, 121, 126, 129–30; housing segregation and, 41–42, 112; inequality and, 115, 169–70; magnet schools and, 30, 56, 66–68, 111, 113, 114, 118–22, 123; open enrollment and, 56, 69, 71, 115–18, 132, 143, 146; private schools and, 111, 112, 113, 114, 205 (n. 98); Richmond and, 56, 61, 62, 69; school desegregation and, 7, 61, 62, 66–68, 112, 113, 114, 128–29, 132; school district boundaries and, 7, 142, 144–45, 209 (n. 40); school segregation and, 115, 116, 117, 123–24, 202–3 (n. 69); values and assumptions and, 113–15. *See also* Louisville

School desegregation: academic achievement and, 17–18, 49–50, 63; benefits and, 16–18, 51, 99, 130, 133, 159, 171; busing and, 25, 26, 28, 37, 46, 48, 62–63, 64, 65, 68, 69, 89, 130; "collaboratives" and, 129–32, 206 (n. 113); community and, 133, 134; court oversight ending and, 48, 63, 64, 66, 68, 71, 73, 80, 82, 103, 112, 124, 131; diversity and, 17, 51, 70–71, 86, 101; federal government and, 140–41, 145, 147–48, 150–51, 153–54, 168–69; free transportation and, 69, 70, 137, 143, 146, 147; grassroots action and, 129, 131, 150, 154–57, 171–72; magnet schools and, 27, 30, 66–68, 121, 122, 141, 143; media and, 156, 179 (n. 35), 212 (n. 88); metropolitan areas and, 1, 5, 7, 27–28, 35, 36–37, 50–51, 52, 55, 73–74, 101, 133, 160, 161–64, 183 (n. 93); multi-racial and, 70–71, 102–3, 134; pairing schools and, 25, 62–63, 142–43; racial discrimination and, 122–23, 137–38, 202 (n. 63); research and, 153–54, 155, 166; resistance to and, 7, 28, 30, 61, 111, 149, 159, 205 (n. 98); school choice and, 7, 61, 62, 66–68, 112, 113, 114, 128–29, 132; urban/suburban consolidation and, 1, 2, 27–29, 51, 71–72, 86–87, 99–100, 134–35, 138–40; urban/suburban transfers and, 27, 67, 80, 115, 116, 117, 119, 128, 129–32, 143, 145, 146, 160; voluntary efforts and, 7, 63, 66–68, 107, 114, 140–41, 147, 160; "white flight" and, 28–29, 48, 60, 64, 136. *See also* Charlotte; Chattanooga; Louisville; Richmond, Va.

School desegregation and housing segregation, 6, 47, 51; busing and, 63, 64, 65; policies and, 49–50, 65–66, 68–69, 87, 89, 138–39, 146–48, 151–52, 165–69, 175 (n. 29); segregation declines and, 1, 2, 38, 99–100, 101; urban/suburban transfers and, 46, 131–32

School district boundary lines: academic achievement and, 32; charter schools and, 125, 143, 145, 146; "collaboratives" and, 129–32; courts and, 23–27, 46–47; diversity and, 60, 71, 75, 103; educational regionalism and, 35, 139–46; elasticity and, 139–42; fragmentation and, 18–20, 33, 35, 43–44, 139; housing segregation and, 12–13, 26–27, 35, 42, 47, 99, 162; inequality and, 11, 13, 18; metropolitan areas and, 1–3, 5, 18–23, 24, 55, 56, 57; permeability and, 142–46, 150, 209 (n. 40); school choice and, 7, 142, 144–45, 209 (n. 40); urban/rural consolidation and, 27, 59; urban/suburban consolidation and, 5, 6, 11–12, 20–22, 27–29, 51, 57, 58–60, 87, 139–40, 141–42, 174 (n. 9), 191 (n. 1); urban vs. suburban schools and, 18, 24, 45, 78, 80, 111–12; U.S. Supreme Court and, 1–2, 5, 23, 24–26, 48, 56, 58, 59, 134–35. See also *Milliken v. Bradley*; School desegregation; School segregation

School enrollment, 127, 195 (n. 3); Asian students and, 3, 38, 75, 76, 77, 102; Latino students and, 74–77, 98, 102; open enrollment and, 56, 69, 71, 115–16, 132, 143, 146; racial diversity and, 3, 6, 7, 73, 74–77, 102, 103, 115–16, 134; school district boundaries and, 143, 145, 146, 155; student assignment and, 61, 67, 69, 86, 112, 155–56

School Improvement Grants, 145, 146

School integration. *See* School desegregation

School segregation: academic achievement and, 13, 16, 32–33, 80; buildings and, 14–15, 70; charter schools and, 126–27, 128, 151; crime and, 15, 80; harms of and, 1, 7, 13–16, 80, 82; Latino students and, 3, 38, 42, 80, 86, 93, 103, 104; poverty and, 13, 15, 74, 75, 93, 94, 95, 136, 171; private schools and, 30, 111, 159, 205 (n. 98); recent times and, 3, 4, 7, 13, 18, 38, 44, 68–70, 75, 133; resegregation and, 37, 38, 64, 68, 71, 80, 82, 104–6, 111–12; school choice and, 62, 115, 116, 117, 123–24, 202–3 (n. 69); school district boundaries and, 3, 18–33, 45, 47, 48, 55, 57, 58–59, 78, 111, 134–35, 174 (n. 14); student assignment and, 61, 68, 80, 86; teachers and, 14, 68; urban/suburban transfers and, 18, 26, 60, 61, 115–16, 117. *See also* Charlotte; Chattanooga; Louisville; Richmond, Va.; School and housing segregation; School desegregation

Shame of the Nation, The (Kozol), 14–15

Sheff v. O'Neil, 150

Smarter Charter, A (Century Foundation), 125

St. Louis, 27, 130, 160

Student Assignment Plan (Charlotte), 124

Swann v. Charlotte-Mecklenburg Board of Education, 46, 48, 63, 68

Taylor, William, 27

Teachers, 14, 32, 68

Texas Department of Housing and Community Affairs v. The Inclusive Communities Project, 152

Thomas, Clarence, 48–49

Time magazine, 24

Title IX of the Education Amendments Act of 1972, 30

Twin Cities, 34, 117. *See also* Minneapolis

Unitary status, 48, 64, 71, 151, 153; Charlotte and, 68, 80, 82, 98, 100, 123, 124, 139, 147; Charlotte and Louisville and, 69, 87, 89, 93

U.S. Census, 73, 155

U.S. Commission on Civil Rights, 27

U.S. Constitution, 50, 129

U.S. Department of Education, 44, 103, 121, 127, 145, 147; Office for Civil Rights (OCR), 60, 70, 140–41, 150–51, 157, 191 (n. 14), 208 (n. 25)

U.S. Department of Health, Education and Welfare, 41

U.S. Department of Housing and Urban Development, 151, 157

U.S. Department of Justice, 47, 58, 121, 140, 150, 151, 208 (n. 25)

U.S. Supreme Court, 152; housing segregation and, 151–52; school and housing segregation and, 46, 48–49; school desegregation and, 27, 57, 61,

62, 63, 64, 68, 70, 103, 122, 123, 150, 161, 164; school district boundaries and, 1–2, 5, 23, 24–26, 48, 56, 58, 59, 134–35. See also *Brown v. Board of Education*; *Milliken v. Bradley*; *Parents Involved in Community Schools v. Seattle District No. 1*; *Plessy v. Ferguson*; *Swann v. Charlotte-Mecklenburg Board of Education*
University of Virginia, 155
Urban renewal, 22, 23, 34–35, 44–45

Veteran's Administration, 22

Warren, Elizabeth, 111, 112
Washington D.C., 125
Weldon Cooper Center for Public Service (University of Virginia), 155
Wells, Amy Stuart, 145
Welner, Kevin, 126–27
"White flight," 28–29, 48, 60, 64, 136
Wilmington, 27, 160